Heritage Management
In New Zealand and Australia

*To Jo and Treve who have had to tolerate slideshows,
late-night phone calls, and many diminished visitor experiences*

and

*to our parents, who don't really know what we do,
but love and support us anyway.*

Heritage Management in New Zealand and Australia

Visitor Management, Interpretation and Marketing

Edited by
C. Michael Hall and Simon McArthur

Auckland
OXFORD UNIVERSITY PRESS
Melbourne Oxford New York

Oxford University Press, Walton Street, Oxford OX2 6DP
Oxford   New York   Toronto
Delhi   Bombay   Calcutta   Madras   Karachi
Kuala Lumpur   Singapore   Hong Kong   Tokyo
Nairobi   Dar es Salaam   Cape Town
Melbourne   Auckland   Madrid
and associated companies in
Berlin   Ibadan

Oxford is a trade mark of Oxford University Press

© the contributors 1993
This edition first published 1993

All rights reserved. No part of this publication may be reproduced,
stored in a retrieval system, or transmitted, in any form or by any means,
without the prior permission in writing of Oxford University Press.
Within New Zealand, exceptions are allowed in respect of any fair dealing for the
purpose of research or private study, or criticism or review, as permitted
under the Copyright Act 1962, or in the case of reprographic reproduction in
accordance with the terms of the licences issued by Copyright Licensing Limited.
Enquiries concerning reproduction outside these terms and in other countries
should be sent to the Rights Department, Oxford University Press,
at the address below.

National Library of New Zealand
Cataloguing-in-Publication Data

Heritage management in New Zealand and Australia: visitor management,
interpretation, and marketing / edited by C. Michael Hall and Simon
McArthur. Auckland, N.Z. : Oxford University Press, 1993.
1 v.
Includes bibliographical references and index.
ISBN 0–19–558274–8
1. Cultural property, Protection of—New Zealand. 2. Natural resources—
New Zealand—Management. 3. Tourist trade—New Zealand.
4. Conservation of natural resources—New Zealand. 5. Cultural property,
Protection of—Australia. 6. Natural resources—Australia—Management.
7. Tourist trade—Australia. 8. Conservation of natural resources—Australia.
I. Hall, Colin Michael, 1961–   II. McArthur, Simon.
363.690993 (363.690994)   zbn93–001287

ISBN   0 19 558274 8

Cover designed by Nikolas Andrew
Typeset in Bembo by Egan-Reid Ltd
Printed in New Zealand by GP Print Ltd
Published by Oxford University Press
1A Matai Road, Greenlane
PO Box 11–149, Auckland, New Zealand

CONTENTS

Contributors	vii
Preface	ix
New Zealand Natural Heritage Foundation	xi
1. Heritage Management: An Introductory Framework C. Michael Hall and Simon McArthur	1
2. Visitor Management and Interpretation at Heritage Sites Simon McArthur and C. Michael Hall	18
3. The Marketing of Heritage C. Michael Hall and Simon McArthur	40

Natural Perspectives

Introduction	49
4. Writing Environmental and Park History Steven Mark	51
5. The Interpretation of New Zealand's Natural Heritage Les Molloy	59
6. Theme-based Interpretation: Taking Rainforest to the People Simon McArthur	70
7. 'Walk Softly': The Effectiveness of the Tasmanian Minimal Impact Bushwalking Campaign Tim O'Loughlin	82

Senses of Place: Indigenous and Integrated Perspectives

Introduction	93
8. Māori Heritage: Visitor Management and Interpretation Ngawini Keelan	95
9. Aboriginal Heritage and Visitor Management W. E. Boyd and G. K. Ward	103
10. Landscape, Heritage, and Identity: Stories from the West Coast V. G. Kirby	119
11. Marketing a Sense of Place Graham Brown	130
12. Marketing Indigenous Heritage: A Case Study of Uluru National Park Josette Wells	137

13. Presenting History *in situ*: Historic Site Management on Public Land in Victoria 147
    Jane Lennon
14. Waldheim Chalet: A Link Between Tasmania's Cultural and Natural Heritage 157
    R. E. Saunders

Cultural Perspectives: European Culture and the Built Environment
Introduction 167

15. Institutional Arrangements for Cultural Heritage Management in New Zealand: Legislation, Management, and Protection 169
    David J. Butts
16. Cultural Tourism, History, and Historic Precincts 188
    Martin Davies
17. A Regional Approach to Heritage Management: A Case Study of Otago 197
    G. W. Kearsley
18. Napier, The Art Deco City 209
    Robert McGregor
19. Perspectives on Urban Heritage Tourism in New Zealand: Wellington in the 1990s 218
    Stephen J. Page
20. Hobson Wharf: A New Museum 231
    T. L. Rodney Wilson

Future Directions: Strategic Heritage Management

21. Strategic Planning for Visitor Heritage Management: Integrating People and Places through Participation 241
    Simon McArthur and C. Michael Hall
22. Evaluation of Visitor Management Services 251
    Simon McArthur and C. Michael Hall
23. Towards Sustainable Heritage Management? 274
    C. Michael Hall and Simon McArthur

Index 279

Contributors

Bill Boyd is Senior Lecturer, School of Resource Science and Management, University of New England—Northern Rivers, Lismore, New South Wales, Australia.

Graham Brown is Senior Lecturer, Centre for Tourism, University of New England—Northern Rivers, Lismore, New South Wales, Australia.

David Butts is Director, Museum Studies, Massey University, Palmerston North, New Zealand.

Martin Davies is Senior Historical Archaeologist, Department of Parks Wildlife and Heritage, Hobart, Tasmania, Australia.

Michael Hall is Senior Lecturer, Tourism and Recreation Programme, Massey University Albany, Auckland, and Senior Research Fellow, New Zealand Natural Heritage Foundation, Palmerston North, New Zealand.

Geoff Kearsley is Director, Centre for Tourism, University of Otago, Dunedin, New Zealand.

Ngawini Keelan - Department of Property Studies, Massey University, Palmerston North, New Zealand.

Val Kirby is Senior Lecturer, Department of Landscape Architecture, Lincoln University, Canterbury, New Zealand.

Jane Lennon is Manager Historic Places, Department of Conservation and Environment, Melbourne, Victoria, Australia.

Steven Mark is Historian, United States National Park Service, Crater Lake National Park, Crater Lake, Oregon, United States of America.

Simon McArthur is Interpretation and Recreation Planner, Forestry Commission, Hobart, Tasmania, Australia.

Robert McGregor is President, Art Deco Trust, Napier, New Zealand.

Les Molloy is Interpretation Coordinator, Department of Conservation, Wellington, New Zealand.

Tim O'Loughlin is Wilderness Recreation Research Officer, Department of Parks, Wildlife and Heritage, Hobart, Tasmania, Australia.

Steven Page is Senior Lecturer and Course Director, Centre for Tourism Studies, Christchurch College, University of Kent, Canterbury, United Kingdom.

Rob Saunders is Manager, Communications, Department of Conservation and Environment, Melbourne, Victoria, Australia.

Graeme Ward – Institute for Aboriginal and Torres Strait Islander Studies, Canberra, Australian Capital Territory, Australia.

Josette Wells is Lecturer, Tourism, University of Canberra, Australian Capital Territory, Australia.

Rodney Wilson is Director, Hobson Wharf Auckland Maritime Museum, Auckland, New Zealand.

Preface

Heritage preservation is a major issue in Australia and New Zealand. However, the passing of legislation to protect a heritage site or the establishment of a national park is only the beginning of the conservation story. Heritage can only be preserved for future generations if appropriate management policies and processes are developed and implemented.

This book is a result of the editors' interest in the interpretation, promotion, and management of heritage areas. Unfortunately, many heritage sites in Australia and New Zealand are poorly interpreted and managed, with a resultant loss in the quality of both the heritage and the visitor experience. Nevertheless, some innovative work is being conducted.

The present work aims to bring together practitioners and researchers in order to identify issues and solutions related to heritage management in Australia and New Zealand. A visit by the editors to Port Arthur in January 1991, which highlighted the problems of poor interpretation and visitor management, provided the catalyst for this book. An overheard comment that 'all it is, is a bunch of ruins', reinforced the editors' conviction that interpretation and appropriate marketing activities must have a central role in visitor management at heritage sites. Fortunately, the editors have been able to assemble a range of contributors who can indicate ways in which we can overcome the failure of many politicians, management agencies, and tour operators to understand the interrelationship between heritage and visitors. However, it must be emphasized that this work is only a beginning. Nevertheless, we hope it will go some way in assisting managers and students of heritage to find means by which visitor experiences and heritage management practices can be improved. Without appreciation and understanding by visitors and the community in general, the political support for heritage will not be forthcoming or maintained.

This book has been undertaken under the auspices of the New Zealand Natural Heritage Foundation. The Foundation has an ongoing concern for the development of appropriate visitor management strategies at heritage sites and has been especially helpful in providing an environment conducive for research and in providing special assistance in the completion of this particular project. Special thanks must also be given to the Directors of the Foundation, Brian and Delyse Springett, for their support and encouragement of our endeavours.

Support for our work has come from numerous quarters. Dick Butler, Richard Flanigan, Jane Foley, Tim Gardner, Steve Mark and Rob Saunders have been invaluable in assisting us in our understanding of the complexities of heritage management. Institutional support has been gratefully received from the Forestry Commission, Tasmania, and the Massey University Research Fund, while the provision of a Canadian Airlines International Canadian Studies Award enabled Michael Hall to examine heritage management issues in Canada. Treve McCarthy assisted with the preparation of the final manuscript, while the secretarial staff of the Department of Management Systems, Massey University, helped out with the all-important photocopying. Finally, we wish to extend our thanks to Oxford University Press, especially Anne French, for their support for the project; and to our friends, families, and partners, who put up with our critical interpretive eye on every weekend escape.

C. Michael Hall,
Senior Research Fellow, New Zealand Natural
Heritage Foundation, Palmerston North, New Zealand.

Simon McArthur,
Forestry Commission Tasmania, Hobart, Tasmania, Australia.

New Zealand Natural Heritage Foundation
MASSEY UNIVERSITY PALMERSTON NORTH

The New Zealand Natural Heritage Foundation is a national non-profit environmental education trust situated at Massey University in Palmerston North.

Launched in 1988, the Foundation's overall mission is to educate New Zealanders and others about the importance of the natural heritage to our spirituality, health, prosperity, and life-style. The concepts of sustainability and education for sustainability imbue all areas of the Foundation's work.

Supported by a Board of Trustees comprising eminent New Zealand educators, decision-makers, and business people, and with former Governor-General, Sir Paul Reeves, as Patron, the Foundation is run on effective and efficient, lean administrative lines, with specialist work completed on contract by experts.

In a short period of time, the Foundation has assumed a leading role for several areas of environmental education in New Zealand, working in both the formal and non-formal areas of education, awareness-raising, and training.

The flagship television series, 'Moa's Ark', and the book of the series, *Moa's Ark—the Voyage of New Zealand*, topped viewing and reading figures in 1990. The Foundation has produced publication and resources for schools and the general public, including resources in Māori; has developed a curriculum overview for environmental education at schools level; has a successful course operating through Massey University—'New Zealand's Natural Heritage'; and is active in the area of sustainable tourism and education and training for sustainable tourism.

A strong international profile has been achieved in a short time, through the Foundation's products, through international conferences organized by the Foundation in New Zealand, and as a result of the Foundation's presentations at key international fora, including the Earth Summit, June 1992, and the World Congress on Education and Communication for Environment and Development (ECO-ED) in Toronto, October, 1992.

The Foundation provides a model of an efficient, independent educational organization which works closely with educational institutions, government departments, and, importantly, with the managers, practitioners, operators, and the community who have the ultimate influence upon the operation and achievement of the goals of education for sustainability.

For further information about the activities of the Foundation contact:
The Director
New Zealand Heritage Foundation
Massey University
Palmerston North
New Zealand

1

Heritage Management
An Introductory Framework

C. Michael Hall and Simon McArthur

The conservation and management of heritage have become major concerns in western society in recent years. Wilderness preservation, national parks, species conservation, the protection of indigenous artefacts and cultural activities, and the conservation of buildings, historic sites and townscapes have all become prominent issues. However, broad-scale awareness of heritage and concern for its conservation are recent phenomena, particularly in frontier societies such as Australia and New Zealand. Indeed, it is only since the Second World War that positive attitudes have started to be expressed towards protecting the past, be it cultural or natural. Several reasons can be put forward as to why such concerns have emerged. First, a rapidly changing society has meant that people have sought to retain buildings, townscapes and objects which help to maintain a link with the past and therefore build a sense of continuity in their lives. Second, heritage helps forge individual, community and national identities which enable us to define who we are. Third, heritage may have scientific and conservation significance and be representative of certain natural and cultural environments. Finally, heritage has assumed economic importance as people increasingly want to visit heritage sites and experience what has been preserved.

That people are now interested in heritage and its conservation is beyond dispute, even if there is no agreement about exactly what should be kept and why it is significant. The editors have argued elsewhere that heritage is an explicitly political concept, but the present book will not detail this issue, although heritage managers must be aware of the values that heritage represents (Hall and McArthur 1991). Instead, this book focuses on the processes by which heritage is managed and the means by which visitors can have access to and can experience heritage without damaging what they have come to see. This first chapter provides an introduction to many of the concepts and issues which heritage managers face and provides a framework to help understand the components of the heritage management system. The chapter will outline three basic issues that we need to understand in the management of heritage: first, the nature and meaning of heritage; second, the significance of heritage; third, the elements of the system by which heritage is managed and experienced.

The Paradox of Managing Heritage

The management of heritage presents a paradox. How do we allow people to visit and experience heritage without the heritage becoming so degraded that it loses its value and attraction? Or, to put it another way, how do we ensure that we don't love heritage to death?

There are some people who would argue that many heritage sites should not be available for visitation. Undoubtedly, there are some areas which are so fragile, so sensitive to human impacts and so valuable that they must be left untouched. However, if heritage is to be protected, public support is vital and substantial support can only come through visitation. Vicarious appreciation through television documentaries and books is an important element in public education and awareness, but it is not sufficient by itself to ensure that areas, objects, or cultural practices are conserved. Therefore, it is only through the provision of positive visitor experiences that heritage preservation can, in the long term, be ensured and heritage passed on to future generations. As the following sections will explain, the nature of heritage and its significance mean that people's experience of heritage is the core component in its management, marketing, and interpretation.

The Nature of Heritage

Heritage represents the things we want to keep. Heritage is defined by the *Macquarie Dictionary* as '1. that which comes or belongs to one by reason of birth; an inherited lot or portion. 2. Something reserved for one . . .'. The notion of inheritance is also emphasized in the wording of Article 4 of the World Heritage Convention where each party to the Convention recognizes 'the duty of ensuring the identification, protection, conservation, presentation and transmission to future generations of the world's cultural and natural heritage'. Therefore, heritage is the things of value which are inherited. If the value is personal, we speak of family or personal heritage; if the value is communal or national, we speak of 'our' heritage. More often than not, heritage is thought of in terms of acknowledged cultural values. For instance, a residence is not usually deemed as heritage unless it can be seen as part of the symbolic property of the wider culture or community, as an element of that culture's or community's identity.

The linkage of heritage and identity is significant. References to heritage typically propose a common cultural heritage. Distinguished old buildings are spoken of as being part of 'our' heritage. It is suggested that 'we' metaphorically own them and that their preservation is important because they are part of our identity. But who is the we? (Wellington City Art Gallery 1991).

The notion of heritage is presently being shaped and defined to meet the changing needs and expectations of Australian and New Zealand societies, nations which are undergoing substantial self-examination in terms of identity and cultural composition. Post-war migration from southern Europe and, more recently, from Asia has led to a reduction in the significance of British heritage ideals and values. In addition, the renaissance of Aboriginal and Māori culture has led to a far greater appreciation of indigenous cultural values by the European majority. Therefore, heritage has assumed a role by which a wide range of groups and communities within society are able to assert their identities within a broader national culture. Society, in turn, has grasped on to various symbols, icons, and mythologies in order to try and fashion a collective national identity.

Twenty years ago, the concept of heritage was relatively narrow and centred on architectural preservation, archaeology, archives, and other collecting institutions. However, the term 'heritage' has now come to represent 'a network of interrelated elements—tangible and intangible, natural and cultural (human), personal and collective' (Ministry of Citizenship and Culture 1987: 6).

International heritage agreements and concerns have played an important part in the way we perceive heritage in Australia and New Zealand (Davison 1991; Hall 1992). For example, the World Heritage Convention has played a significant part in the development of the way in which Australians have defined the 'National Estate' and perceived the quality of their own heritage (Griffiths and Bruce 1985). The term 'National Estate' has been described as 'the things that you keep' (Committee of Inquiry into the National Estate 1975: 20). Under the Australian Heritage Commission Act 1975, the National Estate is defined in section 4(1) as consisting of 'those places, being components of the natural environment of Australia or the cultural environment of Australia, that have aesthetic, historic, scientific or social significance or other special value for future generations as well as for the present community'.

The World Heritage Convention identifies heritage as being either cultural or natural in character, although World Heritage sites may be universally significant in terms of both cultural and natural attributes (e.g. Kakadu National Park, South-West Tasmanian Wilderness Parks). However, the split of heritage into natural and cultural components is somewhat artificial, as the values which are associated with natural areas such as national parks, wilderness, and scientific reserves are cultural. To retain an area as a national park is as much a cultural decision as it is to make the land available for grazing or intensive agriculture, and so the 'natural' landscape is itself as much 'cultural' as 'natural'. Indeed, the legitimacy of the cultural practices of indigenous peoples in areas now set aside as national parks and reserves is increasingly being recognized by governments and conservation agencies. Therefore, from this perspective, two overlapping understandings of heritage can be perceived: first, a Western (European or Pākehā) concept of heritage which identifies specific elements of the landscape or built environment as constituting heritage, i.e. humankind as separate from the landscape; second, an indigenous (Aboriginal or Māori) notion of heritage which emphasizes that humankind is not separate from the landscape but is part of an indivisible whole, i.e. heritage as an everyday lived experience. While these perceptions of heritage may be regarded as ideal types, they do affect the manner in which government, agencies, students, and visitors perceive and manage the heritage around them and, as the following section outlines, the extent to which heritage may be regarded as significant.

The Significance of Heritage

The significance of heritage varies according to the values and attitudes of different groups and individuals and the nature of the heritage resource itself. However, four broad and interrelated areas of significance can be identified: economic, social, scientific, and political (Figure 1.1).

Economic Significance
One of the main justifications for preserving heritage, especially from the point of view of government and the private sector, is the value of heritage for tourism and recreation (Hall and Zeppel 1990; Zeppel and Hall 1992). The expenditure of visitors to heritage sites and the associated flow-on effects have meant that heritage tourism is now big business. For example, heritage is given considerable prominence in New Zealand's domestic and international tourism marketing strategies. The New Zealand Tourism and Publicity Department's 1989 domestic travel segmentation study categorized 21 per cent of the New Zealand population (12 per cent of annual holiday volume) as 'heritage minded' with preferred holiday activities including visits to historic sites, museums, and art galleries, and exploring national and forest parks (New Zealand Tourism and Publicity Department 1990). The scale of heritage visitation in New Zealand is indicated in Table 1.1.

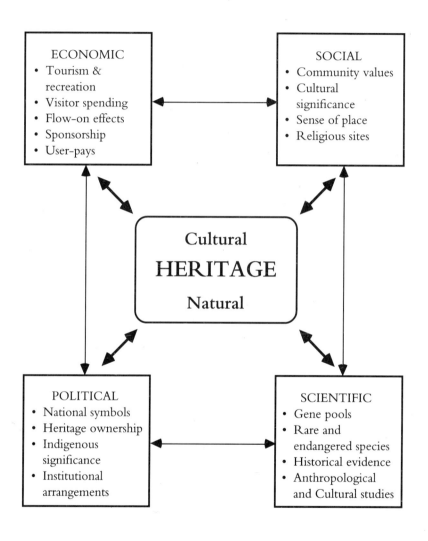

Figure 1.1: The significance of heritage

Table 1.1: Visitation to New Zealand heritage attractions 1991

Region	Museums/ Art Galleries	Gardens and Urban Parks	Historic Buildings	Natural Attractions
Northland	164.1	19.0	58.6	20.0
Auckland	240.1	302.5	15.8	70.0
Waikato	267.1	400.6	–	137.1
Bay of Plenty	482.4	649.9	0.5	130.0
Hawkes Bay/ Gisborne	26.6	11.2	4.0	N/A
Taranaki	85.6	148.5	4.6	N/A
Manawatu	443.2	29.1	5.2	–
Wellington	651.3	6.6	66.5	12.7
Nelson	126.3	–	11.0	9.0
West Coast	29.3	–	–	647.8
Canterbury	702.3	1225.0	1.2	220.0
Otago	216.2	N/A	65.2	–
Southland	199.7	N/A	–	–
Total	3634.2	2792.4	232.6	1246.6

Source: Adapted from Deloitte Ross Tohmatsu 1991, p. 39.

Heritage is also a major attraction in Australia for both domestic and international tourists (Hall 1991). For example, in 1988–89 there were 12,951,794 visitors to national and state museums and art museums and 4,375,997 visitors to regional, local, and private museums and art museums (Australia Council 1990a) (Total attendance on a state-by-state basis is shown in Table 1.2.) Cultural and heritage sites are also major attractions for international visitors, with sites such as Kakadu, Uluru, and Port Arthur contributing substantially to Australia's overseas tourist image. Furthermore, the high profile of Aboriginal art and performance in North America, Europe and Japan has aroused a substantial level of visitor interest in indigenous culture (Table 1.3).

In addition to the perceived economic benefits of tourism and recreation, sponsorship has increasingly become a significant source of income for heritage sites. Sponsorship can be used by the private sector as a

Table 1.2: Total attendance at Australian museums and art museums, 1988–89, by State

State	Art Museums No.	Art Museums Attendance	Museums No.	Museums Attendance	Total No.	Total Attendance
NSW	27	1,745,683	27	4,425,568	54	6,171,251
Vic	24	1,111,358	23	2,875,447	47	3,986,805
Qld	19	975,986	4	779,410	23	1,755,396
SA	9	395,404	6	1,018,992	15	1,414,396
WA	10	574,010	6	721,094	16	1,295,104
Tas	6	44,719	7	513,471	13	558,190
NT	2	40,350	1	217,633	3	257,983
ACT	3	336,169	4	1,552,936	7	1,889,105
Totals	100	5,223,679	78	12,104,551	178	17,328,230

Source: Australia Council 1990a, p. 4.

Table 1.3: Level of international visitor interest in Aboriginal arts and culture, by country of residence (%)

	New Zealand	Japan	Other Asia	USA/ Canada	UK/ Ireland	Europe	Other
Very or fairly interested	34	49	39	59	46	64	42

Source: Australia Council 1990b, p. 2.

supplementary marketing tool to reach specific target audiences and to create a 'socially responsible' or 'green' corporate image, while heritage sites can also use sponsorship funds to assist in conservation or to present certain cultural activities to visitors (Roux 1987; Danilov 1988).

Another recent reason for the increased economic significance of heritage is the development of a user-pays approach, particularly in national parks, museums, and art galleries. In a political environment which has meant a reduced role for government in 'non-essential' areas, heritage is increasingly having to pay its own way in terms of visitor fees and through mechanisms such as sponsorship. The development of a user-pays philosophy will therefore have substantial implications for the manner in which heritage is perceived and used, and how it is marketed and promoted to current and potential visitors.

Social Significance
Although heritage is presently seen in substantially economic terms, the personal and collective associations of heritage cannot be ignored (see Chapter 10). Indeed, although economics is often the decisive factor in determining whether or not heritage is preserved, it is the social significance of heritage that will typically first arouse interest in preservation. As noted above, heritage is important in assisting us to define who we are as individuals, a community, a culture, and a nation, not only to ourselves but also to outsiders. Therefore, heritage can be both a means of appreciating what we have inherited and a motive to cultivate it.

Heritage is also important in determining our sense of place (see Chapters 10 and 11). A sense of place arises where people feel a particular attachment to an area in which local knowledge and human contacts are meaningfully maintained (Hall 1991). It is the place where we feel most comfortable and where we feel we belong. 'People demonstrate their sense of place when they apply their moral or aesthetic discernment to sites and locations' (Tuan 1974: 235). Heritage is therefore something which is retained to ensure that certain elements of people's senses of place remain essentially unchanged.

Scientific and Educational Significance
Heritage may have substantial scientific and educational significance. Natural heritage such as national parks or nature reserves may hold important genetic material and provide a habitat for rare and endangered species. Within these areas various kinds of research on ecological processes can also occur (see Chapter 5). Research may consist of ecosystem dynamics, comparative ecology, surveys of fauna and flora, and the relationship of base ecological data to environmental change, including climatic change and human impacts. Social sciences such as anthropology and cultural studies may also conduct research on artefactual heritage or cultural heritage as presented in folkloric traditions or dance.

Heritage is also important in terms of its educational values. Heritage sites can provide a living history lesson for students and visitors. Natural heritage may serve as a foundation for environmental education programmes, while cultural heritage can convey to students and visitors a greater understanding of their own and other cultures, a particularly important educational concern in multicultural societies such as Australia and New Zealand.

Political Significance

The relationship of heritage to identity has meant that the meaning and symbolism of heritage may serve political ends. Indeed, the very definition of what constitutes heritage is political. For example, the conservation and interpretation of certain heritage sites over others may serve to reinforce a particular version of history or to promote existing political values. In addition, heritage may be politically significant for indigenous peoples as it represents the ability of that culture to endure despite colonization and attempts to destroy indigenous identity.

The ownership of heritage is political at two different levels. First, ownership helps to reinforce possession and interpretation of the past. Second, the idea of heritage 'asserts a public or national interest in things traditionally regarded as private' (Davison 1991: 7). Therefore, the rights and wishes of private owners of heritage may come into conflict with government or public interests. The institutional arrangements which surround heritage will also have a political dimension. Furthermore, the organization of heritage management authorities, their legislative basis, their relationships with other government departments and the private sector, and their relative freedom from ministerial interference, are all affected by a variety of political values and interests.

The acknowledgement of the significance of heritage to society in general and to various groups and communities in particular is a precursor to its protection. However, the long-term conservation of heritage is almost entirely dependent on its formal recognition as heritage under government legislation, such as the processes which relate to National Estate listing and the National Trust in Australia or the Historic Places Trust in New Zealand. The registration of artefacts, sites, or landscapes as heritage requires formal mechanisms which determine local, regional, national, or international significance. Tables 1.4 and 1.5 record some of the factors and some of the sources of information which are used to determine the significance of cultural and natural heritage. The list is not exhaustive, and a range of other considerations may influence the listing decision. In addition, it should be noted that legislation has tended to focus on tangible heritage rather than intangible traditions and practices.

The listing of rock art, a building or a forest as heritage is only the first stage in its conservation. The formal recognition of something as heritage implies the need for management if such heritage is to be preserved. Therefore, it becomes essential for us to understand the processes by which heritage is experienced and managed.

Table 1.4: Factors in the determination of the significance of cultural heritage

Cultural Heritage Type	Some Factors Determining Significance	Select Sources of Information
Artefacts e.g. stone tools; rock art; colonial furniture and clothing	• Rarity • Condition of artefact • Cultural significance • Designer • Materials • Level of technology • Relative age • History of use	• Museums • Libraries • Past and present members of the local community • Archives • Photographs and sketches • Comparison with other artefacts • Auction plans and notices
Buildings e.g. The Treaty House, Waitangi; Presbyterian First Church, Dunedin; Te Tokanganuianoho (whare-runanga), Te Kuiti; Victoria Barracks, Brisbane	• Rarity • Representativeness of building style • Architect • Builders, e.g. convict-built • Cultural significance • Significant owners or occupants • Local or regional significance • Materials • Relative age • Condition • History of use	• Directories • Rate books • Title office records • Special interest groups, e.g. historical societies • Managing authority personnel • Libraries • Museums • Members of the local community • Archives • Building permits • Tender notices • Early maps • Architectural plans/artwork/ photographs • Auction plans and notices • Remaining flora and fauna • Comparison with other buildings • Management plans
Sites (collection of buildings, artefacts, and/or site of historical event) e.g. Port Arthur, Tasmania; former University of Canterbury site, Christchurch; Eastwoodhill	• Condition • Rarity • Materials • Integrity of landscape • Builders e.g. convict-built • Cultural significance • Relative age • Significant owners or occupants • History of use	• Photographs • Early maps • Community information • Archives • Remaining flora and fauna • Artwork, e.g. paintings • Tender notices • Building permits • Drainage plans

Table 1.4 *continued*

Cultural Heritage Type	Some Factors Determining Significance	Select Sources of Information
Sites *continued* Arboretum, New Zealand	• Universal significance	• Comparison with other sites • Examination of refuse sites • Special interest groups, e.g. historical societies • Management plans • Auction plans and notices
Townscapes e.g. Wellington waterfront; West End Fremantle; Salamanca Place, Hobart; Maldon, Victoria; The Rocks, Sydney	• Cultural significance • Condition • Integrity of constituents, e.g. cluster of dwellings retained in original condition • Relative age • Universal significance	• Photographs • Early maps • Community information • Archives • Comparison with other areas • Examination of refuse sites • Remaining flora and fauna • Artwork, e.g. paintings • Special interest groups, e.g. historical societies • Management plans
Landscape e.g. York–Avon Valley, Western Australia; Tasman Peninsula, Tasmania; Bay of Islands Maritime and Historic Park	• Cultural significance • Past and present landuse • Economic significance • Universal significance	• Introduced flora and fauna • Remaining indigenous flora and fauna • Photographs • Early maps • Community information • Archives • Comparison with other areas • Artwork, e.g. paintings • Libraries • Special interest groups, e.g. historical societies • Management plans • Geological records and surveys

Table 1.5: Factors in the determination of the significance of natural heritage

Natural Heritage Type	Some Factors Determining Significance	Select Sources of Information
Specimen e.g. extinct, rare, or endangered species: Lord Howe Island hen; native New Zealand frog *Leiopelma*; giant weta *Deinacrida*	• Rarity • Ability to reproduce naturally • Ability to reproduce in captivity • Relationship to other species • Remaining habitat • Cultural significance • Economic significance • Scientific significance • Indicator species	• Libraries • Arboretums • Film recordings • Sound recordings • Artwork, e.g. scientific sketches • Botanic collections and herbaria • Zoological gardens and wildlife parks • Oral histories • Museums • Management plans • Geological records and surveys
Specific sites e.g. Reserve to protect penguin rookery Phillip Island, Victoria; royal albatross breeding site, Taiaroa Head, Otago, New Zealand; Kauri *Agathis notabilis* (Tane Mahuta); Organpipes National Park, Victoria; Rotorua Thermal Reserve	• Scientific significance • Rarity • Ability to reproduce naturally • Ability to reproduce in captivity • Relationship to other species • Remaining habitat • Cultural significance • Economic significance • Integrity • Universal significance	• Oral histories • Libraries • Arboretums • Film recordings • Sound recordings • Artwork, e.g. scientific sketches • Botanic collections and herbaria • Zoological gardens and wildlife parks • Archives and historical records • Management plans • Auction plans and notices • Geological records and surveys
Habitats e.g. wet tropical lowland rainforest or the 'Big Scrub', NSW; Coastal reserve, Hamilin Pool, West Australia; Travis Swamp, Christchurch; Oparara Caves, New Zealand	• Rarity • Integrity • Relationship to other habitats • Cultural significance • Economic significance • Scientific significance • Buffer zones • Universal significance	• Libraries • Studies of similar habitats • Oral histories • Film recordings • Sound recordings • Artwork, e.g. scientific sketches • Surveyors' records • Archives and historical records • Management plans • Auction plans and notices • Geological records and surveys
Ecosystems e.g. Waipapa Ecological Area, Pureora Forest, New Zealand; Southwest National Park, Tasmania; Fiordland National Park, New Zealand; Great Barrier Reef Marine Park	• Integrity • Relationship to other ecosystems • Cultural significance • Economic significance • Scientific significance • Universal significance	• Libraries • Oral histories • Film recordings • Sound recordings • Artwork, e.g. scientific sketches • Surveyors' records • Archives and historical records • Management plans • Geological records and surveys

Heritage Management: An Introductory Framework

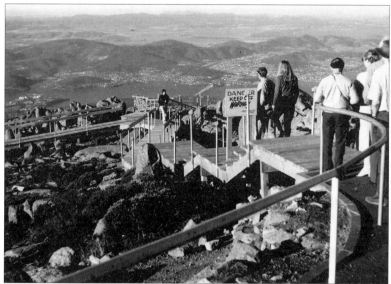

Plate 1.1: Visitors ignoring signage and using boardwalk still under construction at Mount Wellington, Hobart, Tasmania

The Heritage Visitor Management System

Traditional heritage management has focused on the heritage resource as the central element in the management process. However, this approach is deficient because it generally takes inadequate account of the human element in heritage management and especially the significance of visitors. For many heritage managers, the old cliché that the site would run smoothly as long as there were no visitors would certainly apply! Instead, we propose that the visitor experience should be placed at the centre of any heritage management process. We argue that by providing high-quality experiences which satisfy visitors' expectations, motivations, and needs, we can modify and influence the behaviour of visitors in such a way as to ensure that the values of the heritage resource are maintained (Figure 1.2).

In order to understand the quality of the visitor experience we need to recognize the characteristics of both the demand and supply sides of the heritage management system. Traditional heritage management has primarily focused on the supply side. However, in order to maintain heritage values effectively and to provide appropriate visitor experiences, we need to identify demand and integrate it with the provision of the heritage resource.

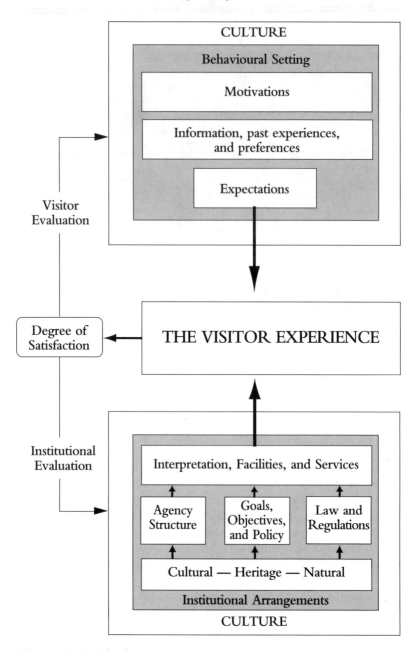

Figure 1.2: The heritage visitor management system

The demand and behavioural setting for heritage experiences are determined by the cultural background of the visitor. Different cultures have different values as to what is heritage. For example, cattlemen in the alpine country of Australia perceive the heritage value of the high country to be related to its ability to sustain their lifestyle, while conservationists (primarily urban-based) want to preserve the alpine areas in a perceived natural state without the presence of competing values. In order to understand what current and potential visitors may be seeking at heritage sites we need to identify their motivations, past experiences, preferences, and expectations. Having this information can allow heritage managers to alter the manner in which the visitor experience is provided. For example, in the case of a visitor evaluation conducted at Liffey Falls in Tasmania, the Forestry Commission discovered that the principal motive for visitation was simply to access and experience the Falls rather than use the range of other recreation facilities available. Therefore, considerable savings were made in the allocation of the Commission's human and financial resources, thereby allowing them to be refocused into what was required to satisfy the visitors and maintain the heritage values of the site (McArthur and Gardner 1992).

The supply and institutional arrangements for heritage experiences also need to be recognized as occurring within a cultural dimension. Different cultures have different ways of presenting their heritage to outsiders. Furthermore, the nature of the institutional arrangements which surround heritage management is often inadequately considered. The structure of management agencies, policy, and the legal framework all directly and indirectly influence the delivery of visitor management services and facilities, including interpretation. For example, in the case of Liffey Falls, several different land tenures occur within a World Heritage area, and each tenure is managed by a different agency with its own objectives and management strategies. Therefore, despite there being a common heritage resource, the experiences available to visitors within each of those tenures are substantially different, even though visitors did not identify the different tenures within the area (McArthur and Gardner 1992).

Evaluation plays a critical role in the heritage visitor management system. Evaluation is conducted by both visitors and institutions. Visitors informally evaluate their experience in terms of their degree of satisfaction. Institutions conduct their evaluations in a number of ways and at different levels. First, and most commonly, the annual budget process will determine the degree of support for visitor programmes. Second, proposals for new projects will often lead to an evaluation of previous programmes. Third, agency staff will often conduct their own informal and formal evaluations of programme delivery in terms of time, resources, and future developments. Fourth, and most critically, institutions evaluate the visitor experience through examination of visitor characteristics and feedback. However, this last form of evaluation, while perhaps being the most significant, is also often the most neglected by heritage management agencies because it is typically regarded as 'unimportant' (Beckmann 1988).

On the supply side, evaluation provides feedback to improve the delivery of the visitor experience and maintenance of heritage values. On the demand side, evaluation creates a new set of visitor expectations, preferences, and desired experiences. Therefore, as the following set of chapters present, the challenge for heritage managers is to meet the changing demands of visitors while maintaining and perhaps enhancing the integrity and values of heritage sites.

Conclusion

This chapter has explored the values and significance of heritage and its relationship to the visitor experience. Values are central to our understanding of heritage. All heritage is based on human values. Therefore, the accommodation of these values is critical to successful heritage management. Traditional heritage management practices focused on the resource and neglected the visitor experience. However, the increasing significance of heritage in our society means that the fundamental role that visitors play in supporting heritage conservation can no longer be ignored.

References

Australia Council 1990a, *Museums, Arts Museums and Public Galleries: Report of a Survey, 1988–89*, Research Paper No. 3, Policy and Research, Strategic Development Unit, Australia Council, Redfern.

Australia Council 1990b, *International Visitors and Aboriginal Arts*, Research Paper No. 4, Policy and Research, Strategic Development Unit, Australia Council, Redfern.

Beckmann, E. 1988, 'Interpretation in Australia—current issues and future prospects', *Australian Parks and Recreation*, vol. 28, no. 2, pp. 6–14.

Committee of Inquiry into the National Estate 1975, *Report of the Committee of Inquiry*, Parliamentary Paper No. 195, Government Printer, Canberra.

Danilov, V. J. 1988, 'Corporate sponsorship of museum exhibits', *Curator*, vol. 31, no. 3, pp. 203–230

Davison, G. 1991, 'The meanings of "heritage"', in *A Heritage Handbook*, eds. G. Davison and C. McConville, Allen & Unwin, North Sydney, pp. 1–13.

Deloitte Ross Tohmatsu 1991, *New Zealand Tourist Attraction Survey 1991: An Analysis of New Zealand Tourist Attractions*, Tourism and Leisure Consulting Group, Deloitte Ross Tohmatsu.

Griffiths, C. and Bruce, R. 1985, 'The Australian Heritage Commission and the Register of the National Estate', *Environmental and Planning Law Journal*, vol. 2, pp. 169–175.

Hall, C. M. 1991, *Introduction to Tourism in Australia: Impacts, Planning and Development*, Longman Cheshire, South Melbourne.

Hall, C. M. 1992, *Wasteland to World Heritage: Preserving Australia's Wilderness*, Melbourne University Press, Carlton.

Hall, C. M. and McArthur, S., 1991, 'Whose heritage, whose interpretation, and whose quality tourism?: perspectives on the politics and sustainability of heritage tourism', in *Heritage and Quality Tourism, Proceedings of the Third Conference of Heritage Interpretation International*, University of Hawaii, Honolulu.

Hall, C. M. and Zeppel, H. 1990, 'Cultural and heritage tourism: the new grand tour?', *Historic Environment*, vol. 7, no. 3–4, pp. 86–98.

McArthur, S. and Gardner, T. 1992, *Forestry Commission Visitor Manual*, Forestry Commission, Hobart.

Ministry of Citizenship and Culture 1987, *Giving Our Past a Future*, Queen's Printer for Ontario, Toronto.

New Zealand Tourism and Publicity Department 1990, *Domestic Travel Segmentation Study*, New Zealand Tourism and Publicity Department, Wellington.

Roux, S. 1987, *Up Market with the Arts*, Policy and Planning Division, Australia Council, Sydney.

Tuan, Y-F. 1974, 'Space and place: humanistic perspectives', in *Progress in Geography* 6, ed. C. Board *et al.*, Edward Arnold, London, pp. 211–52.

Wellington City Art Gallery 1991, *Inheritance: Art, Heritage and the Past*, Wellington City Art Gallery, Wellington.

World Heritage Committee 1984, *Operational Guidelines for the Implementation of the World Heritage Convention*, WHC/2 Revised, UNESCO, World Heritage Committee (UNESCO, Intergovernmental Committee for the Protection of the World Cultural and Natural Heritage), Paris.

Zeppel, H. and Hall, C. M. 1992, 'Review. Arts and heritage tourism', in *Special Interest Tourism*, eds. B. Weiler and C. M. Hall, Belhaven Press, London, pp. 47–68.

2

Visitor Management and Interpretation at Heritage Sites

Simon McArthur and C. Michael Hall

Introduction

This chapter addresses some of the dominant issues facing visitor management at heritage sites. It will provide an assessment of several commonly used visitor management techniques. While conventional heritage management practice has focused on the resource, the authors' approach emphasizes the use of interpretation and education as a more appropriate long-term technique to manage both heritage and the visitor experience. The chapter concludes with the need for effective monitoring and evaluation using a dynamic framework which is able to adapt to changing visitor demands, a point which will be discussed in more detail later in the book.

As noted in Chapter 1, people need heritage as a reference point by which to add perspective and meaning to their lives. This perspective and meaning come from the direct experience of heritage. There is a two-way or reciprocal relationship between heritage and visitor. It is not possible for a visitor to have an experience in a heritage site without causing some sort of impact upon that area, be it physical, biological, chemical, or social. In varying degrees this impact can reduce the quality of heritage values and the visitor experience, as shown in Plate 2.1. Conversely, conserving heritage is dependent on a political process influenced by community attitudes. These community attitudes are in turn influenced by the experiences of individuals and groups who visit heritage sites. Visitors and heritage must engage in a mutually beneficial relationship.

The practice of heritage visitor management is the practice of ensuring that the visitor achieves a quality experience in an environmentally sustainable manner. It is:

> The management of visitors to a heritage site in a manner which maximizes the quality of the visitor experience and minimizes the impact of visitation on the heritage resource.

Plate 2.1: The impact of bushwalking on sensitive environments

Plate 2.2: The use of hardening to reduce visitor impact upon heritage values

Effective visitor management is being made more difficult by issues relating to increased use, time constraints, financial constraints, smaller group size, and higher visitor expectations. Many heritage sites have undergone enormous increases in visitation (see Chapter 1). For example, visitation to Australia's national parks in the past five years has substantially increased in the light of growing interest in and awareness of the environment. The characteristics of this increased use place considerable stress on heritage managers. Many areas receive nearly all of their visitation during very short time frames (McArthur and Gardner 1992). These time frames require an experience to be supplemented with 'high performance' facilities and services that respond to intense use. Studies have also shown that group size in both commercial and non-commercial user groups has decreased (McArthur 1992a; McArthur and Gardner 1992). The relationship between an increase in use and a decrease in group size tends to suggest a greater demand for individual space and facilities. In addition, many people visiting natural areas bring along expectations that reflect a growing and diverse range of experiences. These issues are likely to intensify further with increases in population, mobility, and interest in heritage.

Plate 2.3: In the heart of the State Forest, a steel boardwalk crosses Keogh's Creek, Geeveston, Tasmania

To cope with these issues, and to lighten pressure on other areas, the traditional response by management is the 'hardening option'. Hardening usually involves the surfacing of access routes (e.g. walking tracks) and associated facilities (e.g. picnic areas) and increasing the number and range of facilities (see Plate 2.2). This option may allow the immediate environment to become more sustainable, but it comes at a cost. Hardening changes the nature of the experience, and despite the best intentions and 'environmentally sound' materials and techniques, hardening may compromise heritage values. In an effort to reduce pressure elsewhere and to achieve some sort of economic value for works, hardened sites tend to be heavily promoted. Consequently, they access new markets that attract increases in visitation and changes in visitor profile. Earlier visitors take one look at the promotion, the increase in numbers, and the change in clientele, and move elsewhere—a situation generally known as 'recreational succession'. Examples are the Milford track in New Zealand and the Overland track in Tasmania, which until the 1980s were receiving unsustainable impact directly as a result of significant increases in visitation. The implementation of techniques such as strict schedules and extensive surface hardening have some 'purists' (who once frequented the walks) now scoffing at both experience and participants in terms such as 'training tracks' and 'walking freeways for yuppies'. When the 'purists' move elsewhere, they take the original impact with them, in Tasmania's case to the Arthur Ranges in the South-west National Park.

Hardening sometimes fails to blend in with the surrounding environment, compromising the original values of the heritage, as shown in Plate 2.3. It is the most commonly used visitor management technique at heritage sites, but its success is uncertain and it is by no means a long-term solution.

The Relationship between Visitor Management, the Resource, and the Visitor

Perhaps the greatest challenge for visitor management is defining just what each experience should be, who it should be for, and how many visitors should be catered for. This is a significant challenge given the dynamic nature of both heritage and visitor.

There is a direct relationship between visitor management, visitor experience, and the condition of the resource, as shown in Figure 2.1. Placing visitor management between the resource and the visitor experience, we see that it can only be effective when both the resource is adequately conserved and the visitor is adequately satisfied. Therefore, it is the responsibility of managers to identify appropriate management strategies.

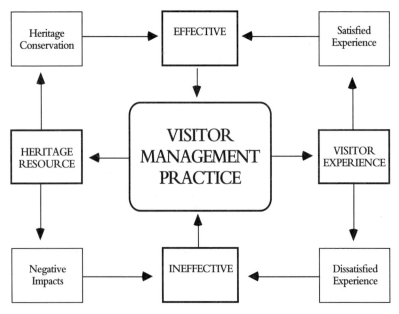

Figure 2.1: The relationship between visitor management, visitor experience, and the condition of the resource

Hardening
As discussed earlier, making the resource 'bomb proof' to visitor impact can come at the expense of the experience. Techniques such as boardwalks confine visitor flow and thus impact, yet they also modify the type of visitor and increase the level of crowding. For example, on the Gordon River in Tasmania, a boardwalk was created to serve as an 'attraction trade off' to restricted river access further upstream. For commercial reasons the tours contain large group sizes in excess of 50 people per boat. While the boardwalk and surrounding rainforest appear to cope with this sudden influx, the groups are nevertheless confined at key stops. Visitors interested in photographing the famous 2000-year-old Huon pine struggle against limited time and fellow photographers, and most of their photographs will include the backs of others in front of them. Interpretation signs along the way were installed to enrich the experience and communicate an important management message. Brief tests on several tours indicated a strong desire by many visitors to learn more of their experience, yet less than half of these groups had managed to read more than one sign, and less than one in five had read all of them (McArthur 1992a). Similarly, many tours of historic sites suffer from excessive channelling and partitioning of visitor flow. Hardening also presents visual impacts which can detract from the aesthetics of the heritage, as is shown in Plate 2.3.

Many heritage managers have improved the aesthetics of hardening with more sympathetic materials and design. However, site hardening places considerable demands on financial and human resources. For example, World Heritage sites tend to have a superior quality and quantity of site hardening because these sites have the benefit of increased government funding. Conversely, just as heritage can be conserved at the expense of the experience, it is quite conceivable that a visitor can have a high-quality experience while leaving the resource in poor condition. For instance, cultural heritage managers are constantly at pains to prevent visitors souveniring artefacts such as stone implements or building materials from sites (Gale and Jacobs 1987). Similarly, how many recreational fishing parties return home with bags full, oblivious of remaining stock? They may well have had a great time, but perhaps have just taken the last remnants of the lake's breeding stock. The following year this scenario could turn into a 'lose–lose' situation, where the resource is exhausted, no fish are caught, and the party are eaten alive by mosquitos!

There is of course the possibility of achieving that 'win–win' situation, but it can only occur with a change in visitor understanding and behaviour. Hardening is a fairly drastic method of altering behaviour. Another is by controlling the number or type of visitors to a site.

Controlling the Level of Visitation

One of the more radical techniques sometimes applied to heritage sites is their closure for a period of time. The seasonal or annual closure of camping grounds is common practice and appears to reduce impact. However, the technique fails to manage demand, with visitor discontent and alternative sites receiving additional visitation. There may also be an increase in demand as soon as the site is reopened.

In Victoria, Wilson's Promontory National Park is a classic example of using camper number restrictions during the popular Christmas school holidays, to maintain the goals of heritage management. The limit is based on a defined camping area and number of sites, and camping in other areas is strictly controlled. The success of the scheme appears to be the result of limited access to alternative areas and a general acceptance by the community of the goal and technique being used. Nevertheless, people must book months ahead and the consequence is that a significantly high proportion of well-organized visitors find ways of returning year after year, and others less well organized are excluded. This observation has been supported by Birrell and Silverwood (1981), who found that increased scarcity and competition for coastal holiday sites caused changing patterns of access, with a tendency for the experience to be monopolized.

Imposing any sort of limitation often runs against visitors' need for freedom, self-expression, and escape. Birrell and Silverwood (1981: 119) claimed that 'The Victorian coast now has to be patrolled by a growing body of police and rangers to ensure compliance with access restrictions. Unregulated movement on the coast is a privilege of the past. Even the joys of sunbaking in wind protected sand dunes . . . have become a rarity as rangers try to protect dunes from further vegetation erosion.' A growing number of battles are being fought between some users of natural heritage and various management bodies. Some of these groups who regard themselves as 'traditional' users (off-road vehicles, shooters, and vehicle-based camping) have witnessed a change in conservation values which now excludes them from conducting their activity in certain areas. These groups reject recreational succession as an insult to their very culture, and are becoming a political force in places like the Central Plateau and West Coast of Tasmania. Perhaps the principal reason why this technique fails is because of a failure in communication and understanding between parties.

Controlling the Visitor by Indirect Means

The second technique is controlling the type of visitor by indirect means, such as selective marketing and provision of strategic information, regulations, cost, selective provision of facilities, selective maintenance, and management

Table 2.1: Techniques for influencing/controlling the type of visitor to a natural heritage site

Technique	Example
Selective marketing	• Promotion of one site over a neighbouring one. • Promotions aimed at a specific market deemed to be most desirable.
Selective provision of strategic information	• Publications that omit certain sites. • Publications that omit certain experiences at a site. • Use of advance warning signage to promote one site while removing signage to another.
Implementation and enforcement of regulations	• Restrictions on duration of experience e.g. day use only, overnight only. • Restrictions on access e.g. zoning, confinement to certain road and track networks, fencing, and natural barriers. • Restrictions on equipment e.g. fuel stoves. • Restrictions on group size. • Restrictions on experience e.g. guide required, certificate required. • Restrictions on behaviour e.g. must take all faecal waste out of site, bag limits for fish.
Cost	• Implementation of a user pays system. • Bring in/throw out commercial operators e.g. kiosk or caravan park. • Available only to commercial groups.
Selective provision of facilities	• Camping facilities only. • Access points e.g. tracks, boat ramps. • Interpretation e.g. visitor centre. • Substitution of experience by moving facilities to another site.
Selective maintenance	• Allow site to fall into apparent disrepair. • Maintain one site at a higher standard than another.
Management presence	• Change the type and/or level of management profile.

presence. Table 2.1 indicates some examples of the techniques currently in operation. Well-known examples of this tactic are often found where there is limited access to the experience, such as the Australian and New Zealand sub-Antarctic Islands, Fraser Island, the Milford track, Uluru, Point Nepean, Willandra Lakes, Carnarvon Ranges Aboriginal art sites, and the Maori Arts and Cultural Institute at Rotorua.

The restraints imposed by available time and regulations imply a degree of substitution in an individual's choice of a natural heritage experience. Experiences that include a high degree of regulation tend to increase the cost (equipment, transportation, and entry fee) while reducing the duration of the experience. Sites which continue to offer a quality experience without increasing costs, limiting time and imposing regulations are likely to receive an influx of visitors who have transferred their choice from a previous site.

Conventional heritage management practice has focused on the conservation of the resource, sometimes at the expense of the experience. Instead, we advocate an approach which emphasizes the use of interpretation and education to maximize visitor experience while conserving the resource. Therefore, interpretation is a tool to manage both experience and impact.

Interpretation as a Tool in Visitor Management

The idea of using of interpretation as a management tool is not new. Some twenty years ago McMichael (1972: 9) argued that 'the most important method of managing our (Australian) National Park resources is to implement a well-designed interpretation programme, which seeks to inform the visitor of the values of the park and of nature conservation, not by direct teaching but by experience'. However, the implementation of this idea has not occurred due to:

- Preoccupation by managers towards the purchase and 'securing' of heritage;
- The infancy and slow development of interpretation throughout the 1970s and 1980s;
- A lack of experimentation and conceptual thinking by interpreters; and
- A lack of feedback and value system for interpretive programmes (Beckmann 1988).

The evolution of interpretation at heritage sites has occurred as a by-product of the fusion of recreation with education. The longstanding and generally accepted definition of interpretation was laid down by Tilden (1977: 9) as 'an educational activity which aims to reveal meaning and relationships through the use of original objects, by firsthand experience, and by illustrative media, rather than simply to communicate factual information'.

The principles laid down by Tilden were created at a time when most interpretation was based in national parks, historic homes, and monuments, concentrating on the promotion of the preservation ethic, of the 'things of great beauty'. Today, interpretation is used by a much wider clientele, moving for instance from national park agencies to ecotourism operators to extractive industries. Heritage managers regularly use interpretation to achieve a number of objectives (Sharpe 1982; McKechnie 1984; O'Brien 1985; Roggenbuck 1987; O'Laughlin 1986, 1989; Beckmann 1988; Howes 1989; Alcock 1991; Barrow 1991; Trapp et al. 1991; Saunders 1992; Forestry Commission 1992):

- To enrich the visitor's experience;
- To assist the visitor to develop a keener awareness, appreciation, and understanding of the area being visited;
- To accomplish management goals through encouragement of thoughtful use of the resource by the visitor, thereby:
  —reducing the need for regulation and enforcement;
  —enabling careful distribution of visitor pressure so that environmental impacts on fragile natural resources are minimized (e.g. through minimal impact recreation programmes); and
- To promote public understanding of the agency and its programmes.

The order of the above objectives is deliberately listed from the visitor's perspective of importance, yet currently it is practised inversely by some sectors and agencies. This reversal reflects the political, social, and economic realities of the 1990s. It has seen many programmes add another chapter to their copies of Tilden—the theory of advertising. When one moves from the principles of interpretation to its delivery, the resemblance is clear because both advertising and interpretation:

- Seek to be noticed—to attract attention, since they accept the limited time and attention span of their audience;
- Regard novelty and humour as powerful forms of communication; and
- Accept the demand to be frank and honest, to 'tell the whole picture,' despite this being the most difficult task of all.

The use of interpretation in visitor management primarily stems from the desire to change behaviour. While such a goal is a noble and simple principle, it is by no means understood by many who wield it. A model developed by Prior (1992) is useful in illustrating the series of complicated stages that visitors go through in facing the challenge to change their behaviour (Table 2.2). The model shows that the mere presentation of an interpretive experience goes only part of the way towards changing behaviour, and that a number of other variables influence the decision-making process. Many of these variables are not followed up by those involved in interpretive programmes.

Table 2.2: Stages within an interpretive programme to change visitor behaviour

Stage	Dependence	Examples
1. Recognition that an issue is real and serious	Interpretation (personal preferred) that directly relates to an issue, ideally using visitor's own social networks	Guided tour through a wetland threatened by urban encroachment and degradation
2. A decision that action is necessary	Visitor is provided with methods to adopt action response	Visitor introduced to a volunteer education and planting programme
3. Perception of individual effectiveness	Visitor has and believes he/she has mental and physical skills necessary to adopt methods offered	Knowledge of planted seedlings and doesn't mind getting feet wet and muddy
4. Appraisal of the likely outcome of action	Visitor believes action will 'make a difference', that issue is not too overwhelming	Evidence that last year's planting stopped erosion of higher banks containing high tidal wetland vegetation
5. Calculation of the consequences of action	Individual reward from action can be measured externally (financially) and/or internally (e.g. self-esteem or confidence)	Visitor knows that maintaining wetlands as a major tourist attraction will maintain profitability of hotel operation.

Source: Adapted from Prior 1992.

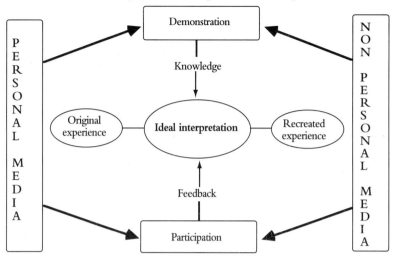

Figure 2.2: The two big players in the world of interpretation —demonstration and participation

There are countless ways in which to interpret heritage, yet in essence, under the accepted definition, they all strive to use techniques associated with either demonstration or participation. Demonstration is a powerful way of communicating *to* an audience, while participation communicates *with* an audience. The difference of feedback makes participation a more powerful technique. Figure 2.2 shows that the most successful programme will have achieved a combination of both demonstration and participation, and will draw from either an original experience or one that has been recreated.

Interpretive techniques use either personal and non-personal media, or a combination of both. By their very definition, personal techniques require individuals to act in varying capacities such as:
- Information duty: responding to demand either roving or at a fixed point;
- Organized talks/discussions: at a fixed point or along a tour;
- Organized entertainment: play, musical, puppet show;
- Organized activities: making things, measuring things, games; and
- Theme parks: living/breathing recreation of a setting.

Non-personal media have fewer dimensions and lack the opportunities for feedback that are associated with personal techniques. Consequently, although they are not usually as successful as personal interpretation, they are used far more because of their lower short-term costs (particularly with respect to salaries). Examples of non-personal media include:

- Publications;
- Signs;
- Self-guided activities;
- Visitor Centres;
- Audiovisual devices;
- Indoor and outdoor exhibits (e.g. walks, drives, and snorkelling).

While the art of delivering interpretation has been around long enough to have evolved into some very clever, effective programmes, planning for interpretation has been slower to mature and countless interpreters continue to 're-invent the wheel'. Like any other management tool, because of pressures of time and constraints on funds many have adopted a rather *ad hoc* form of interpretive planning. In fact, many interpreters continue to operate without identifying fundamental messages or target audiences. In the world of visitor management, they continue to find themselves on the decorating rather than construction team—'filling' a visitor centre with exhibits or 'decorating' a walk with signs. If planning is weak then evaluation programmes are nearly impossible to implement, and without the insights of evaluation, strategic planning is further weakened. There are three essential ingredients to consider when planning for interpretation at a natural site: the product, the operating environment, and the resource (Table 2.3).

Whether an agency's visitor management programme is established or still in its infancy, and regardless of time and funds, it must plan to be effective. Sound interpretive planning should follow a number of key steps for the implementation of new products and for the review of existing ones. Clearly, much of this work is required in the initial stages and later serves as a useful reference point for review. An idealized flow diagram for the key steps in interpretive planning is shown in Figure 2.3. Strategic planning is the most important stage and should represent the largest investment in effort. Sound strategic planning will reduce the amount of time and funds required for implementation, and provides the essential background for monitoring and evaluation. Unfortunately, such an emphasis is rarely achieved, with most effort being immediately focused on implementation (the development of a product or service).

The lack of strategic planning is weakest in stages three to five, although agencies do sometimes conduct broad-scale planning and resource assessment exercises. Given that audience analysis and evaluation will be discussed in Chapter 22, this chapter will explore the need for improved message definition. The ideal communication structure should identify and respond to all the major relevant issues. A lack of understanding of issues will encourage the use of blindly adopted myths regarding the principles and practice of effective interpretation, thereby reducing the effectiveness of visitor management in general.

Table 2.3: Considerations in the planning of natural heritage interpretation sites

Level	Factors
Product	• Access is available to target audience. • Site is close to significant population. • Site indicates likelihood of achieving appropriate visitation levels and audience. • Site offers a range of visitor experiences. • Site has qualities which promote project objectives. • Other tourist and recreation sites exist in close proximity. • Adequate facilities are available on site. • Facilities are adequate and well maintained. • Construction constraints are minimal. • Ongoing maintenance is minimal. • Interpretation is suitable to be integrated with other sites. • Interpretation is suitable to be differentiated from other sites. • Major feature/theme available for interpretation. • Promotional possibilities exist for pre-visit information and ongoing visitation.
Operating Environment	• Managing authority will allocate appropriate financial, labour, and physical resources. • Managing authority is supportive of interpretation proposal. • Prospective interest and/or support of local government, other relevant government agencies, special interest groups, and local community. • Technology exists to develop proposed interpretative facilities. • The proposed project is within the management authorities policy guidelines. • Proposed project is able to be effectively implemented because of a supportive organizational culture.
Resource	• Nature and characteristics of heritage. • Heritage site contains elements of interest relevant to the project's objectives (e.g. a natural site represents a specific habitat, is largely undisturbed, and/or contains geomorphological features, ecologically significant fauna and flora). • The site can tolerate proposed level of visitor impacts and development of interpretive infrastructure.

Figure 2.3: Flow diagram representing key steps in interpretive planning for visitor management

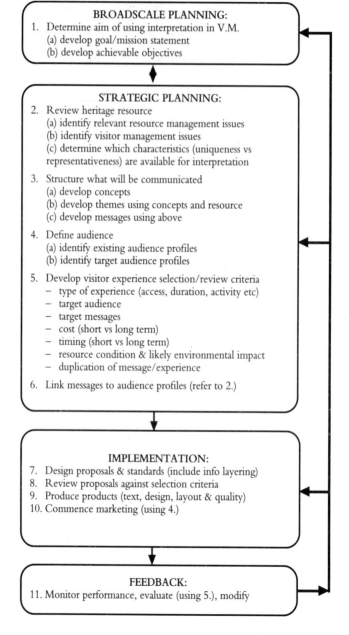

Once the issues have been identified, they should be blended into three components:
- *Concepts*: A strong idea underlying a group of common messages.
- *Themes*: A group of characteristics drawn from a region's natural and cultural heritage.
- *Messages*: What is actually planned to be said.

This structure can be metaphorically represented in a play: where the concept is represented by the writer's original idea, the theme by the stage and its set, and the messages by the script. Themes are comparatively easy to create and apply since they should reflect the characteristics of the heritage. The use of a theme ensures that the interpretation is relevant to the heritage which the visitor is experiencing. However, themes are often stretched beyond their limit when interpreters attempt to make them into concepts.

It is the concept which provides the central educational message, the 'meaning' which Tilden (1977) referred to in his definition of interpretation. Accordingly, interpretation should originate from the concept, using the combination of theme and technique to communicate a message. Unfortunately, even in recent times many experienced interpreters continue to plan for interpretation by identifying a theme and technique without a solid interpretive concept (for some examples of this omission see Field 1989; Howes 1989; Howroyd 1991; Tatnell 1991; Saunders 1992; Fox and Warnett 1992; Stone et al. 1992).

A failure to develop and adopt concepts is a failure to broaden the visitors' horizons beyond the heritage site and a failure to make them aware of their place in the total environment (MacGillivary 1984). This broadening process allows people to have a better understanding of the complexities of coexisting with the environment, and allows them to make informed decisions on matters relating to heritage management. This oversight has been very apparent in the interpretation of World Heritage Areas in Australia and New Zealand (Saunders 1992; see also Chapter 5). The powerfully emotive associations associated with World Heritage status tend to tempt some managers and interpreters into relaxing and thinking that their 'battle to convince is won', that all they now need do is 'find something pretty to interpret'. Yet some of the most comprehensive and stimulating interpretation has recently come from agencies who are regularly being forced to justify themselves (Beckmann 1992). As tightening economic policy and changing political values force trade-offs to be made in the management of natural heritage, the need to identify and utilize concepts as well as themes in interpretation is becoming more and more critical.

A current example of an agency which has adopted this approach is the Tasmanian Forestry Commission, which is currently using it to develop its

Heritage Management

Table 2.4: The allocation of concepts to messages through various 'vehicles' and specific interpretive techniques

Implementation of Forest Concepts for Arve Road Visitor Strategy

Concept	Theme	Message	Vehicle	Technique
Forests are naturally dynamic ecosystems	Forest Ecology	• What is a forest?	Interpretation	Display at Esperance Forest & Heritage Centre
		• Forests are complex natural systems	Interpretation	Display at Esperance Forest & Heritage Centre
		• Parts of the forest are continually dying & growing	Interpretation	Interpreted walk (signs) along Huon pine track (Tahune Forest Reserve)
			Interpretation	Interpreted walk (signs) along Zig Zag Track
	Forest distribution	• Variation in the environment causes variation in the type of forest	Interpretation	Display at Esperance Forest & Heritage Centre
			Recreation & interpretation	Interpreted walk (signs) at Southwest Gateway
			Recreation & interpretation	Interpreted walk (signs) along Keogh's Creek
		• There are many different types of forest	Interpretation	Display at Esperance Forest & Heritage Centre
	Natural impacts	• Fire shapes the diversity, structure & complexity of forests	Recreation & interpretation	Interpreted walk (signs) at Southwest Gateway
			Recreation & interpretation	Interpreted walk (signs) along Keogh's Creek
			Recreation & interpretation	Interpreted lookout (signs) at West Creek Lookout
Managing people and the environment	Forests have changing values	• People have different needs from forests	Recreation, information & media	Provision, acknowledgement & promotion of active recreation - non-commercial (sightseeing, walking, fishing, 4WD'ing & camping) - commercial (4WD tours & rafting) Tahune Forest Reserve poster
		• People's needs change over time	Recreation & interpretation	Interpreted walk (signs) along Huon pine track (Tahune Forest Reserve)
	Managing the forests	• Different uses for different lands	Information	Visiting forests in Southern Tasmania Arve Road Brochure Tahune Forest Reserve poster Information Booth along early part of Arve Road Multiple use routed road signage
			Media	Promotions, formal reactions to speculators
			Information	Visiting forests in Southern Tasmania Arve Road Brochure Information Booth along early part of Arve Road
			Media	Promotions, formal reactions to speculators
		• The role of the Forestry Commission	Interpretation	Display at Esperance Forest & Heritage Centre
			Recreation & interpretation	Self-guided drive along Arve Loop Road
		• Using science	Interpretation	Display at Esperance Forest & Heritage Centre
		• Sustainability	Recreation & interpretation	Self-guided drive along Arve Loop Road
Sustaining the globe	Interrelationships	• Your forest or ours	Recreation & interpretation	Interpreted lookout (signs) at The Big Tree
	Your decision	• Forest consumerism	Interpretation	Display at Esperance Forest & Heritage Centre
		• Personal responsibility	Interpretation	Display at Esperance Forest & Heritage Centre

Source: McArthur 1992b

interpretive programmes (Forestry Commission 1992). For a long time the Commission had relied on its reserves to attract people to learn about the forests which it predominantly managed for timber production. These reserves offered a range of picnic and short walking opportunities that tended to represent the 'cute and cuddly' side of forestry. However, this only served to exacerbate visitors' feelings of confusion, frustration and sometimes anger when driving home through a clear-felled forest. The resentment indicated that the technique was fundamentally flawed not only by a lack of interpretation, but reliance upon the wrong theme to convey a message. At the time of writing the Commission had completed the strategic planning stage of the above process, and were allocating concepts, themes, and messages to designated natural heritage experiences (McArthur 1992b) (Table 2.4).

The crime of ignoring concepts is perpetrated above all by politicians and by some managers who relate only to technique. A prime example of this is the way in which proposals for visitor centres have been put forward and accepted (Beckmann 1988). Some of these individuals have supported interpretive projects which use a structure such as a visitor centre in preference to personal services which do not offer the same opportunities for gaining recognition—how do you install a plaque and 'open' a personal service? Many management agencies continue to be susceptible to this and other 'popular' techniques without asking some hard questions through defined criteria, such as those suggested in stage five of Figure 2.3.

Establishing a Framework for Visitor Management

Whether management decides to use hardening, controlling numbers and type of visitor, or interpretation/education, or even a combination of these, the vital ingredient is a framework for visitor management at heritage sites. Over the past twenty years the Canadian Parks Service has been developing a system to ensure that the recreational use of natural heritage is actively included in the planning process (Payne and Graham 1984; Graham et al. 1988). Today the system is known as VAMP (Visitor Activity Management Programme), and it is particularly useful in evaluating the interpretation needs of heritage sites and for ensuring that all aspects of the trip cycle (awareness, pre-trip planning, en-route, reception/orientation, on-site activities, departure and reflection) are taken into account (see Chapter 21 on strategic planning). The components of the simplified framework shown in Figure 2.4 are not unusual. The distinguishing characteristics are its emphasis on the central role of synthesis and the constant need for close integration of input and feedback at every stage of planning. This means setting up systems that are receptive to such input and escaping the 'now we've had our participation process, we can get on with the job' syndrome.

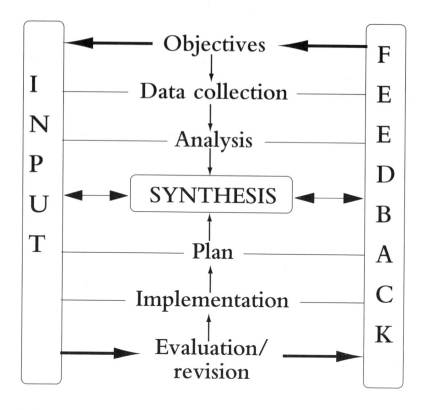

Figure 2.4: Visitor management framework to adapt to changing visitor demands

In order to achieve such a framework, the current and desired audience needs to defined, and this requires a visitor evaluation programme. Such a programme need not be a huge task. Frequently agencies have at their disposal a number of sound sources of information just waiting to be tapped. Not least of these are the individuals in charge of daily management. There is no substitute for experience—the trick with this resource is to treat it professionally. Information should be gathered through a pre-set series of questions, and answers should be recorded for later analysis. The principles and techniques of visitor evaluation are dealt with in more detail in Chapter 22.

The 'visitor market' for heritage sites is not restricted just to those who actually visit. Latent demand represents a strong component of community feelings towards these areas. Furthermore, there is a wider public interest to be considered in the way heritage values are managed. For example, often some of the strongest political support for the preservation of wilderness areas (e.g. the south-west of Tasmania and New Zealand, Kakadu, and the Daintree), comes from people who reside thousands of kilometres away and will never visit the area they feel for. Most people extrapolate their experiences of natural areas into their own general principles which they apply to heritage sites as a whole. To this end, visitor management must go beyond using interpretation with its own direct market, and into the world of public participation.

Public participation allows the community to contribute to the development of visitor management plans and often encourages both parties to be more constructive. The public participation process is not a matter of releasing draft management plans for people to comment on if they have the inclination and time to do so. It requires a clear mandate from management and a clear awareness of objectives. Some of the key factors in the process may include:

- Acknowledging that involving the public means you are asking them to perform a service for you;
- Specifically identifying what you need from the public, and what you can offer them in return;
- Identifying key groups and their relative importance to the management process;
- Developing individual strategies for each group that includes the opportunity for 'feedback on the feedback process'; and
- Implementing the strategies and commencing review.

Some of the techniques used in the public participation process include: media advertisements, hotlines, trained personnel for enquiries, public meetings (general and specific), focus group discussions, surveys, polling, and information sheets. Within each of these techniques should be specific messages targeted to specific audiences. The public participation programme represents the essence of an appropriate visitor management framework because it is the logical extension of a successful interpretation programme.

Conclusion

This chapter has only begun to address the complexities of heritage visitor management. It has suggested that many of the traditional visitor management techniques have met with only limited success because they have failed to understand the dynamic relationship between the visitor and the heritage resource. The use of interpretation can be a highly successful technique towards achieving effective visitor management, and several of the case studies in this book illustrate this. However, interpretation on its own will never be a complete success unless it is closely integrated with other dimensions of visitor management, such as marketing, evaluation, and strategic planning. Heritage is concerned with people's values. Therefore, unless we can manage people, we cannot manage heritage.

References

Alcock, D. 1991, 'Education and extension: management's best strategy', *Australian Parks and Recreation*, vol. 27, no. 1, pp. 15–17.
Barrow, G. 1991, 'Spreading the load', *Environmental Interpretation*, (October), pp. 14–16.
Beckmann, E. 1988, 'Interpretation in Australia—current status and future prospects', *Australian Parks and Recreation*, vol. 23, no. 6, pp. 6–14.
Beckmann, E. 1992, 'Educating the community in Australia', *Australian Parks and Recreation*, vol. 28, no. 2., p. 5.
Birrell, R. and Silverwood, R. 1981 'Social costs of environmental deterioration: the case of the Victorian coastline', in *Outdoor Recreation: Australian Perspectives*, ed. D. Mercer, Sorrett Publishing, Melbourne, pp. 118–24.
Field, G. 1989, 'Milyering visitor centre—a case study in interpretive design', *Australian Ranger Bulletin*, vol. 5, no. 3., pp. 16–19.
Forestry Commission 1992, Communication Strategy for Education and Visitor Services Branch, Unpublished report, Forestry Commission Tasmania, Hobart.
Fox, A. and Warnett, M. 1992, 'An interpretive haven in the desert—Yulara Information Centre', *Australian Parks and Recreation*, vol. 28, no. 2, pp. 19–20.
Gale, F. and Jacobs, J. 1987, *Tourists and the National Estate*, Australian Heritage Commission, Canberra.
Graham, R., Nilsen, P., and Payne, R. J. 1988, 'Visitor management in Canadian national parks', *Tourism Management*, vol. 9, no. 1, pp. 44–62.
Howes, M. 1989, 'Interpreting Point Nepean in Australian', *Ranger Bulletin*, vol. 5, no. 1., pp. 32–3.
Howroyd, L. 1991, *Interpretive Prospectus for Esperance Initiative*, Esperance Municipality, Geeveston.
McArthur, S. 1992a, Tasmania's Gordon River Cruises: wilderness experience or cattle drive? Unpublished report from visitor studies on Gordon River Cruise 1991/92, Questions and Answers, Hobart.
McArthur, S. 1992b, Arve Road Visitor Strategy, Unpublished report, Forestry Commission, Hobart.
McArthur, S. and Gardner, T. 1992, *Forestry Commission Visitor Manual*, Forestry Commission, Hobart.
MacGillivary, R. 1984, 'Visitor programs for all occasions', *Australian Ranger Bulletin*, vol. 2, no. 4, pp. 120–22.
McKechnie, P. 1984, 'National parks and tourism', *Australian Ranger Bulletin*, vol. 2, no. 4, pp. 109–10.
McMichael, D. F. 1972, 'Management of people and facilities for recreation', in *Management of Conservation Reserves*, Australian Conservation Foundation, Parkville, pp. 9–12.

O'Brien, C. 1985, Current status of interpretation in Australia, Paper presented at First World Congress on Heritage Interpretation and Presentation, Canada.

O'Laughlin, T. 1986, 'Communicating with the public. Minimal impact bushwalking: A way through the wilderness?', *Australian Ranger Bulletin*, vol. 4., no. 1., pp. 38–9.

O'Laughlin, T. 1989, 'Walk softly—but carry a big education campaign', *Australian Ranger Bulletin*, vol. 5, no. 3, pp. 4–7.

Payne, R. J. and Graham, R. 1984, 'Toward's an integrated approach to inventory, planning and management of parks and protected areas', *Park News*, vol. 20, no. 4, pp. 20–32.

Prior, M. 1992, 'Responding to threat: psychology and environmental issues', *Habitat Australia*, April, pp. 12–14.

Roggenbuck, J.W. 1987, 'Park interpretation as a visitor management strategy', in *Proceedings of the 60th National Conference of the Royal Australian Institute of Parks and Recreation*, Royal Australian Institute of Parks and Recreation, Canberra, pp. 24.1–24.14.

Saunders, R. 1992, 'Voices in the wilderness—interpreting Tasmania's World Heritage Area', *Australian Parks and Recreation*, vol. 28, no. 1, pp. 16–19.

Sharpe, G. W. 1982, 'An overview of interpretation', in *Interpreting the Environment*, ed. G.W. Sharpe, John Wiley, New York, pp. 3–26.

Stone, A., Hill, D., and Wrench, C. 1992, 'A rainforest in a town: rainforest interpretation centre, Orbost', *Australian Parks and Recreation*, vol. 28, no. 2., pp. 21–3.

Tatnell, A. 1991, Planning an interpretive exhibit: Namadgi National Park Visitor Centre, Unpublished paper for Namadgi National Park Visitor Centre, A.C.T. National Parks Service, Canberra.

Tilden, J. 1977, *Interpreting Our Heritage*, 3rd. ed., University of North Carolina Press, Chapel Hill.

Trapp, S., Gross, M., and Zimmerman, R. 1991, *Signs, Trails and Wayside Exhibits: Connecting People and Places*, University of Wisconsin Stevens Point Foundation Press, Stevens Point.

3

The Marketing of Heritage

C. Michael Hall and Simon McArthur

Marketing is a critical element in the management of heritage. However, to many people involved in heritage management, marketing is a dirty word, because marketing is often confused with selling. Within the tourism context, selling is typically focused on 'bums on seats', using 'hard sell' techniques. Marketing aims at providing customer satisfaction as the end result of a process which is focused on understanding the wants, needs, and expectations of customers. In heritage management our customers are our visitors.

To modify Kotler and Levy's (1969) definition of marketing in heritage management terms: marketing is that function of heritage management that can keep in touch with the site's visitors (consumers), read their needs and motivations, develop products that meet these needs, and build a communication programme which expresses the site's purpose and objectives. Marketing for non-profit service agencies, such as those which typically manage heritage sites, may be described as a set of voluntary activities aimed at achieving agency objectives by facilitating and expediting exchanges with target markets who have particular wants or who are seeking certain benefits (Howard and Crompton 1980). A heritage site offers something of value, such as the experience of rainforest, in exchange for something else of value, such as the visitor's money, time, opportunity costs, and/or support (Weiler 1990). Therefore, marketing involves the effective management of a heritage site's resources in a manner that is of mutual benefit to both the site and the visitor. Certainly selling and influencing will be large components of heritage marketing; but, properly seen, selling follows rather than precedes management's desire to create experiences (products) which satisfy its consumers. Market research must therefore be an integral part of heritage management and planning.

A successful heritage marketing plan will focus on the development of a marketing process which revolves around five stages:

- Internal and external situation analysis
  —Who are the visitors?
  —How is the heritage site presently meeting their needs and motivations?

- Setting marketing objectives and strategies
  —Where would the heritage site management like to be?
  —Which visitor segment do we want to serve?
- Marketing activities
  —What can management do to get there?
- Marketing management
  —How will management get there?
- Marketing evaluation
  —How will management know it has arrived at where it wanted to be?

Unfortunately, many heritage sites are managed without the benefit of a marketing plan or strategy. Nevertheless, there are numerous benefits to visitors, management, and the heritage resource, in the development of a market orientation in heritage management (Table 3.1).

Situation Analysis: Market Segmentation and Internal Analysis

Visitors to heritage sites may appear to managers to be a diverse market. However, no heritage site can be all things to all people. Therefore, it is essential that managers should incorporate an understanding of the behaviour of visitors into their marketing and promotional strategies. For example, in many instances interpretation has a tendency to aim for the 'average' visitor, since different people respond in different ways to different forms of interpretation. However, the result can often be bland, repetitive, or superficial, satisfying few people. Visitors are remarkably diverse and so we cannot expect a standard interpretive message to provide a satisfying experience. Therefore, an understanding of the market can enable managers to tie specific interpretive material to specific visitor groups. Heritage managers must identify market segments which are in tune with the nature and the degree of resilience of a site or, alternatively, the site should be developed in such a way as to meet the needs of the market (Prentice 1989). Therefore, heritage site managers need to conduct an internal situation analysis which identifies existing management objectives, market position, resource management issues, and interpretation. For example, an assessment of the tourism potential of the Australian Alps noted that several key issues would need to be addressed in any marketing strategy:

1. we are dealing with a finite and fragile resource;
2. this resource is unique in Australia in providing specific recreational opportunities not available elsewhere on the continent;
3. the economic and political climate is such that tourism is considered an asset to the community; and conservation is more of a luxury than it has been in the past;

Table 3.1: Benefits of a marketing-oriented approach in heritage management

Group	Benefits
Visitors	• Heritage management becomes customer-oriented, aimed at visitor satisfaction for selected visitor segments • Visitor travel and trip planning to heritage site is improved • Visitors are aware of the range of experiences available at a heritage site • Visitors can select a desired heritage experience • Visitors experience heritage themes in a manner consistent with their expectations, motivations and needs
Management	• Specifies and prioritizes financial and human resource management requirements and assists in determining how resources should be allocated • Provides justification for financial resources and their allocation • Identifies specific visitor information needs • Improves marketing of heritage sites • Encourages a strategic planning approach in management • Assists the development of appropriate interpretation strategies, concepts, themes, messages, and techniques
Resource	• Limits the likelihood of inappropriate on-site visitor activities • Limits the likelihood of inappropriate facilities and infrastructure • Minimizes visitor impact on heritage site • Encourages appropriate on-site behaviour

Source: After Canadian Parks Service 1988.

4. the resource of the Australian Alps is greater as a whole than as the sum of the parts, and hence greater opportunities are available for tourism and for conservation (Mackay and Virtanen 1992: 163).

A market segment is identifiable by grouping together all those potential participants and visitors with similar motivations and/or propensities towards particular types of heritage sites or site features and/or particular ways of promoting and supplying them. Segments may be identified along four main lines:

- *Geographical segmentation*: Managers should know how many people there are in the 'catchment region' of both existing and planned heritage sites and what distances people are away from sites in terms of different public and private modes of transport.
- *Demographic segmentation*: Heritage markets may be segmented along the lines of such variables as age, sex, occupation, level of income, ethnic association, religion, level of education, and class.
- *Psychographic segmentation*: Markets may be identified in terms of people's motivations and self-images.
- *Product/benefit segmentation*: Markets can be identified by the particular product characteristics they prefer, such as a particular type of cultural or heritage experience or visitor activity.

Nevertheless, however the market is segmented, it should be emphasized that an attractive market for a heritage site will be one in which:

- The market segment is of sufficient size to make the site viable;
- The market segment is compatible with the nature and characteristics of the heritage site;
- The market segment has the potential for growth or maintenance of visitation levels;
- The market segment is not 'taken' or 'owned' by existing sites; and
- The market segment has a relatively unsatisfied interest or motivation that the site can satisfy.

Marketing Objectives and Strategies

Planning is the most basic function in heritage management. 'To be effective, managers must know what they intend to accomplish' (Pearce and Robinson 1989: 163). Most fundamentally, managers must set and use objectives to guide the planning and development of heritage sites.

An objective is an intended end. It is a statement of where heritage managers want to go in satisfying visitor market segments. In the case of heritage visitation, a variety of measurable and non-measurable objectives can

be identified. Objectives can range from raising the profile of a site or increasing awareness of a particular endangered species to bringing income into a park or a local community. Clearly defined objectives can improve the management of sites in a number of ways:
- By providing guidance towards appropriate organizational behaviour;
- By reducing uncertainty and lack of direction in the development of an event;
- By motivating people to work toward specific ends;
- By providing a measure with which to gauge the success of site management; and
- By providing a focal point for co-ordination of the site organization.

The role of objective setting in the marketing of heritage visitation can be seen in the tourism marketing and promotion strategy for the Australian Alps. The strategy 'identifies promotional objectives and management objectives. These provide a focus for tourism management across the whole of the Alps, but do not supersede the role of the individual agencies' (Mackay and Virtanen 1992: 163). The mission statement recommended in the strategy was:

> The principal marketing goal of the national parks management is to encourage public understanding, appreciation and enjoyment of the natural and cultural heritage in ways which leave it unimpaired for future generations.

There are two principal purposes to the tourism marketing and promotion strategy:

> 1. to identify strategies to assist park management agencies in their planning and management of tourist services, programs and facilities
> 2. to increase public awareness of the [Australian Alps National Parks] as a desirable holiday and travel destination for both international and domestic markets (Mackay and Virtanen 1992: 163).

Objectives should be formulated through the involvement of all levels of site management with due consideration of the results of the situation analysis and, where appropriate, input from relevant stakeholder groups external to site management, e.g. friends of parks associations. Opportunities and issues arising from the situation analysis should be prioritized by the type of marketing action required, the decision level required to implement such actions, and the long- and short-term effects of actions on the heritage resource. This will enable managers to identify what can be achieved, within what time span, and what the costs and benefits of specific marketing actions will be.

Marketing Activities
Having established a set of heritage marketing objectives, it is essential to determine how these objectives can be achieved. This will require the determination of a set of marketing activities in a strategic plan which indicates how existing visitor services and products should be altered or maintained in order to supply the desired experiences to specific market segments.

The design of an appropriate marketing strategy for heritage sites consists of analysing market opportunities, identifying and targeting market segments, and developing an appropriate market mix for each segment. The traditional 'four Ps' of the marketing mix are: product/service characteristics; promotional decisions concerning channels and messages; prices to be charged for products/services; and places and methods of distribution of products/services. In addition to the traditional four Ps of marketing, tourism, analysts such as Morrison (1989: 37–8) suggest another four Ps that may be considered relevant to the marketing of heritage sites: people, programming, partnership, and packaging.

Target market identification involves three stages: first, a decision regarding how many market segments a site wishes to target given its management objectives and the nature of the heritage resource; second, the development of a market profile for each segment; third, the development of a marketing strategy that is appropriate to the profile of the selected segments. Heritage sites may select a 'concentrated' strategy by which they focus on a single segment. Indeed, this will be the likely strategy for many cultural heritage sites. However, national parks, for example, will have a range of environments and experiences available to visitors. Therefore, park managers may be able to target a number of visitor segments (a differentiated strategy), each with their own set of expectations, motivations, and desired experiences and activities. For example, in the Australian Alps marketing and promotion strategy discussed above, the identified target markets (Mackay and Virtanen 1992: 163) were:

- holiday markets;
- bushwalking and camping enthusiasts;
- specific recreation seekers;
- Australian Alps National Parks management and staff;
- tourism industry operatives and associations;
- residents.

Marketing Management

The development of marketing strategies with clearly identified target markets and product mix is not the end of the marketing process. Heritage managers also have to ensure that marketing strategies can be implemented and the target market reached through the development of appropriate management strategies and mechanisms. Therefore, managers have to ensure that human and financial resources are available for the development and promotion of marketing product. Staff may have to be hired and/or trained. Existing staff may be given new responsibilities, while new relationships may have to be formed with stakeholder groups such as tour operators. For every major management action or responsibility that is required to give effect to the marketing strategy, plans of action should be developed. The plan of action will outline the required action, tasks, responsibilities, timeline for implementation, cost estimates, and relative priority. Therefore, the plan of action becomes a valuable mechanism for ensuring not only the effectiveness of the marketing strategy but also that it is undertaken in as efficient a manner as possible (Canadian Parks Service 1988).

Marketing Evaluation

Evaluation is the often forgotten element in heritage management. However, it is crucial that heritage managers determine whether or not a marketing strategy was a success in the light of the initial marketing objectives. Indeed, it may well be the case that some goals were met while others remained unfulfilled. The success or otherwise of a marketing strategy will only remain hearsay and conjecture unless a formal evaluation occurs.

Evaluation should not be regarded as an afterthought. The costs of evaluation should be built into any project budget, as it should be regarded as a basic strategic management tool which assists heritage managers to find out where they have been, to decide where they want to go in future marketing strategies, and to identify how they are going to get there.

Conclusion

Marketing has for too long been regarded as an inappropriate activity for heritage managers to engage in. However, as Moulin (1990: 85) noted in the case of the packaging and marketing of cultural heritage resources: 'Marketing or commercialisation do not necessarily destroy the meaning of cultural products although they might change or add new meanings to old ones'. Instead, 'danger lies in the marketing and promoting of cultural resources without planning for their sustainability. Visitor numbers should not be the yardstick for successful tourism.'

As noted at the beginning of this chapter, marketing is not selling. Marketing is concerned with effective communication with visitors and with the development of heritage products, including value-added products such as interpretation, for a specific target market. Effective heritage management requires the matching of product with audience. Marketing is the tool which achieves that goal.

References

Canadian Parks Service 1988, *Getting Started: A Guide to Park Service Planning*, Canadian Parks Service, Ottawa.

Howard, D. R. and Crompton, J. L. 1980, *Financing, Managing and Marketing Recreation and Park Resources*, Wm. C. Brown, Dubuque.

Kotler, P. and Levy, S. J. 1969, 'Broadening the concept of marketing', *Journal of Marketing*, vol. 33, pp. 10–15.

Mackay, J. and Virtanen, S. 1992, 'Tourism and the Australian Alps', in *Heritage Management: Parks, Heritage and Tourism, Conference Proceedings*, Royal Australian Institute of Parks and Recreation, Hobart, pp. 159-65.

Morrison, A. M., 1989, *Hospitality and Travel Marketing*, Delmar Publishers, Albany.

Moulin, C. 1990, 'Packaging and marketing cultural heritage resources', *Historic Environment*, vol. 7, no. 3/4, pp. 82–5.

Pearce, J. A. and Robinson, R. B. Jr. 1989, *Management*, McGraw-Hill, New York.

Prentice, R. C., 1989, 'Visitors to heritage sites: a market segmentation by visitor characteristics', in *Heritage Sites: Strategies for Marketing and Development*, ed. D. T. Herbert, R. C. Prentice, and C. J. Thomas, Avebury, Aldershot, pp. 15–61.

Weiler, B. 1990, 'The international tourist and the coastal destination: matchmaking through marketing', in *Environmental Management of Tourism in Coastal Areas*, eds. I. Dutton and P. Saenger, University of New England—Northern Rivers, Lismore, pp. 72–83.

Natural Perspectives

Introduction

The four chapters in this section highlight major themes in natural heritage management in Australia and New Zealand. Mark (Chapter 4) discusses the value of environmental history as both a management tool and as a basis for interpretation in parks and reserves. While environmental histories are few and far between in Australia and New Zealand, Mark notes the issues encountered in the North American experience and the potential role of environmental history in parks.

Molloy (Chapter 5) provides a national perspective on the development of interpretive strategies in New Zealand, while McArthur (Chapter 6) highlights the role of interpretation at a regional and site level. Both chapters note the significance of using themes as a basis for interpretation and the importance of developing a clearly defined interpretation strategy to meet management objectives (see Chapter 2).

Chapter 7 by O'Loughlin provides a case study of a specific management issue in national areas, namely the minimization of visitor impacts. The chapter examines the success of the minimal impact bushwalking campaign in Tasmania and the difficulties that managers have had in conveying appropriate messages to walkers.

The four chapters indicate the role that values play not only in determining what needs to be interpreted but also what actually is heritage. Increasingly, natural heritage managers are having to consider the cultural dimensions of 'natural' heritage sites and their implications for management and interpretive strategies, a point which will be taken up in greater detail in the section on senses of place.

4

Writing Environmental and Park History

Stephen Mark

Introduction

History is storytelling. A historical narrative tries to find meaning in a sometimes chaotic chronological reality. As a result, the scholar makes value judgments in the story to give it unity. The aim is clarification of a past that would otherwise lack order and meaning (Cronan 1992: 1349).

There was a time when history largely focused on the élite. Scholars analysed the papers and other written records of 'great' people in the military, political, or social spheres to discern the stories most important in shaping the 'world'. This approach to history served to validate the social order through commemoration. As a method of recounting the past, however, traditional history has limited appeal because it is a fairly narrow band on the storytelling spectrum.

Sources for traditional history are largely found in the archival record. By contrast, social history's methods have significantly widened the scope of historical narrative over the past thirty years. In aiming at the wider community, it incorporates into the story non-traditional sources like oral history, aerial and historic photographs, material culture, census data, and weather records. These sources have helped to build a forum for the 'inarticulate', a term for subjects who have been left outside the realm of traditional history.

Widening the scope of historical narrative has frequently resulted in more complex interpretation of the past and should point the way to better heritage management. Parks continue to be a major focus of heritage management but have been a relatively quiet backwater in traditional historical narrative. The relatively new field of environmental history, however, can place them within the larger context of interaction between nature and culture. Environmental historians have tackled a wide range of subjects with an eagerness to embrace social history's techniques of assembling source material.

Environmental history is a field concerned with the role and place of nature in human life (Worster 1977). The first section of this chapter identifies potential sources useful in reconstructing historic environments. It is followed by an overview of methodological problems related to the question of change in nature. Cultural landscape reports and administrative history are subsequently outlined because they have specific application to park and heritage settings and can draw from the sources identified for environmental history.

Reconstructing Past Environments

Since historians have generally limited their study of the past to the period associated with a written record, 'prehistory' has been left to other disciplines like archaeology, geology, palaeontology, and physical geography. Where historians involved themselves with prehistory, it was usually to trace the development of scientific theory through traditional sources.

Travel accounts written during the period of initial European settlement have been used by scholars interested in historic environments. They hope to establish a presettlement landscape as a baseline from which to assess subsequent changes. One difficulty with using travel accounts, however, is that they are written in places where the journalist is not actually travelling; instead the writer is summarizing past events at a convenient place. Another problem is how to tie the usually limited detail (little of which could be used quantitatively) to specific localities. The paucity of locality information is often present in even the best accounts, such as those left by collectors of natural history specimens.

The only site-specific records available in many areas about presettlement landscapes are land survey notes. These have been helpful in establishing a historic condition of some forests, riparian habitats, and grasslands. Their reliability varies, however, because there can be limitations associated with insufficient description, bias in recording data, contract fraud, and land use prior to survey (Galatowitsch 1990).

Repeat photography is one way to document landscape change. The presence or absence of conspicuous natural features is the main component needed for use in an accompanying narrative (Rogers, Malde, and Turner 1984). An investigator will locate previous photo points and replicate them, sometimes in a series.

Cross-dating techniques are useful in assessing historic disturbances by fire or other agents. Fire histories are usually based on comparisons of fire scars with tree ages obtained from increment cores or wedges. Similarly, soils can be used to date historic disturbances from logging, grazing, or human occupation. Through soils referencing, the disturbed site is compared with the profiles of adjacent control areas. This method may help date removals of forest cover, the introduction of exotic flora, or occupation sequences at a historic site.

Despite the array of potential sources and techniques, scholars are still debating the validity of environmental history's method. Cronan (1990: 1123) asserts that good work in environmental history incorporates three levels of analysis. These are the dynamics of natural ecosystems in time (ecology), the political economies that people erect within these systems (economy), and the cognitive lenses through which people perceive those systems (the history of ideas). One major problem is that ecology is a very fractured discipline, where there is not a consensus for a definition of nature. The ecosystem model, with its emphasis on biodiversity and complexity, is not universally accepted because some ecologists argue that there are no systems in nature (Worster 1977).

Ecology has turned out to be a swamp for environmental historians, not the rock upon which they could build their stories. Its fractured condition has led critics to ask how, if past conditions are so difficult to quantify or assess, historians can identify change in nature. This is a crucial question because environmental historians generally need to identify change and its social and economic effects before proceeding with a discourse on ideas.

Cultural landscape documentation has some advantages over the broader sweep of historic environments because the question of nature's character is not so central. Adaptable to a park setting, its points of emphasis are design, material, change, function, and use. One of its main effects has been to broaden the focus of historic preservation beyond buildings to the associated landscape.

Cultural Landscapes

Broadly defined, a cultural landscape is any geographical area that has been impacted by human activity. The term can be applied to a park setting, and therefore managers and staff should take note of values associated with cultural landscapes in their planning and maintenance activities. Generally thought of as a landscape having historic value, it is classified as at least one of four types: historic sites, historic designed landscapes, historic vernacular landscapes, and ethnographic landscapes.

Historic sites are associated with what has traditionally been understood as important events, activities, or people. Existing features and conditions are interpreted primarily in terms of what happened there at significant times in the past. Managers of these areas would most likely aim to preserve a specific appearance because uncontrolled change might damage the landscape's commemorative value or integrity.

Historic designed landscapes are deliberate artistic creations traceable to recognized styles. They are valued because of their aesthetic qualities and are associated with significant people, trends, or events in landscape architecture. Management involves identifying the types and degrees of change that can occur without harming character-defining features. Examples of these types of landscapes range from formal gardens to naturalistic design (where the features are sublimated to the surroundings) in larger park areas.

Historic vernacular landscapes illustrate values and attitudes towards the land and reflect settlement patterns. Associated with a nation's demographic, social, and economic development, vernacular landscapes have more often been associated with rural areas. Physical change may be essential to the continuation of uses that made the landscape significant, so that it may be necessary to implement some form of landscape management.

Ethnographic landscapes are used by ethnic groups for traditional activities that range from subsistence hunting and gathering to religious ceremonies. These are landscapes seen through the eyes of one or several cultures. An understanding of an ethnic culture's folklore, as well as thorough linguistic and ethnographic research, are essential for an appropriate management response, especially in sensitive areas.

A cultural landscape report is an approach developed during the late 1980s for the documentation and evaluation of a landscape's character-defining features, materials, and qualities. Usually interdisciplinary in scope and character, it incorporates documentary materials familiar to the historian, an interpretation of the archaeological record for the site, and a thorough physical investigation of the extant landscape. The intent is to minimize the loss of character-defining features and materials, and therefore its key components are a physical history and site analysis upon which treatment and development alternatives are based.

A good research design and source material are clearly vital to the success of any project. The research design puts forth the investigator's goals, summarizes existing knowledge of the topic, identifies research questions, and discusses the methods to be employed. The physical extent of the study area should be delineated, as should the amount of information to be gathered. In providing for interdisciplinary study where appropriate, the research design will also clearly define the relationships among disciplines.

The narrative history should describe the historical context, key developments, design intent, primary design principles, patterns, features, and significant events or individuals associated with the landscape. Research into the archival record (such as manuscripts, diaries, correspondence, and newspaper articles) has been the traditional basis for this type of writing and generally should precede field work. Documentation of the historic period(s), however, would not be complete if oral history, maps, and photography (aerial, infrared, and historic) are ignored (Gilbert 1991: 5).

The primary purposes of field work are to identify resources, define their exact locations, determine their integrity and condition, and evaluate their significance. In documenting cultural landscapes, this may entail sampling, excavation, examination of architectural fabric, or ethnographic study. An inventory of character-defining features, along with documentation of existing conditions and related site information at the appropriate scale(s), follows the narrative history. As an example, a site-specific typology might be developed for designed landscapes located in a park setting. On a site characterized by naturalistic plantings and rustic structures, the typology could encompass circulation (roads, parking, walkways, trails), vegetation (planting concepts and materials), structures (buildings and rockwalls), small-scale features (signs, fountains, kerbing, benches), and include stonework, planting, and paving as construction technologies (Gilbert and Luxenberg 1990).

Recommendations in the cultural landscape report should be aimed at how best to perpetuate the integrity of character-defining features. If organized by topical areas, the recommendations can include a set of historic design principles based on precedents cited in the narrative history. These principles can be generalized, but will furnish direction for any new development in park settings; the aim is to ensure continuity between new and historic design, both in function and material. Planners, managers, and staff will also benefit from a history of the park as a park, especially if the story successfully synthesizes the available source material into key questions behind ongoing and recurring issues.

Administrative History

A park administrative history has been described as an explanation of the unit's conception and establishment, as well as its management to the present (Mackintosh 1991: 1). As a guide for more informed decision making, its main audience consists of park staff. The more valuable administrative histories will resist the temptation to indulge in an exhaustive account of a park area's early history, relating only what new staff would need to know as they assumed their duties.

An administrative history will usually include five types of information (Mackintosh 1991). The first is a brief descriptive statement about the park for initial context. It should incorporate the park's location, purpose, significance, and primary resources. Following the introductory statement is an account of area use and management prior to its acquisition by the present park authority. Important aspects should be further developed where they have bearing on current administration. A national park, for instance, might once have been managed by a local association, administered under another government department, or purchased from private holdings. An account of the movement to establish a park is one vital part of an administrative history, because it can provide critical insight about legislative intent. Emphasis in this section should be the motivations of key organizations and people promoting (as well as opposing) the park's establishment. Special care should be taken to note the positions taken by legislators and government agencies (including the park authority) on the proposal.

Once the conditions behind the park's establishment have been delineated, the bulk of an administrative history should be a synthesis of the major events and activities subsequently affecting the area's management. Broad topics such as land acquisition, facility development, planning, and resource management should be addressed separately as chapters or sections. The work's scope should be comprehensive, but there is no need to think of it as 'finished' once a volume is printed. Chapters can be added periodically to keep the administrative history updated, or when topics not covered in previous work need to be addressed (Mark 1991: 703).

Appendices containing copies of important legislation, agreements, and studies will increase an administrative history's value as a management reference. An index is important where the reader might have to do some cross-referencing, as in a chapter on scientific research.

Administrative histories can draw from a variety of sources, but the most basic are legislative documents (available in libraries) and the park authority's files. The latter may be in the park, central office, or the respective state or national archives. Collection of the needed government records or papers pertaining to important individuals or organizations can be a long and sometimes expensive process. Once assembled, however, this material can be an enormous asset to park management by forming the basis of a working archives or data base.

Oral history can supplement traditional sources, though it is no substitute for the written record. It plays an important role in illuminating themes not always apparent in the mass of documentation collected for an administrative history, and can sometimes lead the researcher to additional source material. Reliability is a great concern in oral history and can depend on the relationship between the interviewer and the narrator (Lang and Mercier 1991: 104).

If the narrator is a former or present park employee, the level of information provided may be contingent on the interviewer's knowledge of the bureaucratic terrain that shaped past administrative actions. Researchers sponsored by the park authority usually have an advantage in this regard, but they may not be able to analyse some problems critically enough because of their sensitivity to the agency. 'Outsiders' such as Runte (1990), Twight (1983) and Hall (1992) have succeeded in providing useful accounts about park concessions, inter-agency conflict and wilderness preservation, respectively—topics that would stifle the house historian. All too frequently, however, what could have been a solid contribution to park history is undone by an author simplifying the institutional context of parks in favour of a sweeping thesis of questionable validity (Schrepfer 1983; Chase 1986; Lien 1991).

Conclusion

A good history is a structured narrative without distortions told in an interesting manner. To the professional receptive to historical narrative, it is an analytical system for understanding time and space. That system is dependent upon chronology for its organization, something which has had no widespread appeal among the general public.

If historians want to impart concepts and analysis to the public, they must understand the citizen's interest in the past being largely social utility. A real or imagined association, whether through family genealogy or the conversion of historic structures to new uses, is how most people locate themselves or their community selectively in time and space. This reference point to history can be a sovereign territory from that of the professional's. For a bridge to be built from environmental and park history to public interpretation requires that people become an organizing device in historical narrative. There can be more than an abstract character, as public uses of oral history or so called 'living history' have at times demonstrated. If the message is clear and tailored to its audience, it should become easier to mass support for programs to protect the collective heritage.

References

Chase, A. 1986, *Playing God in Yellowstone: The Destruction of America's First National Park*, The Atlantic Monthly Press, Boston.
Cronan, W. 1990, 'Modes of prophecy and production: placing nature in history', *Journal of American History*, vol. 76, no. 4, pp. 1122–31.
Cronan, W. 1992, 'A place for stories: nature, history, and narrative', *Journal of American History*, vol. 78, no. 4, pp. 1347-1376.
Galatowitsch, S. M. 1990, 'Using the original land survey notes to reconstruct presettlement landscapes of the American west', *Great Basin Naturalist*, vol. 50, no. 2, pp. 181–91.
Gilbert, C. 1991, 'Tools of the trade: methodologies in landscape preservation', *The George Wright Forum*, vol. 8, no. 2, pp. 2–12.

Gilbert, C. and Luxenberg, G. 1990, *The Rustic Landscape of Rim Village, 1927–1941: Crater Lake National Park, Oregon*, U.S. Department of the Interior, National Park Service, Seattle.

Hall, C. M. 1992, *Wasteland to World Heritage: Preserving Australia's Wilderness*, Melbourne University Press, Carlton.

Lang, W. and Mercier, L. 1991, 'Testing for reliability in oral history', in *Interpreting Local Culture and History*, eds J. S. Sanford and J. Austin, University of Idaho Press, Moscow, pp. 103–18.

Lien, C. N. 1991, *Olympic Battleground: The Power Politics of Timber Preservation*, Sierra Club Books, San Francisco.

Mackintosh, B. 1991, *National Park Service Administrative History: A Guide*, U.S. Department of the Interior, National Park Service, Washington, D.C.

Mark, S. R. 1991, 'Administrative history', in *Planning and Development at Rim Village, Crater Lake National Park*, U.S. Department of the Interior, National Park Service, Seattle.

Rogers, G. F., Malde, H. E., and Turner, R. M. 1984, *Bibliography of Repeat Photography for Evaluating Landscape Change*, University of Utah Press, Salt Lake City.

Runte, A. 1990, *Yosemite: The Embattled Wilderness*, University of Nebraska Press, Lincoln.

Schrepfer, S. 1983, *The Fight to Save the Redwoods: A History of Environmental Reform, 1917–1978*, University of Wisconsin Press, Madison.

Twight, B. 1983, *Organizational Values and Political Power: The Forest Service Versus the Olympic National Park*, The Pennsylvania State University Press, University Park.

Worster, D. 1977, *Nature's Economy: A History of Ecological Ideas*, Cambridge University Press, Cambridge.

5

The Interpretation of New Zealand's Natural Heritage

Les Molloy

> New Zealand is as close as we will get to the opportunity to study life on another planet (Diamond 1990).

Natural Character of New Zealand

Any successful interpretation of the natural character of the diverse group of islands that make up New Zealand must engender both awe and a profound sense of loss. Awe at the ancient lineage of much of the biota, with its curious life-forms which evolved in long isolation from the major continental land masses and awe, too, at the dynamic geological and climatic environment of these islands, sitting astride a major active boundary of the earth's crustal plates and lying in the path of the 'West Wind drift' (Stevens, McGlone and McCullock 1988). The feeling of a profound sense of loss stems from the knowledge that so much of this priceless natural heritage has been destroyed in the 1200 years since humans arrived. This is particularly so for the last 150 years since the beginning of European settlement—a minuscule fragment of geological history compared with the preceding hundreds of millions of years of evolution in isolation (Enting and Molloy 1982).

But interpretation of the indigenous New Zealand landscape needs to probe beyond the products of long isolation. It has to reveal the dynamic setting that has resulted in diverse rock types and a very hilly and mountainous terrain; it has to invoke the powerful agents of environmental change, such as widespread volcanism, uplift, glaciation, changeable weather, and the occasional arrival of a new organism riding the West Wind. New Zealand has been described as having continental-scale diversity of landforms and ecosystems crammed into relatively small islands—islands that extend across twenty-three degrees of latitude, from the subtropical Kermadecs (29°S) to the sub-Antarctic Campbell Island (52°S), within a diverse marine environment, and with an intricate coastline of more than 15,000 km. Despite its rather strange biological cargo of mainly ancient origin, 'Moa's Ark', as David Bellamy has so aptly described it (Bellamy and Springett 1990), is really a very youthful-looking vessel in terms of its superstructure of constantly rejuvenated landforms and soils (Molloy 1988). This youthfulness is a further sharp contrast with New Zealand's nearest continental neighbour, Australia, with its old, dry, flat, worn-down landscape characterized by red soils and open eucalypt woodland. Furthermore, all these environmental differences have contributed to the cultural individuality of our two nations (Fleming 1976).

Natural Heritage Interpretation 1887–1987

1887 is a convenient starting point for looking at the origins of natural heritage interpretation in New Zealand; for 1887 was the year in which the first national park, Tongariro, was gifted to the nation by the Māori owners, the Ngāti Tuwharetoa tribe (Thom 1987). Over the following century, eleven more national parks (eventually covering an impressive nine per cent of the land area) were created, and became the 'crown jewels' of New Zealand's protected area system and inevitably the focal point for most natural heritage interpretation.

The tradition of guiding visitors to New Zealand's 'scenic wonderlands' and natural phenomena was already established by 1887. In that year local Māori began guiding in the Waitomo Caves; by the mid-1870s the Rotorua geothermal areas (again with Māori guides) were well-established tourist attractions, particularly the famed Pink and White Terraces (subsequently destroyed by the Mount Tarawera eruption of 1886) and the Whakarewarewa geyserfield. Cruising the fiords of Fiordland and the Whanganui River was becoming popular and the 'Finest Walk in the World', the Milford Track, was opened in 1890. The first of the great alpine guiding schools began with the opening of the first Hermitage hotel at Mt Cook in 1884, followed by tourist guiding on the Franz Josef and Fox Glaciers in Westland at the turn of the century. While this early tourism primarily catered for recreational pursuits, there are many accounts of the appreciation that visitors felt for the heritage knowledge and personal commitment of the guides—New Zealand's first professional 'interpreters' (Harper 1991).

It was not until 1952, and the passing of the first National Parks Act, that a co-ordinated system of national park management began to emerge within the Department of Land and Survey. By 1987, through a citizen board structure and a well-trained field staff, a national park system had evolved that was the envy of the rest of the world (Thom 1987). The organizational backbone for this management success were the park rangers, many of whom, as early as the late 1950s, had shown keen interest in developing specialist skills in the educational art of interpreting their park. The influence of the United States National Park Service in stimulating this interest in park interpretation was paramount. By the mid-1960s, most parks conducted a field interpretation programme over the summer months ('summer visitor programme') and park ranger staff were supplemented by science advisers from the Education Department and volunteer seasonal interpreters.

Throughout the 1970s the interpretive services within the national parks grew impressively; by 1976 all parks had a visitor centre (many with sophisticated audiovisual presentations); a specialist departmental interpretation design and production unit was set up in 1978; and the introduction of a five-year diploma in park ranger management at Lincoln College (now University) in 1976 allowed most park rangers (who could now re-enter Tertiary education through a 'block course' arrangement) wide exposure to contemporary interpretive philosophies and techniques. By 1980, it is probably fair to say that, given the relative youthfulness of its park system and the very limited budgets, New Zealand had a system of national park-based interpretation comparable to that of North America (Harper 1991).

Environmental Reorganization—1987

The year 1987 was a landmark in natural heritage management in New Zealand. Park circles celebrated the centennial of New Zealand's national park system in an atmosphere of uncertainty, as government instituted the most far-reaching departmental reorganization in New Zealand's history—within which the new Department of Conservation (DOC) attempted to come to grips with its extraordinarily wide mandate (Cahn and Cahn 1988). DOC had been given responsibility for much more than the national parks; it had also inherited the management responsibilities previously undertaken by a variety of public agencies for reserves, forest parks, and other state forests, wildlife and native plants (especially endangered species), historic places, foreshores, seabed, lakes and rivers, marine resources, and marine mammals. This translated into responsibility for managing thirty per cent of the area of the country. In addition, DOC was given the radical new role of advocating the protection of natural and historic resources anywhere in New Zealand, and in educating the public about the importance of conservation. Furthermore, all this was to be done within the spirit of the Treaty of Waitangi; in effect, by forging partnerships (including interpretation of heritage) with the iwi (tribes) of Aotearoa.

Review, Consolidation, and New Directions
The infrastructure of natural heritage interpretation inherited by DOC had become unco-ordinated and run-down with the uncertainties of the

governmental restructuring of the mid-1980s. In the short term, matters became even worse under DOC because of more urgent corporate priorities. These problems were recognized in a further restructuring during 1989, and a strategic departmental response (Molloy 1992a) was launched, including a comprehensive review of all interpretive facilities and services. The main weaknesses identified in this review are listed in Table 5.1, as well as the perceived strengths of natural heritage interpretation in New Zealand.

Many of the weaknesses listed in Table 5.1 are hardly surprising given the historically fragmented institutional framework and lack of co-ordination from a national perspective. The traditional 'crown jewels' emphasis left DOC with a dilemma: that of risking the alienation of park interest groups by redirecting advocacy and interpretive efforts to other conservation lands—such as wetlands, rivers and coastal/marine areas—many of them under much higher risk of environmental damage than the mountainous national parks.

Another important outcome of the review was an increased awareness that DOC, while still the dominant player as manager of New Zealand's publicly owned natural heritage, just did not have the skills and resources to interpret it all satisfactorily. There were now many other players in the heritage interpretation game—museums, zoos, ecotourism operators, university educators like the New Zealand Natural Heritage Foundation, and many iwi who were continuing to assert their rights under the Treaty of Waitangi and explore heritage management and interpretation partnerships with DOC. The remaining sections will highlight the strategic directions being followed by DOC and the implications for the interpretation of natural heritage from a Māori perspective.

A National Heritage Interpretation Plan

A cornerstone of DOC's new strategic approach is the first attempt to develop a truly national Heritage Interpretation Plan for all the publicly owned natural heritage of New Zealand. The objective of such a comprehensive plan is to tease out the different natural heritage themes and prioritize the opportunities for telling the stories relating to that theme, through an assessment of key sites, their accessibility to different audiences, and their suitability for different interpretive approaches.

What to interpret—and where?
A major advance is DOC's desire to take a more biogeographical approach to the interpretation of the New Zealand landscape, over time absorbing the former narrow or *ad hoc* emphasis upon individual species or non-representative sites. This more holistic approach has been assisted by the

Table 5.1: Natural heritage interpretation in New Zealand: assessment of weaknesses and strengths of DOC facilities (1990)

Weaknesses	Strengths
• Past concentration on 'Crown Jewels' (national parks) • Over-emphasis on past exploitation and settlement • Site- or species-specific (rarely dealing with processes, communities, or ecosystem representativeness) • Lack of heritage themes network • Minimal interpretation from Māori perspective • Avoidance of conflict (especially 'Conservation Battlegrounds') • Little recognition of 'agents of change' (including animal pests and weeds) • Minimal catering for children and non-English speakers (virtually no interactive displays) • Lack of on-site interpretation along Heritage Highways • Some repetitive displays in visitor centres • Little collaboration with interpreters in tourist industry	• DOC already located at most key heritage sites • Comprehensive conservation mandate of DOC allows co-ordination and integration of stories and consistent standards of design and production • New Zealand has outstanding natural heritage (including two World Heritage sites and many smaller sites of international significance) • Some heritage elements already well interpreted (but usually only in visitor centres) • Potential for partnerships with iwi in telling the story of Māori heritage • Increasing public interest and involvement in conservation and visitor demand for real 'conservation experiences' • Increasing economic importance of tourist industry and awakening interest of 'adventure tourism' sector in heritage interpretation • Summer visitor programmes of longstanding and good reputation

Heritage Management

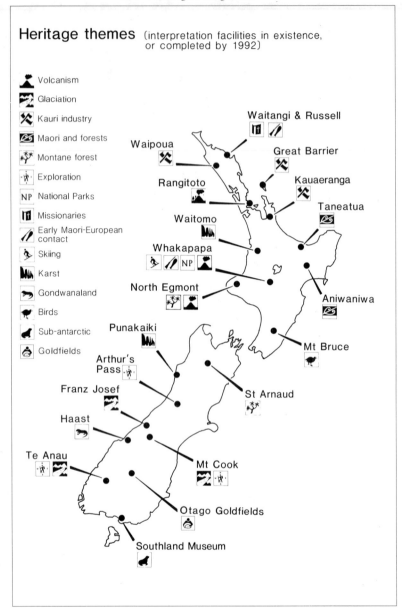

Figure 5.1: Heritage themes

adoption of a framework of 'ecological regions and districts' (McEwan 1987; Simpson, Evans, and Geden 1988) each varying in ecosystem character and distribution. Other resource inventories, compiled by DOC and scientific agency associates, will also be used in assessing sites of national (or international) and regional significance for features like landforms, geothermal, volcanic and karst phenomena, fossils, coastal resources, soils, and rare and endangered species.

However, successful interpretation needs much more than a framework of necessary scientific information. The plan will also need to incorporate comprehensive data on site potentials for development of environmentally acceptable visitor facilities (e.g. visitor centres, boardwalks, interpretive trails, observation hides, and on-site panels), on the proximity of sites to major tourist routes and the expected number of visitors, and on the opportunities provided for group environmental education and guided interpretation programmes, including joint ventures with iwi or sectors of the tourism industry.

Some natural heritage themes are currently told quite well in a number of DOC visitor centres and associated natural areas (Figure 5.1). These include: the Gondwanaland heritage story in the new South Westland World Heritage visitor centre at Haast, and at the associated interpretation sites along the heritage highway between the 'gateway' visitor centres at Franz Josef Glacier and Makarora (Bathgate 1990; Molloy 1992b); volcanology, and the relationship of the iwi with the volcanoes of New Zealand's other World Heritage site—Tongariro National Park—at Whakapapa on Mt Ruapehu; the glacial imprint of the Ice Ages at Franz Josef Glacier; and the story of limestone (karst) landscapes at Waitomo and at Punakaiki in Paparoa National Park. But there are many natural heritage themes whose stories are not told adequately—either on-site, or in visitor centre displays, audiovisuals, publications, or through visitor programmes. Some of these are listed in Table 5.2, and they present a real challenge for DOC and its interpretation associates over the next decade.

How to interpret most effectively?
There is far less agreement on how New Zealand's national heritage can be most effectively interpreted. The traditional approach has reflected the dominance of the central government management agencies—static displays and audiovisuals (usually in park visitor centres), supplemented by live interpretation on summer visitor programmes (usually of the order of 1000 events at sixty different locations over the months of December and January). In addition, there is no strong tradition of role playing or 'campfire-storytelling' so popular in North American programmes.

Participants in summer visitor programmes have consistently expressed a high degree of satisfaction at their value for money, but it has proved difficult to make an objective assessment of the quality of the nature interpretation provided. This is the universal challenge for interpretation administrators—how to make the creations from this educational art more vibrant, more moving, and the recipients more aware (and ultimately more supportive) of nature conservation; this at a time when most of these interpretive staff are part-timers not specialists, often lacking experience in the performing arts, sometimes lacking field knowledge, and always having only a sketchy outline of the receptivity of their audiences. However, to try and improve this situation, real efforts are being made by both museum and DOC interpreters to incorporate more understanding of the learning process into interpretive programmes (Cassels 1992).

Māori Perspectives on Natural Heritage Interpretation
The interpretation of the natural heritage of Aotearoa from a Māori perspective is one of the greatest communication challenges facing DOC and the rest of New Zealand's tourist industry. Just as New Zealand's geological history is being reinterpreted in the light of recent scientific knowledge, so too is our colonial history having to be rewritten with a new sensitivity towards the claims of the Māori people for a redressing of past injustices in terms of their rights under the Treaty of Waitangi. More New Zealanders are coming to appreciate the acute sense of loss felt by the Māori at the alienation of their traditional mana whenua, the 'Lands and Estates, Forests, Fisheries and other properties' guaranteed to them by Article 2 of the Treaty.

It is the spiritual dimension of this relationship of the Māori with their traditional natural resources which makes any attempt by an outsider to interpret it fraught with cultural pitfalls. Knowledge of the natural world was deemed by traditional Māori to be taonga—a treasure entrusted to only a select few, passed on orally from generation to generation to those worthy enough to have this 'food basket of knowledge' opened to them. This reverence for the natural world reflects the belief in a common ancestor for mankind, trees and birds; that forests, rivers and the sea have, like humans, their own life force or 'mauri' which had to be acknowledged. Furthermore, the shadows of tipuna (ancestors) were across all the land, some places (urupa) being particularly sacred (tapu). To interpret such places, and the exploits of tipuna whose memory is associated with them, in the conventional European manner could border on the sacrilegious; even oral interpretation could be deemed an unworthy action. As one Māori interpreter has stated:

When Māori visit a sacred place, they go to feel rather than to see. Interpretation panels are an encumbrance, there for the use of the ignorant, those who cannot see with their minds nor feel with their hearts.

Many Māori have expressed the hurt that they feel at the diminution of the mauri of taonga locked away in sterile museum cases, their life force slowly ebbing away through the absence of affirmation through the nurturing of proper use; so, too, much hurt has probably been unwittingly caused through insensitive interpretation, by Pākehā, of the natural world of the Māori. A few attempts to interpret this world appropriately from a Māori perspective have been made on conservation lands; the forests of Te Urewera National Park were interpreted in Taneatua and Aniwaniwa visitor centres only after consultation with the Tūhoe and Kahungungu iwi; likewise, Tuwharetoa and Atihaunui a Paparangi have become full partners in telling the story of the volcanoes of Tongariro National Park, and the gift to the nation of the park itself.

The Future

In the prevailing economic climate of static, or diminishing, financial and staff resources, the dilemma facing heritage administrators is: what can we sacrifice in order to free up resources to redirect or focus on the very best natural heritage interpretation opportunities? For every expansion of the visitor facilities network means a greater maintenance burden, and this is already a very comprehensive infrastructure for DOC to manage: over 40 park visitor centres, 7500 km of tracks, almost 1000 huts and probably over 1000 outdoor interpretive displays or panels. Moreover a number of important natural heritage elements are in urgent need of interpretation from a national perspective, particularly coastal, marine, lowland podocarp forest, kauri forest and tussock grassland ecosystems, as well as the impact of introduced animals and plants upon our indigenous vegetation and wildlife (Table 5.2). The appropriate locations and interpretive media for these missing natural heritage themes will be a major outcome of DOC's heritage interpretation planning.

There are two other initiatives which imply a high degree of uncertainty for future natural heritage interpretation in New Zealand: the rapid growth in tourists and the shape of partnerships with iwi as Treaty of Waitangi claims are settled.

The New Zealand Tourism Board has set itself the ambitious target of tripling the current annual number of overseas visitors to three million by the year 2000. We know that 55 per cent of all current tourists visit a national park during their stay; it is inconceivable with such an increase in visitor

Table 5.2 : Natural heritage elements not yet interpreted adequately

- Coastal ecosystems
- Marine ecosystems
- Geothermal areas
- Podocarp forests (North Island)
- Rivers and fresh water wetlands
- Tussock grasslands
- Rare and endangered species
- Kauri forests of Northland
- Alpine plants
- Wild introduced animals and plants (and their influence on indigenous biota)
- Major conservation battlegrounds (e.g. Manapouri, Pureora, Whirinaki, Maruia)

numbers that current standards of estate management will be able to be maintained without a significant increase in resourcing.

Currently, there is very little interpretive treatment of everyday Māori use of natural resources, such as the use of the forests or the gathering of kaimoana from the sea; most of what there is deals with the early contact with Europeans (especially missionaries and traders), or the painful events of history, including the dispossession of their lands and forests. As part of DOC's obligation in the spirit of the Treaty of Waitangi, it is intended that local iwi will be involved in all new interpretation centres. Indeed, such involvement is part of the treaty claims of the Ngāi Tahu iwi whose land claims extend across most of the South Island.

In summary, then, the departmental response will have to address all the above issues. Consequently, future natural heritage interpretation on the conservation estate is likely to include: repositioning of visitor centres, better matching of visitor character with interpretive media, a requirement for more tourist concessionaires to provide heritage interpretation, more cost recovery for visitor services (especially DOC summer visitor programmes), more reliance on volunteers, and more joint ventures with district information centres and iwi.

References

Bathgate, J. 1990, *Interpretation Strategy: South Westland*, Department of Conservation, Hokitika.

Bellamy, D. and Springett, B. 1990, *Moa's Ark: The Voyage of New Zealand*, Viking, Auckland.

Cahn, P. and Cahn, R. 1988, 'New Zealand Parks', *National Parks*, September–October, pp. 26–31.

Cassels, R. 1992: 'Mind, heart and soul: towards better learning in museums and heritage parks'. Paper presented to Australian Heritage Parks Conference, Warrnambool, Victoria.

Diamond, J.M. 1990, 'New Zealand as an archipelago: an international perspective', in *Ecological Restoration of New Zealand Islands*, eds. D. R. Towns, C. H. Daugherty, and I. A. E. Atkinson, Conservation Sciences Publication No. 2. Department of Conservation, Wellington.

Enting, B. and Molloy, L. 1982, *The Ancient Islands: New Zealand's Natural Environments*, Port Nicholson Press, Wellington.

Fleming, C. A. 1976, 'The biogeographical basis of national cultures', *Proceedings of the Linnean Society of New South Wales*, vol. 101, no. 4, pp. 218–36.

Harper, R. K. 1991, Interpretation in the national parks of New Zealand, unpublished M.Appl.Sci. thesis, Lincoln University.

McEwan, M. W. (ed) 1987, *Ecological Regions and Districts of New Zealand*, 3rd rev. ed, Department of Conservation, Wellington.

Molloy, L. 1988, *Soils in the New Zealand Landscape: The Living Mantle*, Mallinson Rendel and New Zealand Society of Soil Science, Wellington.

Molloy, L. 1992a, 'Environmental education and Interpretation: a New Zealand perspective', in *The Way Forward: Proceedings of the New Zealand Natural Heritage Foundation International Conference on Environmental Education*, eds. D. Springett and C. M. Hall, New Zealand Natural Heritage Foundation, Palmerston North.

Molloy, L. F. 1992b, 'Te Wahipounamu: an approach to the interpretation of World Heritage Wilderness' in *Joining Hands for Quality Tourism: Interpretation, Preservation and the Travel Industry: Proceedings of the Third Global Congress of Heritage Interpretation International*, eds. R. S. Tabata, J. Yamashiro, and G. Cherem, University of Hawaii Sea Grant Extension Service, Honolulu, Hawaii.

Simpson, P., Evans, B., and Geden, B. 1988, 'Ecological districts as a framework for landscape interpretation in New Zealand', *Earth-Science Reviews*, vol. 25, pp. 509–19.

Stevens, G., McGlone, M., and McCullock, B. 1988, *Prehistoric New Zealand*, Heinemann-Reed, Auckland.

Thom, D. 1987, *Heritage: The Parks of the People*, Lansdowne Press, Auckland.

6

Theme-based Interpretation
Taking Rainforest to the People

Simon McArthur

Introduction

This chapter outlines the approach and products resulting from a project designed to promote the conservation of Tasmanian rainforest. The project applies the interpretive principles of Tilden (1977) and uses a variety of innovative visitor management and interpretive techniques to provide stimulating and educational experiences. It has been used as a benchmark by many visiting managers and interpreters, and has been nominated and awarded several design, educational, and tourism awards. Perhaps more importantly, the project represents a strong emphasis on planning and illustrates the use of a number of management techniques, including a conceptual framework, selection criteria for interpretive sites, and evaluation methods for product improvement.

Conserving Tasmania's Rainforest

The controversies over the preservation of Tasmania's natural heritage since the mid-1960s have highlighted the significance of effective environmental education (Hall 1992). The growing reliance upon interpretation as a key educational technique has meant that it has had to develop and mature at a rapid rate. Nowhere is this more apparent than recent interpretive developments in Tasmania's forests (McArthur & Gardner 1992).

It was only a few years ago that the world's rainforests were identified as a resource requiring special attention. The 'apple isle' contains the largest continuous tract of cool temperate rainforest in the world—some ten per cent of the State's area. Most of these forests are preserved and a considerable amount are in World Heritage national parks. Continuing political support for these areas requires public support, which is based on understanding, which, in turn, relies on effective interpretation. However, there is a poor level of understanding about Tasmania's forests and their management, and in some sectors, a lack of interest (McArthur and Gardner 1992).

In 1988 the Tasmanian component of an Australian National Rainforest Conservation Program (ANRCP) was established to run for four years. Under the general guise of rainforest conservation, strategies were developed that sought to provide a greater understanding of rainforest at scientific, managerial, and general public levels (McArthur 1990; 1991a, b).

Planning for Rainforest Interpretation

In response to the ANRCP an interpretation project was devised to promote the conservation of Tasmania's rainforests by:
- Providing an enjoyable and satisfying rainforest experience where education is complemented by recreation;
- Assisting the general community to develop a keener awareness, appreciation, and understanding of Tasmanian rainforest;
- Educating and informing a wide range of persons of the need to conserve Tasmanian rainforest; and
- Stimulating ongoing interest and actions that will facilitate an improved ability to conserve rainforest.

The project ran for eighteen months, with the first four being devoted to planning. This period culminated in a detailed strategy report which:
1. Provided a basic grounding of interpretation as it would relate to the project.
2. Identified a set of key rainforest concepts that would ensure that the breadth of content available was adequately dealt with.
3. Assessed and created a wide range of interpretive locations and media for use within the project. These media were to:
   —be individually distinctive yet complementary;
   —be incorporated within a person's general understanding of rainforest;
   —encourage visitation/usage of alternative sites/media; and
   —complement contemporary scientific information.

Short, positive statements about rainforest were compiled by the interpreter using various reference materials. These statements were then referred to specialists for comment and support. Once they were accepted, the interpretive content of the project was settled. The concepts contributed towards a strategic approach to interpretive planning by:
- Forming the basis to select the interpretive medium, location, and technique;
- Avoiding unplanned duplication of messages; and

Table 6.1: Concepts and messages to interpret Tasmanian rainforest

Concepts	Layered messages
Rainforest is a very old community	• Rainforest can tell us many things about the past. • Rainforest relicts remind us that the world is changing; they are a time capsule. • Rainforest can tell us about the earth's climate, even before people lived here. • Where does rainforest come from? What was Gondwana, and what did it look like? What happened to it and why? • Relationship between rainforest and Eucalpyts, geological time/lifespan. • If rainforest is so old, and used to be so widespread, why is there so little left?
Tasmania has a very different type of rainforest from that in most parts of the world	• Cool temperate rainforest: how is it different from tropical and subtropical forms? • Reasons for cool temperate rainforest distribution.
Rainforest creates its own environment	• It is complex, and provides many 'environments within environments'. • Plant and animal adaptations to cool, dark, wet conditions • Some rainforest species help each other to live. • It is a water reservoir. • Rainforest requires a lot of water to survive. • It can maintain itself without many other influences. • Recovery following disturbance (succession). • Rainforest recycles much of its waste.
Tasmania has some very special types of rainforest	• Types can be classified by their plant species. • Rainforests have a distinct structure. • Altitudinal changes re species structure and size.
Rainforests are highly diverse	• Many plant and animal groups contain species still unknown to us [invertebrates and fungi]. • Some types of cool temperate rainforests [and their plants] are only found in Tasmania.
Threats to rainforest are mostly caused by humans	• Rainforests have always received natural threats. • Lightning/fire, disease, drought, climatic change. • Today there are new threats that rainforests must attempt to cope with: agriculture; logging; pest species; and recreation. • New threats increase older natural effects. • Rainforests cannot cope with the extra pressure and regularity of threats that we induce.
How we can help rainforest to survive	• One of rainforest's values is simply being there. • Rainforest prefers to be left alone.

- Serving as a defensive back-up to critics during the project's implementation.

The concepts are by no means perfect and the messages lack structure (Table 6.1). Nevertheless, they were considered innovative at the time, and they certainly assisted in the line of defence against interfering specialists.

In essence, the project can be divided into two main components: on-site and off-site. On-site refers to the development of four walks and a viewing platform located in various rainforest settings. Off-site refers to a mobile display and several publications that included a site promotional brochure, interpretive poster and children's book. The focus of the present chapter is on the on-site component of the interpretive programme.

Table 6.2: Part of a Goals Achievement Matrix used in the selection of rainforest sites for interpretation development

SELECTION CRITERIA	OBJECT INDEX	Weld borough Pass	Sandspit River
Rainforest exists and is largely undisturbed	5	3/15	3/15
Easy access to most vehicles all year round	5	3/15	1.5/7.5
Site is close to a significant population	2	3/6	2/4
Site is guaranteed of good visitation levels	5	3/15	2/10
Tourist sites exist in close proximity	3	3/9	2.5/7.5
Other interpretation exists in close proximity	2	0/0	0/0
Site is located on through road	3	3/9	1/2
Site offers varying time period for visit	3	1/3	3/9
Site already contains facilities	4	1/4	3/12
Facilities are adequate and well maintained	4	1/4	3/12
Construction constraints minimal	4	3/12	0/0
Ongoing maintenance can be minimized	4	3/12	1/4
District management have resources and attitude	4	2.5/10	3/12
Interpretation suitable and integrated with other sites	4	3/12	3/12
Major theme/concept available for interpretation	5	3/15	3/15
Threat/disturbance available for conservation stress	2	3/6	2/4
Promotional possibility for ongoing visitation	4	3/12	3/12
TOTAL SCORE		159	138
RANKING		1	2

N.B. Each site receives an initial score out of three (measuring how it satisfies the criterion), which is multiplied by a score out of five (the weighting for the importance of the criterion). The addition of the seventeen criteria scores yields a total score and a ranking.

Site-based Interpretation

Owing to some thirty sites being offered for development, the project developed a detailed set of selection criteria which were used to assess the appropriateness of each setting. A Goals Achievement Matrix was used to value the selection criteria for each of the potential sites. Table 6.2 illustrates a portion of the matrix for two of the potential interpretive sites.

Themes (characteristics drawn from the region's natural and cultural heritage) from each site were blended with the concepts and represented further in the design of facilities such as tracks and signage. The sites are predominantly walks which average around twenty minutes. They have been carefully designed to be as distinctive as possible in both design and construction techniques, materials ranging from gravel to treeferns to boardwalk. This project approached the design of recreation and interpretive facilities as a single unit. An example of this was the integration of each walk's location, grade and surface with the location, content and style of each interpretive sign.

We need to make interpretation credible yet appealing for our target audience. A format or tone that sounds as if it is coming from the mouth of management is unlikely to be successful. Therefore, the signs use a variety of cartoon characters, comic strips and games to grab and hold attention so that education is combined with an enjoyable experience. Two of the sites feature talking trees and another an alien's first visit to rainforest. Interpretation officers sometimes are accused of 'anthropomorphizing', meaning that they treat rainforest plants and animals as though they were human. This is a deliberate course of action that enables people to relate their own feelings to that which the rainforest might be experiencing. We educate our children in this way, and occasionally apply it to our pets and gardens, with even an old salad being referred to as 'sad'.

Each of the site's signs is layered in its presentation of information, to account for repeat visitors. As an example, one has a fly buzzing around the corner of each sign (eventually the fly is caught in a spider web and tied up by its captor). This is not something the visitor may notice first time round, but that is the key, as there is something for the next visit. Layering also encourages people to look carefully at their environment for what is going on behind the scenes.

Most of the sites do not use species tags, which the author feels have been done to death. However, people still like to know what plants they are looking at. Therefore, at some sites species tags were incorporated within a theme, making them more interesting for the visitor.

At one site, the combination of miserable weather, an audience with little time, high conservation values, and the likelihood of timber poaching (via increased access) favoured the use of a visitor platform rather than a walk. A platform does not provide a very active experience. Instead, the interpretive solution was through positive association. Instead of disguising the constraints, use them to your advantage. Hence, the interpretation was designed around a corny current affairs programme starring 'Rick Rainforest'. Through a more active delivery, the rainforest can come alive, the platform can become a stage, and the visitors an audience. Now the visitors can feel more involved, they are not even watching it on television, they are with Rick live, so they may feel special. This is another example of blending the site and interpretation to provide an integrated quality experience.

With the exception of environmental groups, the use of catch-phrases in environmental education is sadly underplayed. This project not only repeatedly used the phrase 'Retain our rainforest, a refuge, a retreat', but created minor modifications in the wording to stimulate the more perceptive visitors who have had other Tasmanian rainforest interpretation experiences. For instance, at a site containing relict rainforest, the phrase is modified to 'Retain our relicts, a refuge, a retreat'.

Interpreters of heritage sites have the opportunity, which is too little taken advantage of, to promote other destinations and experiences to their 'captive audiences'. There is a need for this kind of promotion, if only in recognition of Clawson and Knetsch's (1966) five-phase experience model. Accordingly, the last sign of each site not only suggests other places to visit and learn about rainforest, but mentions the site booklet as a means of gaining more information. In this manner we link the positive effects gained from a heritage experience, into the return home phase and the planning process for a future experience.

The Creepy Crawly Nature Trail

Rather than provide a detailed account of each site, it seems more useful to cover one in detail—the Creepy Crawly Nature Trail. The Creepy Crawly walk is located in the Southwest National Park, a World Heritage Area. It has received considerable research into the world of invertebrates, and continues to be considered a useful scientific site.

The Tasmanian southwest has long been a magnet for bushwalkers. This group has the greatest access to the region, owing to the area's size and management focus as a wilderness area. Although the Southwest National Park still has limited access and facilities, the publicity and access gained as a result of the damming of Lake Pedder increased numbers and changed the visitor profile (Department of Lands, Parks and Wildlife 1989). While Lake

Pedder probably remains the initial major drawcard for many visitors, it is the mountainous scenery and dramatic changes in vegetation which sustains this interest. Today the majority of visitors to the region are touring 'day trippers' who mainly stay on sealed roads and prefer a short 'sample' of the southwest. Visitation to the area primarily occurs during short intense periods of the year when weather is most favourable. Disposable time is limited and short, so that intense experiences are favoured. Using tourism research (Tourism Tasmania 1991) the three prescribed target groups for the region were noted as societally conscious, conservatives, and young actives. This reflected a desire for stimulating involvement at a physical and cognitive level, suggesting that novelty would attract visitation and stimulate attention.

The walk had existed for some years as a track cut by Hydro Electric surveyors, and had 'evolved' into an interpretive walk that identified various flora and fauna along the way. The combination of weak soils, heavy rainfall and meandering walkers had combined to provide significant impact (compaction of soil, damaged foliage, and light erosion) which also lowered the quality of the experience for many visitors. This is typical of many walks in the region, and today reflects one of the principal human impacts it receives. Upgrading of the walk was preferable to the development of a new one.

Using the research from the site, the theme became 'rainforest invertebrates'. The central concept was that a rainforest food web is intricately balanced and easily upset. The layering of messages allowed a number of concepts from the strategy to be used to drive the theme (Table 6.3). The specific topics covered within the interpretation were:

- The role and close association of rainforest invertebrates via a series of 'role players' within a structured community foodweb;
- The variation in rainforest types that exist on-site (callidendrous, thamnic, and implicate), as a variety of habitats available to rainforest animals; and
- The destruction of habitat by walkers as one of the unpublicized threats to rainforest animals.

The technique selected was a murder mystery, done to attract high levels of visitor involvement. This fits into real life and death struggles that actually occur in rainforest each day. The technique and what is required of the visitor were introduced on the first sign, as was done at other sites using unusual techniques. Following this introduction, the visitor is introduced to a detective, who takes them along the walk and through the murder case. The detective next describes the victim, a Macleay's swallowtail butterfly, selected to heighten a sense of empathy. Following this are six stops known as the log, litter, mossy, open, trunk, and branch neighbourhoods (habitats). Each neighbourhood is represented by three suspects, which are invertebrates

Table 6.3: Concepts and messages to interpret Creepy Crawly Nature Trail

Concepts	Layered messages
Rainforest creates its own environment	• It is complex, and provides many 'environments within environments': —Plants and animals adapt to cool, dark, wet conditions. —Some rainforest species help each other to live. • It can maintain itself without many other influences: —Rainforest recycles much of its waste.
Tasmania has some very special types of rainforest	• Rainforests have a distinct structure.
Rainforests are highly diverse	• Many plant and animal groups contain species still unknown to us e.g. invertebrates. • Some types of cool temperate rainforests [and their plants] are only found in Tasmania.
Threats to rainforest are mostly caused by humans	• Today there are new threats that rainforests must attempt to cope with: agriculture; logging; pest species; and recreation. • New threats increase older natural effects. • Rainforests cannot cope with the extra pressure and regularity of threats that we induce.

known to reside within that habitat. Two of the three suspects are eliminated each time, leaving the final six to be presented at the disturbed neighbourhood, a seriously degraded section of the old trail. Here the question is posed: who is the guilty one? Shortly afterward, the answer is revealed via a large pair of hiking boot soles (printed in red). Underneath is part of swallowtail, and to enhance the impact, the remaining suspects appear to be fleeing themselves. Each of these signs provides a clue via a single word that combined adds up to a sentence that reads 'Look carefully, you might just be the murderer'. An example of one of the interpretive signs is shown in Plate 6.1. Some twelve signs (approximately 850 by 500 cm) were used to convey this interpretation. To increase the dynamic nature of the signs, a deep red was used to highlight certain facets within the artwork, e.g. the stamp 'SUSPECTS'.

Plate 6.1: Interpretive sign from the Creepy Crawly Nature Trail

The Facility

The site's high conservation and scientific values tended to restrict the location and form of visitor services, and actual research sites were avoided. The track was expanded to accommodate several more areas required for the interpretation, and though only 350 m long, its design provides a much longer and more intense experience than one would expect. No branches were removed to build the walkway and visitors must step over logs and duck under branches (see Plate 6.2). The track was purposely built to twist and turn like an invertebrate's trail, enhancing the interpretation considerably. In addition, the structure actually narrows and twists more as the visitor enters denser, tangled forest. The selection of materials for construction had to balance conservation values against aesthetics, cost, and the need for habitats to interpret. The result was different materials responding to the specific conservation value of the area (from a gravel track in the lower value areas, to treated pine or hardwood boardwalk in the moderate areas). In the area representing the highest values, recycled plastic posts were used to support the boardwalk. This fairly new building material is environmentally inert, rot proof, and nearly as easy to work with as wood. Even the upright posts supporting the interpretive signs varied from treated pine to hardwood, depending upon the value of the heritage.

Plate 6.2: Innovative design for boardwalk

Meandering off the pathway by visitors is rare, evidenced by almost negligible impact. Even in the more attractive and enticing areas, visitors appear content with the proximity and angles provided for viewing and photography. Rehabilitation of the old track is well under way. Just eighteen months after the completion of the walk, leaf litter has returned to the original level and several seedlings have sprouted. In some areas the old track is difficult to identify.

The cost of building a walk like the Creepy Crawly Trail is comparatively high. The structure has an almost 'over the top' feel to it, and this is deliberate. Tourism is not an environmental saviour to contrast against other competing uses. People must understand that it too requires extensive resources and community commitment to be sustainable. This walk is an example of integrating every aspect of the visitor experience, with interpretation the focus of visitor management.

Evaluation of Interpretive Sites

Several of these interpretive forest walks were included in a statewide visitor evaluation programme (McArthur and Gardner 1992) and results indicate a general level of success in attracting and holding attention. Timing tests and visitor surveys confirmed that illustrations were always more popular than text and frequently were the sole means for attracting attention and maintaining a conscious memory of the message being portrayed. In this manner, illustrations which communicated the essence of the message in a simplified, enjoyable and symbolic manner were by far the most successful.

Other direct visitor feedback confirmed that the integration of walk and interpretation into one experience paid big dividends. The interpretive experiences produced under this project confirmed that visitors quickly become familiar with a set pattern that links trail surface with the presence of interpretive signage, and can subconsciously prepare themselves for the next sign upon receiving a distinctive change (say from gravel to boardwalk). Visitor numbers have grown annually at most sites by fifty per cent, though the combination of hardening and sensitive design have kept the experience well within the desired limits.

Not all the evaluation was positive, but it was constructive. Most of the problems were detected at Sandspit, the first site to be produced. There were too many signs here (11) and several of these had excessive amounts of text (over 150 words) to keep visitor attention. The last form of evaluation came from 'informal feedback' by way of a small addition to the statement on the first sign: 'For millions of years, rainforests have had to cope with the effects of climate and fire *and woodchipping*'. At least it was neatly scratched in and avoided the usual four-letter words!

Conclusion

Growing access and subsequent use of our natural areas requires a more strategic and up-to-date approach to visitor management and, in particular, an improved understanding of the interactions between people and the environment. Through innovative approaches, interpreters must strive to challenge their audience, their managers, and themselves.

References

Clawson, M. and Knetsch, J. L. 1966, *Economics of Outdoor Recreation*, Johns Hopkins, Baltimore.

Department of Lands, Parks and Wildlife 1989, *Recreation Development Plan Strathgordon-Scotts Peak Area*, Draft report, Department of Lands, Parks and Wildlife, Hobart.

Hall, C. M. 1992, *Wasteland to World Heritage: Preserving Australia's Wilderness*, Melbourne University Press, Carlton.

McArthur, S. 1990, 'Strategy to interpret Tasmanian rainforest'. Unpublished report for the National Rainforest Conservation Program, Tasmanian Department Parks, Wildlife and Heritage/Forestry Commission, Hobart.

McArthur, S. 1991a, 'Changing the look of mobile displays—making people work for their experience'. *Australian Ranger Bulletin*, vol. 6, no. 2.

McArthur, S. 1991b, 'Interpreting Tasmania's natural heritage', in *Our Common Future, International Environmental Education Conference Proceedings*, eds. D. Springett and C. M. Hall, New Zealand Natural Heritage Foundation, Massey University, Palmerston North.

McArthur, S. and Gardner, T. 1992, *Forestry Commission Visitor Manual*, Forestry Commission Tasmania, Hobart.

Tilden, J. 1977, *Interpreting Our Heritage*, 3rd. ed., University of North Carolina Press, Chapel Hill.

Tourism Tasmania 1991, *Tourism in Tasmania—Implications for the Emerging Market*, Tourism Tasmania, Hobart.

7

'Walk Softly'

The Effectiveness of the Tasmanian Minimal Impact Bushwalking Campaign

Tim O'Loughlin

Since the summer of 1985-86 the Tasmanian Department of Parks, Wildlife and Heritage has been engaged in a Minimal Impact Bushwalking (MIB) campaign. The campaign was started to combat environmental impacts caused by increasing numbers of walkers venturing into the Tasmanian wilds. This chapter addresses the campaign's effectiveness.

The Message

The campaign's main message was to leave the least possible trace of each visitor's journey through the wilderness. It targeted two key issues that were causing particular problems in 1986:

- *Gastroenteritis* (diarrhoea and vomiting) This was caused either by faecal waste contaminating water supplies or flies landing on faecal waste and then on food. The advice the Department gave was to use a toilet or go 100 metres away from campsites and watercourses and bury the faecal waste and toilet paper.
- *Campfires* The problem here was twofold: local environmental degradation at campsites and the risk of campfires escaping and causing bushfires. The advice was to use a fuel stove wherever possible and if an emergency fire was necessary to use a small, low-impact fire.

Other issues the Department wanted to address included:
- The 'Carry In–Carry Out' rubbish ethic;
- Where and how to walk (asking walkers to spread out in open untracked areas and to stay on tracks in tracked areas);
- Promoting 'no trace' camping (not using drainage ditches or cutting native vegetation for mattresses and tentpoles);
- Not feeding wildlife; and

- Avoiding the use of detergents or soap in waterways, particularly alpine tarns.

The MIB Materials

The following materials were produced to get the MIB message across to walkers in a variety of forms:
- *Walking the Wilderness* A pamphlet which detailed basic Minimal Impact Bushwalking techniques;
- *50 Million Years Evolving... What will it be like when you leave?* A full-colour poster with an evocative MIB message;
- *Walk Softly* An audiovisual transferred to video detailing MIB techniques in a humorous way;
- *Minimal Impact Bushwalking teacher's kit* Including 'Phantom Walker' activity sheets, modelled on 'the Phantom' comic book character;
- *Minimal Impact Bushwalking* A comic poster. A quick summary of MIB in cartoon format.

The programme also produced numerous newspaper, bushwalker magazine and electronic media items as well as having track rangers in the field informing people about MIB.

Key written material was assessed using qualitative market research techniques (done by Quantum market research in Melbourne). This involved four focus groups, two Tasmanian, and two Victorian. The results radically changed some of the presentation of our ideas and gave us a good understanding of the key points the Department needed to either counter or enforce in walkers' thinking.

Distributing the Materials

Many campaigns are not as effective as they could be because of poor distribution. The programme tried to get its materials distributed as widely as possible while still reaching the target audience.

The materials were distributed to organizations that served as walker information sources. These were found using the results of a walker survey conducted in 1985–86 (Table 7.1). This information was vital to many of the programme's decisions. For example, it stressed the need to put an article in *Wild* (read by ten per cent of bushwalkers surveyed) and to upgrade the information that relates to MIB on the back of National Park maps (consulted by fifty per cent of walkers).

From walker surveys the Department also found that around sixty-five per cent of bushwalkers in Tasmania over summer came from interstate,

Table 7.1: Information sources relevant to walk

Information Sources	No.	%
Friends (word of mouth)	151	62.1
NPWS maps and routeguide	121	49.8
Guidebooks	66	27.2
Gearshops	44	18.1
Magazines	40	16.5
Walking clubs	31	12.7
NPWS pamphlets	29	11.9
Rangers	15	6.2
Conservation groups	13	5.3
Registration points	10	4.1

particularly the southeastern mainland states of Victoria, New South Wales, and the Australian Capital Territory (fifty-four per cent). In some summers there have been more Victorian bushwalkers in Tasmania than Tasmanians! For this reason, and given the lack of any strong MIB campaigns on mainland Australia, it was essential to spread the MIB message interstate as well.

The Department mailed materials out to walking clubs, camping stores, and environmental groups. The project officer visited key organizations in the southeastern Australian capitals, pursued the Tasmanian media, spoke to local walking clubs and environment groups, and used track rangers to take the message to people '*in situ*' in the bush. So how effective was the campaign?

'Gastro'
Over the summer of 1985–86 (the summer before the campaign) there were reports of up to a half of all the walkers on the Overland track in Cradle Mountain–Lake St Clair National Park getting sick with gastroenteritis. At the end of the walking season one of the huts on the track was found to have 100 piles of exposed faecal waste within a thirty-metre radius of the hut.

Before the next summer the Department made a number of improvements to Overland track toilet facilities but was no closer to finding out the cause of the problem. It is still not known whether the medical problem was caused by flies landing on the faecal waste and then on food or food preparation areas, faecal waste polluting the water supply, or another carrier altogether.

The advice the Department gave out the following season (1986–87), to bury the faecal waste 100 metres away from campsites and watercourses, was well accepted and acted upon by walkers. Track rangers, who had as one of their less pleasant duties the task of burying any faecal waste, only found a few 'deposits'—nothing like the problems of the previous year.

Over the 1986–87 summer the Department surveyed walkers and asked them if they had gotten 'gastro'. Around eight to ten per cent of walkers said they had. The track rangers reported observing no cases of full-blown 'gastro', though a few people had minor 'tummy' upsets. It could be that this level of 'gastro', which was relatively stable across all tracks, may be a fairly natural background level. It may be due to changes in walker's diet when walking, drinking the naturally higher organic content of the waters of Southwest Tasmania, or some other factor that occurs on all tracks. This trend has continued, with no major outbreaks of 'gastro' having been reported since the MIB campaign commenced. The combination of the MIB campaign and upgraded facilities appears to have rectified a major problem.

Campfires
Campfires were a more topical issue. The project officer had envisaged that the Department would get reasonable support from walkers on the 'gastro' issue, as the health of other walkers was at stake. However, the campfire issue was less clearcut.

In Tasmania many of the alpine and rainforest species are Gondwana relics, and are not fire-adapted. Over the last thirty years, conservative estimates suggest that sixteen per cent of Tasmania's alpine area and eight per cent of our rainforest has been burnt out. The native pine species are particularly hard hit. A recent study suggests that since white settlement thirty per cent of the King Billy pine population of the state has been burnt. Species such as this rarely regenerate after fire. Another compounding factor is Tasmania's peat soils. These underlie a large amount of the World Heritage Area. Fires lit on peat can burn into the soil and smoulder underground. They are extremely hard to put out and often re-ignite in the next hot weather. A rough estimate suggests that between ten and twenty per cent of bushfires in the Tasmanian World Heritage Area can be attributed to walkers (both in terms of incidence and area burnt). However, walker-lit fires are particularly a problem in some of the most sensitive areas (alpine and rainforest), where walkers are the only human fire source. Other bushfires are caused by arson, escapes from adjacent land, and lightning.

For walkers, the only gain in not having a campfire was the warm inner glow from knowing that you are not adding to environmental destruction at the campsite. The warm outer glow of a campfire is tempting given that campsite degradation takes place gradually over the years and is not readily apparent to most walkers. Walkers rejected the notion that any of their

campfires would escape and cause a bushfire. Therefore, the programme went to great lengths to explain exactly what the problem was, pointing out the local effects at a campsite over time. These effects included:
- Vegetation damage;
- Site expansion as the vegetation is removed;
- Visual scarring of sites (large fireplaces, inappropriately sited fireplaces, too many fireplaces); and
- Rubbish accumulation (walkers attempt to use fireplaces as 'incinerators' for things like freeze-dried wrappers and tins).

Three principal target tracks were looked at to assess the campaign's effectiveness on the fires issue. These tracks were:
- *The Overland track*. Here the education effort was greatest, including pre-walk MIB briefings by rangers, showings of the audiovisual 'Walk Softly', posters in the huts, pamphlets, and a constant track ranger presence;
- *Lowland tracks in the Southwest National Park*. This is an area with a history of campfires and a medium-level education input (track rangers often present, posters in huts and shelters); and
- *The Arthur Ranges in Southwest National Park*. This is a highland area with a history of few campfires and a low education campaign input (posters at the start and finish of the walk and a track ranger in the area for about ten per cent of the time).

The Department trialed an 'educational' Fuel Stove Only Area (FSOA) over the northern (more alpine) end of the Overland track in conjunction with the education campaign. This involved a recommendation from rangers that walkers use a fuel stove instead of a campfire, backed up with signs saying 'Fuel Stove Only Area' in the northern half of the park.

The walker survey asked two questions of walkers that related to fire: 'On how many nights did you or your group light a campfire?' (All, Most, Half, Few, or None) and 'What do you think would be the best policy on campfires for the area you visited?' (No Restrictions, Fuel Stove Only Area in sensitive regions (alpine and rainforest), Fuel Stove Only Area over entire park) (Tables 7.2 and 7.3).

There has been a large and consistent shift from the use of campfires on the Overland track over the four years surveyed. The same swing is evident in walkers' views on campfires policy.

Lowland tracks in the southwest showed a minor shift towards MIB, with the majority of walkers still having a fire on half the nights or more and the majority of walkers favouring bans on campfires only in sensitive regions. In the Arthur Ranges, which received the smallest education programme, there was no statistically significant shift in the fire behaviour of walkers (though the numbers of fires lit here was very low anyway). Reaction from walker

Table 7.2: Overland Track campfire nights

Frequency of campfire nights	1986	% 1987	1988	1989
All	13.8	9.7	5.1	1
Most	11.6	5.7	1.6	–
Half	13.0	5.7	4.3	1.5
Few	31.2	25.8	15.8	7
None	30.4	52.5	72.7	90.5

Table 7.3: Walkers' views on Overland Track campfire policy (% agree)

Policy	1986	1987	1988	1989
No restrictions on fires	18.8	9.9	3.2	2
FSOA in sensitive regions	59.4	54.7	43.9	36
FSOA over entire park	18.8	33.6	50.7	62

FSOA: Fuel Stove Only Area

Table 7.4: Walkers' views on which material best conveys MIB message

Material	%
'Walking the Wilderness' pamphlet	19.4
'Walk Softly' audiovisual/video	79.6
MIB comic poster	34.0
50 million years poster	13.2
'Phantom Walker' kits	21.7
Talking to track rangers	21.4

groups to the trial FSOA on the Overland track was largely positive, with a number of walkers asking why other areas were not covered.

In the Walls of Jerusalem National Park there was a much lower track ranger presence and walker education campaign than in Cradle Mountain. An 'educational' Fuel Stove Only Area sign was installed in the park at the same time as the FSOA on the northern part of the Overland track. However, judging from the evidence of campfires left within the park, the sign had little effect since the number of campfires lit was still very high.

The results indicate that the most effective means of convincing walkers of the need not to have fires is a strong education campaign reinforced by track rangers and backed up with a Fuel Stove Only regulation. Next best is a strong education campaign and least effective is just erecting the Fuel Stove Only Area signs.

Acting on these results the Department declared in 1989 a number of parks or parts of parks Fuel Stove Only Areas. In these areas people can be fined up to $5000 for lighting a fire. These areas were being reviewed in 1992 with a view to expanding them.

Other Issues

Shifts towards MIB practices occurred in terms of minor issues the programme addressed. A statistically significant increase in those carrying out all their rubbish occurred in 1986–87, largely at the expense of those burning and then carrying their rubbish out. These trends continued into following years, with burning, bashing and burying dropping to under two per cent by 1987–88. The Department was partially successful in convincing around twenty per cent of walkers who mostly avoided bogs to walk through muddy sections of track. Nevertheless around sixty per cent of walkers still walked around half or more of the bogs they confronted. Campsite modifications were reduced from around seven per cent in 1985–86 to around five per cent in 1987–88. Soap and detergent use was reduced significantly over the period 1986–88. Those using soap went down from 35.8 per cent in 1985–86 to 13.7 per cent in 1987–88.

What is the Best Education Technique?

The Department also evaluated which were the most effective materials at getting walkers to change to MIB practices. Walkers were asked what MIB education material they thought got the MIB message across best (Table 7.4). Of the materials that people had seen, the video at nearly eighty per cent was more than twice as popular as any other method. The second most popular method was the MIB comic poster (thirty-four per cent), a quick, five-minute-read humorous MIB cartoon.

A problem in interpreting the effectiveness of the programme arises in differentiating users' attraction to the product against their changed behaviour. For example, a track ranger came across two walkers lighting a fire in alpine grassland and asked 'Have you seen the "Walk Softly" video?' One answered 'Yes, I thought it was great', and the second one echoed this by saying 'Yeah, I've seen it twice.' They were doing the opposite of what the video recommended! In this instance a track ranger on the spot had far more impact than a video seen perhaps five days before.

Most walkers appear to like things that are fun, easy, and quick to read. These may grab their attention but the programme suggests that the best way to get the message across is to use educational materials in conjunction with personal methods such as track rangers. Most of the materials produced for the campaign have a long-term role and need to be continued if the MIB campaign is to have a lasting effect. The video is excellent to use with schools and other groups that may have not had much contact with bushwalking. It puts the audience 'live' into the situation and gives people a much clearer idea of how MIB works in practice. It is particularly useful in combination with the 'Phantom Walker' teacher's kit. The next step in the development of these tools needs to be the incorporation of MIB materials into each organization's teaching curriculum, in school courses, and scout badge courses. This is probably the best way of training the next generation of bushwalkers.

The MIB comic poster is a popular, quick and fun way of introducing the MIB concept. It is particularly useful in areas like walker registration booths (and on the back of toilet doors!) where walkers only have a small amount of time to take the message in, and it is very cost effective. The *Walking the Wilderness* pamphlet is the only high-volume written publication that goes into detail about MIB—it is central to the campaign. The track rangers were not particularly popular with walkers, but as pointed out above, being *in situ* has decided advantages. They also have walker safety and other management functions that make them particularly useful. The one element of the campaign that will not be continued is the full-colour poster *50 Million Years Evolving . . . What will it be like when you leave?* This was the least popular of the materials and although it was seen by a number of walkers it is not cost effective enough to warrant reprinting.

Campsite Inventorying

Evaluation of the effectiveness of an educational campaign has always been difficult. The Department relied largely on walker surveys and the opinions of rangers to assess the programme's effectiveness. These are open to a number of different forms of bias. For example, with surveys where the forms are returned to a ranger, there is always the potential that walkers may be saying one thing to please the ranger, but doing another.

One way of getting a more objective view is through the use of campsite inventories. We have commenced using a three-tiered campsite inventory system. At the low end of the system is a ten-minute campsite inventory, which involves taking a series of photos from a known point at the side of the site and joining them together to form a panoramic sweep over the site. A quick 1 to 5 rating system is also employed to rate the site's level of degradation. At the high end of the system the same photo sweep is done, a detailed scale map is produced, and a campsite inventory form filled out. This process can take up to five hours per site for very complicated areas, but averages around two hours. The scale map covers important features such as fireplaces and bare soil areas. The campsite inventory form includes an assessment of the amount of rubbish on site, the amount of faecal waste surrounding the site, the number of fireplaces currently in use, the number of disused fire sites, the amount of tree damage nearby, and the percentage of ground cover that is covered with vegetation, bare soil, and rock.

An intermediate level leaves out the scale map but includes filling out the form, which takes about half an hour per site. This system allows the Department to accurately track the effectiveness of measures such as Fuel Stove Only Areas. If the programme is effective no new fire sites should form and, over time, old sites should become unnoticeable. The system is also used to assess the amount of rubbish on site and the amount of faecal waste left exposed. The Department is still in the early stages of using the system but it is planned to inventory all major tracks and to repeat this every three years for selected indicator sites.

Commercial Tour Operators
Commercial guides are looked to as information sources by less experienced walkers in the absence of rangers. Therefore, it is important to have close ties with commercial operators and for their licence conditions to incorporate MIB provisions. If operators have an understanding of management policies and give them their support, they can pass the information on to others. The Department runs workshops for commercial tour guides that cover aspects of MIB and relevant management issues.

Integration with Other Interpretive Programmes
It is also possible to blend the MIB message in with other messages. The Department has produced a number of walker safety education materials and many of these feature the dual theme of your safety in the environment as well as the safety of the environment. Materials include a sister video to *Walk*

Softly called *Walk Safely*, a bushwalking trip planner booklet called *Welcome to the Wilderness*, and a series of notesheets about major walking tracks.

Conclusion

The MIB campaign has been highly successful in Tasmania. It has been particularly useful, in combination with other measures, in reducing the incidence of gastroenteritis and the risk of campfires in the World Heritage Area. It has succeeded to the point where other states now use the same techniques. New South Wales, Victoria, and the Australian Capital Territory now use the *Walking the Wilderness* pamphlet as the basic MIB advice for walkers in alpine areas. Western Australia and Queensland also use material from the campaign.

The future of MIB education in Australia appears healthy, but it will only be through continued efforts to produce readable and informative materials that are then widely distributed that MIB ideas will pass into bushwalking practice. If the programme is successful, in ten years' time people will not need to be told to take a fuel stove and will not think of walking any other way than 'softly'.

Further Reading

For a more complete explanation of the advice given under the MIB programme see the Tasmanian Department of Parks, Wildlife and Heritage pamphlet *Walking the Wilderness* and O'Loughlin, T. 1989, 'Walk softly—but carry a big education campaign', in *Australian Ranger Bulletin*, vol. 5, no. 3: 4–7.

Senses of Place

Indigenous and Integrated Perspectives

Introduction

The seven chapters in this section examine the attachment of people to heritage and the development of senses of place. The first two chapters by Keelan (Chapter 8) and Boyd and Ward (Chapter 9) discuss the relationship of indigenous peoples to heritage and the implications that this has for visitor management and interpretation. As the two chapters indicate, considerable overlap exists between Māori (Keelan) and Aboriginal (Boyd and Ward) interaction with tourists and the tourism industry, and the difficulties that tourism has created.

People's attachment to place is also the subject of Kirby's examination of landscape, heritage, and identity on the West Coast of the South Island of New Zealand (Chapter 10). Kirby notes that both Europeans and Māori develop strong senses of place and that local notions of heritage can differ substantially from outsiders' perspectives, such as that of the Department of Conservation (see Chapter 5).

The appropriate marketing of senses of place is outlined by Brown (Chapter 11) and Wells (Chapter 12). Brown provides a specific discussion of the idea of a sense of place and its implications for heritage marketing, interpretation, and visitor management, while Wells details a specific case study of heritage marketing (Uluru National Park) and the need to use strategic approaches in the appropriate marketing of heritage.

The last two chapters in this section by Lennon (Chapter 13) and Saunders (Chapter 14) indicate some of the difficulties in integrating cultural and natural heritage values under the same management and interpretive structures. Saunders, in particular, in his discussion of the Waldheim Chalet in Tasmania, highlights the difficulties of reconciling authenticity with visitor expectations, and the conflict of values that occurs in heritage site management.

8

Māori Heritage
Visitor Management and Interpretation

Ngawini Keelan

Heritage is a concept which is currently being shaped to fit the needs and expectations of a multicultural New Zealand society (Hall et al. 1992). In respect to Māori, the issues of ownership and retrieval, compensation for interest foregone and maintenance of heritage, have been pressing concerns for a greater part of the 150 years of British colonization. Today, an eternal conundrum facing political decision-makers is that of reconciling the interests and values of tangata whenua with the national interest. A framework for conciliation is being developed as outstanding Māori claims with the Waitangi Tribunal are worked through. Although Māori have tended to be less than satisfied with the outcomes, their claims set important precedents in case law, and influence the ability of business organizations to deliver a quality service or product. In this respect, the management and delivery of tourism packages is no exception, as Māori claims are all-encompassing and include lands, forests, fisheries, taonga such as greenstone and Māori artefacts, and more recently, the control of national parks, and whale watching ventures in the South Island (Hall et al. 1993).

Heritage Tourism: Issues Relating to Resource Ownership

Heritage tourism has been defined as the desire to experience diverse past and present cultural landscapes, environments, places, and forms (Zeppel and Hall 1992). Specific global trends indicate that tourists are interested in the environment and interaction with local people and customs. These factors have been taken into account in the development of national tourism strategies which promote New Zealand's clean, green environment and the unique nature of the Māori culture and people (Hall et al. 1992). However, the Māori participation in tourism to date has been mainly limited to providing the brown faces, exotic backdrops and cultural experiences for a non-Māori-owned package aimed at the mass tourist market. Although these have had some positive flow-on effects to Māori and to host communities, negative effects such as commodification and cultural bastardization have occurred and need to be addressed if the host–visitor exchange is to be a positive experience for all concerned (Keelan 1991, 1992; Hall et al. 1992).

Some cognizance must also be taken of the fact that Māori and Pākehā values in respect to heritage often differ and conflict. Māori responses to active encouragement by regional authorities, tour operators, and other agencies to develop marae-based visits and homestay packages vary. Within my own tribal area, a number of concerns were voiced in relation to the intrusion of privacy, conflict in values and lack of visitor reciprocation, takatakahi mana, unresolved issues in respect of the ownership of land and resources, the one-sided nature of the host–guest relationship, and the commodification of the culture. Kaumatua were also concerned at the length of time visitors would stay, as they believed that little opportunity for sharing could come from short visits (Nikora, Kaumatua, pers. comm.).

Māori claims in respect to resource ownership are wide-ranging in scope and complexity, and settlement may involve a range of solutions such as monetary redress, return of disputed resources, and restructuring of trusts and leases. However, in most cases, Māori would prefer to have their lands and other cultural properties returned and to be compensated for interest foregone (Keelan 1992). Negotiations in respect of the Ngāi Tahu and Tainui claims provide guidelines for future action and over the next ten to twenty years a number of tribes will be financially well positioned to develop tribal reserves and resources following the settlement of their claims. Some of these tribes will naturally be anticipating entry into the tourist industry. Under these circumstances, the development of Māori-owned, Māori-driven tourist packages will provide unique experiences for the discerning visitor and lessen the risks of cultural commodification and bastardization by placing the responsibility and control back in Māori hands.

Heritage Tourism:
Issues Relating to Traditional Host–Guest Relationships

An analysis of the sociopolitical units of the whānau, hapū, and iwi provides considerable insight into traditional Māori views with respect to tourism. These units were bound together by a complex web of genealogical ties or whakapapa, enabling expansion when under threat or contraction during times of peace.

Mana Tangata
Membership was based on descent or whakapapa. The institution of whakapapa also defined one's social standing in kin groups, i.e. teina or

tuakana. Seniority of descent was an important qualification for leadership as the more senior you were, the closer you were to the gods and the more likely you were to find favour with them (Buck 1982: 337). Attributes such as military and other skills were also important; however, the hereditary chiefs always held absolute authority or arikitanga. Purity of descent was therefore carefully guarded and the ability to whakapapa through a senior line of descent brought a reality of political power which extended into all aspects of Māori life. In the event of death, this mana was succeeded to by the most senior child of the marriage/marriages (Keelan 1991).

Mana Atua

Whakapapa also incorporates a spiritual dimension reaching back to the genesis of time itself and providing explanations in respect to humankind's relationship with the universe, with mother earth, and with matter both animate and inanimate (Keelan 1991). The importance of these spiritual links is perpetuated in the creation myths, and demonstrates the indivisible nature of the Māori people with their environment.

Mana Whenua

The hapū was the most important economic unit, governing geographically defined resources within the iwi boundary. These boundaries would often overlap, creating the potential for conflict. In this respect, the institution of whakapapa provided for a degree of mutual co-operation where scarce resources or highly valued resources were held in common.

Hereditary chiefs held the land in trust for future descendants and oversaw the allocation and utilization of resources. Typically, property rights were well defined and jealously guarded, and any infraction could meet with serious consequences. A well-known Māori proverb adequately demonstrates this characteristic.

> Ma te wahine ma te whenua ka mate te tangata.
> For land and women, men would lay down their lives.

Property rights were also comprehensive in nature and included the right to use what was below, on, and above the ground.

In the Ngāti Porou context, the well-documented case of Ngāti Rakai trespass and poaching in Te Atau territory is an example of the application of both mana whenua and mana tangata in that Te Atau ordered Ngāti Rakai to bear tributes of food to Iritekura, a well-known chieftainess on the East Coast, and to offer themselves up to her as slaves so that they might be saved from certain death. There were a number of purposes served by this decision.

Firstly, the issues of compensation for trespass and the poaching of pigeons was satisfied (utu), and secondly, the issue of homelessness was resolved in that Ngāti Rakai and their descendants were assured a dwelling place. Ngāti Rakai remained subservient to Iritekura and her people as tillers of the soil and bearers of food. This story is well preserved on the carved meeting house belonging to the Iritekura people at Waipiro Bay (Keelan 1991).

Property rights could be acquired by several means. Conquest as a result of war and long-term occupation of so taken territory, by way of a tuku or gift, and by successfully maintaining occupational rights or ahi ka over the long term. The mana of the whānau, hapū and iwi rested on their ability to defend their rights and interests in the land and to fulfil specific social, physical and spiritual responsibilities to both the land and the people over time (Keelan 1991).

These concepts in respect to heritage relating to property have been used in the development of Māori claims before the Waitangi Tribunal and demonstrate the traditionally exclusive nature of Māori resource ownership or tino rangatiratanga, the seriousness with which infractions such as trespass were treated and also the importance of the hapū as a sociopolitical unit. Māori society was composed of an arrangement of genealogically affiliated hapū units with specific property rights over specific boundaries rather than members of an overarching nationhood. The ability to work effectively within these hapū and iwi structures is essential to the success of any tourism project employing Māori resources.

The claims also highlight the attendant loss and deprivation suffered by the people and the extent to which a numerically superior Pākehā government has been singularly effective in drastically reducing Māori land holdings through the application of a plethora of discriminatory legislation and neglect. This trend was furthered by the activities of the Māori Land Court through the creation of individual land titles and vehicles such as Māori land consolidation and leases in perpetuity. By 1975 the area of land under Māori title was less than three million acres from a total of 66 million acres in 1840. Today, the restoration of property rights over ancestral land and resources remains an all-consuming Māori goal.

Sacred Sites: Wāhi Tapu

The concept of wāhi tapu is one that has been embroiled in many Māori claims before the Tribunal. Although the bulk of wāhi tapu claims relate to burial sites, mountain peaks, and shrines, the concept of wāhi tapu can be extended to include all aspects of the environment or papatuanuku, from which Māori base their descent. This view of sacred space holds many similarities with that of other indigenous people:

> Sacred space is a place where human beings find a manifestation of divine power, where they experience a sense of connectedness to the universe ... when one asks a traditional Indian how much of the earth is sacred space? The answer is unhesitatingly all (Hughes and Swan 1986).

Like the Indian people, Māori also 'perceive that earth is a living being, sacred in all her parts' (Hughes and Swan 1986). In modern times, Māori are having to cope with the desecration of wāhi tapu on an ongoing basis. In many cases, this has come about because of the unwillingness of power structures to recognize Māori sovereignty over Māori resources. To this extent, Māori have been largely undermined and ignored in matters relating to environmental planning and management. This freezing-out process has been detrimental to the health of the tangata whenua and to the resources. Mistakes have been made and archaeological sites of historic and cultural value desecrated or destroyed. To Māori, restoration and reinvigoration of these environmental resources is critical, as the wretched nature of the environment is analogous to that of the people.

A Pākehā solution has been to map out wāhi tapu in consultation with Māori and bring them under protection of statute, where applicable. However, Māori have been largely unwilling to cater to these demands for a number of reasons. First, they fear the consequences of Pākehā ignorance and interference. Second, they see all aspects of their environment as wāhi tapu. Third, there has traditionally been little recognition of fundamental Māori concepts such as tino rangatiratanga, tapu, mana, and mauri (Nikora, pers. comm. 1991).

The resolution of Māori land claims will provide opportunities for Māori to revisit wāhi tapu that have traditionally been of significance to tourism, and have direct input into the development of culturally responsive management plans for those resources. In respect to the South Island, Ngāi Tahu Trust Board owns 43 per cent of Kaikoura Tours, 100 per cent of O Tapara Lodge in Milford, 100 per cent of the holiday park and restaurant at Moeraki Boulders, 100 per cent of Ngāi Tahu Fisheries, and a potential compensation package which will make 'Ngāi Tahu one of the biggest businesses in asset terms in the South Island' (Brett 1992). Ngāi Tahu participation as joint custodians of the area's national parks and the possibilities of their acquiring legal title to natural features of special cultural significance, or wāhi tapu such as Aoraki (Mount Cook) and the Takitimu Range in Southland, will no doubt enhance and add value to the management of these resources. The return of tino rangatiratanga may also provide opportunities for further development of potentially valuable tourism resources as in the Ngāi Tahu joint venture deal to 'build a state-of-the-art $80 million monorail link on the floor of the sacred greenstone valley to carry tourists from Queenstown to Milford' (Brett 1992).

Tangata Whenua vs Manuhiri:
Hosting Traditions and Their Implications for Tourism

Political intertribal relationships were often tenuous and at times political marriages between well-born families were arranged to facilitate peaceful coexistence. The practice of journeying outside of one's traditional boundaries was fraught with danger and certainly not lightly undertaken. This degree of caution was still apparent until quite recently. My grandfather spoke about journeying from Port Waikato to the Gisborne area when he was a child, and how the family travelled at night to avoid detection when circumstances forced them to travel over foreign territory.

In Māori terms, therefore, it is the tangata whenua who freely enjoy the spiritual flow of the land. All others are manuhiri who derive their enjoyment at the consent of their hosts. The relationship between the visitor and the host is subject to an elaborate and highly formalized ritual or powhiri aimed at reconciling the mana of the hosts with that of their visitors, and providing opportunities for both parties to test intentions and to overcome their respective spiritual, psychological, social, and physical distance. At the conclusion of the powhiri process, manuhiri may be regarded as honorary members of the kin group and may share in certain tasks such as hosting. However, their activities continue to be regulated by a well-defined code of social conduct and the recognition of the mana of tangata whenua is a highly significant consideration (Keelan 1991; Hall et al. 1992).

The issue of commodification is a critical one in regard to hosting traditions and can be defined as the erosion of cultural products and human relations to a point where they become virtually meaningless to the people who once believed in them, resulting in a form of staged authenticity. Visitor preparation and support is therefore imperative if takatakahi is to be avoided. The ability of the visitor to observe the kawa and the tikanga of the tangata whenua and to reciprocate in an appropriate fashion, and a willingness also to be guided by Māori time and the Māori way of doing things, are critical success factors to the preservation of these unique hosting traditions. Māori hosting requirements should therefore be renegotiated only by the Māori owners of the resource, lest the culture be commodified and bastardized (Keelan 1992).

The concept of carrying capacity is also useful in that it has a degree of applicability for Māori communities such as Rotorua, who have been swamped by the phenomena of mass tourism. 'Carrying capacity refers to the number of people who can visit a site or natural area without detracting or degrading that area in the long term' (Harper and Zell 1990). Carrying capacity could therefore be used in the marketing strategy as a means of regulating and controlling the flow of tourists through host communities.

Heritage Tourism: Issues Relating to Interpretation

The natural world of the Māori provided artistic inspiration and a highly developed appreciation of beauty and quality. 'Even very mundane items, eating bowls and utensils, baskets, gardening tools, mats, fishing sinkers . . . were gracefully designed and pleasing to the eye' (Te Awekotuku 1990: 93). Certain items also had a life of their own and in my particular family, ancient heirlooms like the greenstone earrings Paekura and the adze Waikanae, now of parts unknown, had values which far exceeded their decorative and utilitarian functions.

> Every piece of the well dressed Māori wardrobe had a significance, an essential mauri, or life force, which linked the taonga to the natural world, and in the end to Papatuanuku herself . . . within the plaited complexity of taniko weaving and tukutuku wall panels are the flounder shapes of the patiki, the wavy chevrons of aramoana, the twinkling stars of purapura whetu . . . Artists followed a cycle of acquiring the raw materials . . . making the taonga and then to complete the transformation . . . applying in decorative form a reference to the taonga's source (Te Awekotuku 1990: 93).

The personification of artefacts and natural features of the environment was a characteristic which was deeply rooted in the culture and potently demonstrated in the symbolic relationship of the Māori meeting house to that of a founding ancestor. Māori art forms such as ceremonial speechmaking, karanga, waiata, whakairo, raranga and tukutuku were highly valued by the culture, and subject to a process of public scrutiny which promoted a consistently high standard of quality in the artist's labour for perfection. Such attention to detail has won international appreciation for Māori art and its importance to the tourism industry was aptly demonstrated in the overwhelming popularity of the Te Māori exhibitions. However, the values which Māori place on these taonga has been traditionally underrated, in that little account has been taken of the culture and the people to which that taonga belongs. Māori claims in respect to Māori taonga currently under the control of the Crown and/or national and regional bodies such as museums, libraries and art galleries may set future precedents relating to the management of such taonga. The work of the Tribunal in unravelling and documenting Māori history is also indicative of the extent to which a colonized view of that history has been perpetuated, and the difficulties that Māori people face in ridding themselves of stereotypical distortions, romanticism and myth making.

Interpretation strategies relating to Māori art and culture must therefore be developed from a basis that recognizes the Māori ownership of the product and Māori participation at all stages of the planning and information delivery process. To do otherwise is to misrepresent the product and undermine the culture. Programmes of instruction that have been developed by tribal experts and subjected to tribal scrutiny and testing would yield the most beneficial results for the owners and users of the Māori product and or service.

References

Brett, C. 1992, 'Who are Ngai Tahu?' *North and South*, November, pp. 56–69.
Buck, Sir Peter (Te Rangi Hiroa) 1982, *The Coming Of The Maori*, Whitcoulls, Wellington.
Hall, C. M., Keelan, N., and Mitchell, I. (forthcoming), 'Maori culture and heritage tourism in New Zealand', *Journal of Cultural Geography*.
Hall, C. M., Mitchell, I., and Keelan, N. (forthcoming), 'The implications of Maori perspectives for the management and promotion of heritage tourism in New Zealand', *Geojournal*.
Harper, L. and Zell, R. 1990, 'The role of educational tourism in nature tourism and conservation', paper presented at an international symposium on educational tourism, University of Canterbury, Christchurch.
Hughes, J. D. and Swan, J. 1986, 'How much of the Earth is sacred space?', *Environmental Review*, vol. 10, no. 4, pp. 247–260.
Keelan, N. 1991, 'Heritage Values and their Implications for Tourism', unpublished Master's report, Massey University, Palmerston North.
Keelan, N. 1992, 'International Tourism and its Implications for Maori', unpublished Master's report, Massey University, Palmerston North.
Te Awekotuku, N. 1990, 'Art and the Spirit', *New Zealand Geographic*, no. 5 (March).
Zeppel, H. and Hall, C. M. 1992, 'Review: Arts and heritage tourism', in *Special Interest Tourism*, eds. B. Weiler and C. M. Hall, Belhaven Press, London, pp. 47–68.

9

Aboriginal Heritage and Visitor Management

W. E. Boyd and G. K. Ward

Introduction

Visitor management at Aboriginal heritage sites is an integral part of the wider issues and practices of heritage site management and cultural tourism. Management of heritage sites is becoming an increasingly complex activity, which is placing ever-greater professional responsibilities upon the various management agencies. This complexity is further compounded with increasing involvement of Aboriginal communities and organizations in the process of the management of places which may form an integral part of their contemporary cultural milieu.

This chapter concerns three of the main areas of contemporary interest in relation to the management of visitors to Aboriginal heritage sites. The first reviews sources of issue in Aboriginal heritage management. The second is the range of responsibilities and management activities of those agencies with statutory authority for heritage sites, and their various legislations which provide a foundation for both site and visitor management in Australia. The third deals with the perceptions and activities of Aboriginal custodians of heritage places. This stems from discussions held at a jointly organized Australian Institute of Aboriginal and Torres Strait Islander Studies (AIATSIS) and Victoria Archaeological Survey (VAS) workshop on Heritage Tourism and Aboriginal Sites held in March 1991 (Ward and Boyd, forthcoming). While consideration of the former (legislation and the 'official' agencies) provides a view of the existing management structures, discussions at the workshop introduce wider agenda than are usually considered.

Heritage Tourism and Aboriginal Heritage Management Issues

Aboriginal sites are being exposed to increasing pressure, due primarily to increasing numbers and changing preferences of visitors to such sites. The experience in, for example, Uluru and Kakadu National Parks in the Northern Territory of Australia, in which major sites attract large numbers of visitors, reflects the situation elsewhere (Boyd et al., forthcoming), where the impacts have been found to be complex, entailing not only physical alteration to sites, but also having major cultural, social, and economic implications for communities associated with the sites (Brady 1985; Lawrence 1985; Senior 1987; Altman 1988, 1989; Bogle 1988; Gillespie 1988; Marcus 1988).

'Heritage tourism' or 'cultural tourism' seeks to meet an increasing interest among international tourists in visiting sites associated with cultural activity and experiencing activities with strong cultural, rather than recreational, emphases (Boyd et al., forthcoming). The traditional Western commercial tourism industry is being challenged by a parallel development, the growing empowerment of indigenous peoples in the areas of heritage control (Charles 1984; Hammil and Cruz 1989; Hubbert 1989; Layton 1989; Zimmerman 1989). This is expressed in Australia by, first, a debate centred on the role of Aboriginal involvement in the process of heritage management (Allen 1983; Creamer 1983, 1986a, 1986b; Fesl 1983; Langford 1983; Ucko 1983; Green 1984; Lewis and Rose 1985; Martin 1985; Wright 1986; Beacroft 1987; Mulvaney 1989) and, second, a desire of traditional site owners and custodians, and other Aboriginal people, to become involved in the management of heritage sites, whether in the day-to-day site management, for example as guides and maintenance personnel (Roff 1984), as commercial or administrative managers or business owners (Australian National Parks and Wildlife Service 1982; Kesteven 1987), or in the development of policy, such as in the determination of right of access. Heritage site management, thus, includes a wide range of activities from the strictly resource- or object-oriented activities such as site recording and feature conservation, to predominantly people-orientated activities such as visitor management (Gale and Jacobs 1987a). In practice, these activities are strongly interlinked and rarely separable (Boyd and Dutton, forthcoming), and it is desirable to discuss visitor management within the wider context of site management.

The aims and intent of site and visitor management, and the methods adopted to achieve these aims, reflect and are influenced by the attitudes and philosophies held by the parties involved. The implementation of methods is often specialized, either as so-called 'professional' expertise in, for example, planning, archaeology or art restoration, or as Aboriginal or local community expertise which may provide, for example, in-depth cultural understanding and interpretation of a site. Where active management is seen to be desirable, either by State or Territory statutory authorities or Aboriginal groups (some of which also may be statutory authorities, such as the Northern and the Central Land Councils), generic management principles may be called upon, perhaps adapted from principles and practices already in use in other resource management areas (see Mitchell 1989).

Despite the availability of guidelines for appropriate and suitable on-site management techniques (Schiffer and Gumerman 1977; Pearson 1978; Aten 1982; Hamel and Jones 1982; Sullivan 1984, 1985; Creamer 1986a, 1986b; Gale and Jacobs 1987b; Johnson and Schene, 1987; Lambert 1989; Thorne 1989; Ward 1991a), heritage site management is often conducted in a manner, at worst *ad hoc*, but often within some form of managerial and social context, which reflects either a limited understanding of planning and management options or, perhaps, intercultural conflict. The on-site consequence of these is the emergence of two key problems. Site degradation, first, often follows inappropriate on-site works and limited maintenance. Secondly, and partly as a consequence of the first problem, the quality of visitor experience, especially at publicly accessible and commonly visited sites, is often reduced.

Two main categories of limitations may affect the success of site and visitor management. The first includes the physical characteristics of Aboriginal sites, which frequently make them highly susceptible to impact damage (Flood 1990): (i) dwellings and other constructions were typically slightly built; (ii) the importance of most sites lay not in their physical nature, but in the cultural significance attached to them (Creamer 1980); (iii) most sites are largely non-resilient features, easily damaged by visitor access (Gale and Jacobs 1987a), such as rock paintings and carvings and sacred trees, and occupation sites which are open, surface deposit sites or scatters of artefacts; and (iv) sites are often under threat from economic exploitation, such as shell middens which have been sources for road-base material or agricultural lime. In addition to these characteristics, many heritage sites also occupy locations now favoured for modern tourism development, especially in coastal regions (Sullivan 1975; Morwood 1981; Boyd et al., forthcoming).

The second category of limitations is defined by aspects of the management of such sites (Sorenson and Auster 1989); in particular, changing visitor characteristics and behaviour (Pitts 1986), limited resources, complexity of adopted management structures (Sheppard 1988; Dutton and Hall 1989), and conflicting socio-political demands upon the site. Ultimately, these problems can undermine effective site management and, however site quality is defined (e.g. in terms of 'naturalness', perceived cultural authenticity for the visitor, or sociocultural importance for guardian or custodian communities), there is a reduction in that site quality.

Importantly, from the point of view of visitor management, any diminution in quality of a site may result in reduced public understanding of the site and its cultural context. There are, in essence, three potentially overlapping responses to such a situation, all of which entail a re-examination of management methods. The first focuses on the development of protective legislation which authorizes control over sites and their use (Ward 1983; Prott and O'Keefe 1984; Ministerial Task Force on Aboriginal Heritage and Culture 1988). The second concerns reorganization of management structures (Ministerial Task Force on Aboriginal Heritage and Culture 1988), either within the existing format of statutory authorities, or, more radically, extending beyond government infrastructure and placing the management of Aboriginal sites and visitors with Aboriginal agencies and individuals. The third focuses upon the increasingly rigorous development of management principles and implementation of forward planning methods (Flood 1979; Boyd and Dutton, forthcoming).

Legislation and Administration of Aboriginal Heritage Sites

Since the federation of Australia in 1901, State government has largely controlled matters relating to land. Following the constitutional referendum of 1967, the federal government gained the power to legislate for Aboriginal affairs in the States, although since it has been little used, statutory control of Aboriginal heritage places rests mainly with State and Territory governments. Legislation to protect sites and portable items developed late: the Native and Historic Objects and Areas Preservation Ordinance 1955–1960 of the Northern Territory is the earliest modern legislation to protect Aboriginal heritage items and places. 'Relics' acts in South Australia (1965), Queensland and New South Wales (1967), Western Australia and Victoria (1972) and Tasmania (1975) followed, and subsequently the Northern Territory gained legislation to protect sacred sites (1978). Most States have revised or replaced their statutes, or are doing so, and the Australian Capital Territory finally gained comprehensive legislation in 1991. All States and Territories now have legislation to protect aspects of Aboriginal heritage (Table 9.1), although their provisions and administrative arrangements vary markedly (Ward 1983; Prott and O'Keefe 1984, 1989).

State and Territory heritage legislation has, until recently, focused on archaeological remains, typically providing protection of Aboriginal heritage (defined, for example, in the New South Wales National Parks and Wildlife Act 1974, section 5.1, as '. . . any deposit, object or material evidence (not being a handicraft made for sale) relating to indigenous and non-European habitation . . .') as a class. Thus, places or items do not have to be individually registered or even known to exist to be protected, a blanket protection which is less favoured in more recent legislation. However, the establishment of a register is usually required, administration is guided by an expert committee, sites can be declared protected areas and access to them can be controlled, land can be compulsorily acquired, and penalties can be imposed for damage or destruction. Similarly, artefacts can be protected by making them Crown property, although private ownership may be permitted, and trading and export prohibited or restricted. Often considerable attention is given to controlling archaeological excavation, rather than the major sources of site destruction, mining exploration and pastoral and industrial development, and effective protection is usually only achieved by reference to separate 'environmental protection' or 'impact of development assessment' legislation, where it exists, in conjunction with heritage legislation.

Contrasting with these 'relics' acts are those based in or giving more weight to Aboriginal interests. The Northern Territory's Aboriginal Sacred Sites Act was the first of these (developed to complement the federal Aboriginal Land Rights Act, it was replaced in 1989). It provides an example for new legislation in South Australia (1988), and statutes are being considered in other States. The Northern Territory Sacred Sites Act covers sites of significance to contemporary Aboriginal people and has no direct effect on 'archaeological sites' or other places which might be considered to be of heritage value by non-Aboriginal people. This change in emphasis in legislation has been rightly welcomed by Aboriginal people. However, if it is not paralleled by legislation to protect a more generalized 'heritage', then sites which are solely or predominantly of value to archaeological investigations or education about the past may be left with lessened or no protection. Furthermore, the omission from the Northern Territory's Heritage Conservation Act 1991 of provisions to protect archaeological sites as a class appears to have left such sites without effective protection. Elsewhere in Australia, discussion papers include provision for administration of new legislation by 'Aboriginal Heritage Commissions'; Aboriginal interests tend to be more immediately concerned with cultural significances of heritage sites other than archaeological values and it will be interesting to follow as new legislation is administered by Aboriginal agencies.

There are federal government acts which directly address the protection of Aboriginal heritage and which, as with other federal legislation, take precedence over State legislation. The Australian Heritage Commission Act 1975, which established a Register of the National Estate now including several thousand Aboriginal places, obliges federal ministers to consider and to avoid any action which would adversely affect any place on the Register (unless there are 'no feasible and prudent' alternatives). However, this Act only provides indirect protection against the actions of State governments and of businesses and individuals. The Aboriginal and Torres Strait Islander Heritage Protection Act 1984–1986 (amended 1987), dealing directly with

Table 9.1: Aboriginal heritage legislation and administrative arrangements of the Australian States and Territories

Legislation	Authority
Federal	
Aboriginal and Torres Strait Islander Heritage Protection Act 1984-1986	The Manager, Heritage Protection Administration Branch, Aboriginal and Torres Strait Islander Commission, P.O. Box 17, Woden, A.C.T. 2606
Environmental Protection (Impact of Proposals) Act 1974-1975	The Executive Director, Commonwealth Environment Protection Agency, Department of Arts, Sport, the Environment and Territories, P.O. Box E305, Queen Victoria Terrace, A.C.T. 2600
Australian Heritage Commission Act 1975-1989	The Director, Australian Heritage Commission, Department of Arts, Sport, the Environment and Territories, P.O. Box 1967, Canberra, A.C.T. 2601
Protection of Movable Cultural Heritage Act 1986	The Director, Arts, Film and Cultural Heritage Division, Department of Arts, Sport, the Environment and Territories, P.O. Box 787, Canberra, A.C.T. 2601
Western Australia	
Aboriginal Heritage Act 1972-1980	The Registrar of Aboriginal Sites, Department of Aboriginal Sites, Western Australian Museum, 35 Havelock Street, West Perth 6005
Northern Territory	
Heritage Conservation Act 1991 (Number 39 of 1991)	Heritage Unit, Conservation Commission of the Northern Territory, P.O. Box 496, Palmerston, 0831

Aboriginal Heritage and Visitor Management

Northern Territory Aboriginal Sacred Sites Act 1989 (Number 29 of 1989)	The Chief Executive Officer, Northern Territory Aboriginal Areas Protection Authority, P.O. Box 1890, Darwin, 0801

South Australia

Aboriginal Heritage Act 1988	The Manager, Aboriginal Heritage Branch, Department of Environment and Planning, P.O. Box 667, Adelaide, 5001

Queensland

Cultural Record (Landscape Queensland and Queensland Estate) Act 1988	The Manager, Heritage Unit, Department of Environment and Conservation, P.O. Box 155, North Quay, 4000

New South Wales

National Parks and Wildlife Act 1967-1974	The Director, National Parks and Wildlife Service, P.O. Box 1967, Hurstville, 2220

Australian Capital Territory

Land (Planning and Environment) Act 1991 Heritage Objects Act 1991	The Manager, A.C.T. Heritage and Museum Section, Environment, Culture and Heritage Division, Department of the Environment, Land and Planning, P.O. Box 1119, Tuggeranong, 2901

Victoria

The Archaeological and Aboriginal Relics Preservation Act 1972-1984 Aboriginal and Torres Strait Islander Heritage Protection Amendment Act 1987	The Manager, Aboriginal Heritage Unit, Department of Aboriginal Affairs, P.O. Box 262, Albert Park, 3206

Tasmania

Aboriginal Relics Act 1975	The Secretary, Department of Lands, Parks and Wildlife, P.O. Box 44a, Hobart, 7001

Aboriginal sites and artefacts, can be used to protect sites where a State government has failed to act; an Aborigine can request a declaration of a site which is endangered (Ward 1985). The Protection of Movable Cultural Heritage Act 1986 governs the export and import of artefacts, and is used to control the international trade of Aboriginal items. Other acts, such as the Environmental Protection (Impact of Proposals) Act 1974 (with subsequent amendments) can effect protection of heritage sites, and indeed some States have similar legislation which may provide better site protection than do the original 'relics' acts.

Contemporary Aboriginal Views of Management of Aboriginal Heritage Places

In March 1991, an AIATSIS/VAS Workshop on Heritage Tourism and Aboriginal sites (Ward 1991b; Ward and Boyd, forthcoming) was convened largely in response to the growing debate about the role of Aboriginal people in the management of their own heritage. It was designed to bring together representatives of Aborigines and professional people from the field of heritage management in Australia, to discuss issues of mutual interest. The first group comprised Aboriginal people concerned with the traditional significance and use of Aboriginal sites, and others now involved in developing tourism at these sites. The second group comprised operators and administrators using Aboriginal sites for tourism; members of this group tended to be sympathetic to contemporary Aboriginal aspirations, but might be seen as untypical of tourism entrepreneurs who tend to commodify Aboriginal sites as economic resources (Smith et al. 1992). The third group comprised people, both Aboriginal and non-Aboriginal, concerned with the research into and conservation of Aboriginal sites, including academic and agency archaeologists and site managers; they predominantly are sympathetic to contemporary Aboriginal political aspirations.

These three groups have different perspectives on heritage and heritage management, all having particular interests in such sites, interests which may be in conflict with the interests of other groups. Experience at sites throughout Australia, as highlighted at Mootwingie in western New South Wales (Witter and Bates, forthcoming), indicates that the issues of management, from on-site methods through to determination of policy and implementation of control, has the potential to generate considerable conflict between all or some of the interested parties. These differing agenda reflect differing assumptions and philosophies of each group, and are influenced by exposure to and understanding of, for example, the functioning of the tourism industry, Aboriginal expectations and community processes, and methods for on-site protection. While all groups took the opportunity to make their interests and concerns known to the others, as a consequence of both the aims of the workshop and the character of the participants, much of the discussion tended towards an Aboriginal-centred view of the management of Aboriginal heritage sites. This discussion ranged widely, clearly introducing wider agenda into the discussion of heritage site management than are traditionally invoked. In particular, a broad social and political setting is identified by Aboriginal people as an integral part of the issue of heritage management.

The key issue, currently appreciated in the non-Aboriginal community by archaeologists, site managers and some tourism industry personnel, is that of Aboriginal control of Aboriginal heritage. This does not necessitate ownership in a Eurocentric sense, but requires the development of structures which give communities involvement in the management of sites which they regard as integral parts of their culture, and, ultimately, control, as in the ability to veto proposals. As indicated above, such control may become evident in several ways. Aboriginal input into policy development and management plans may provide the framework by which management is implemented, whereas Aboriginal involvement as employees at and managers of sites provides a direct association of people with the sites. For example, the production of new heritage sites in the Newcastle area of New South Wales (Gordon, forthcoming) represents not only a management response to pressure on existing sites, but a statement of cultural identity and strength, as is the 'refurbishment' of Aboriginal heritage (e.g. Gartside 1992; Morris 1992; Ward 1992). A key issue, which may be addressed by increasing Aboriginal responsibilities for site management, is that of identifying the role of heritage sites, including recording sites and their functions and discussing their significances as part of the living culture of local people, and, in some cases, as an economic resource available to the tourism industry.

At the root of this approach to site management there are antithetical views of heritage management. The view commonly held by Aboriginal people is that current practice is part of the exploitative social processes which have been predominant in Australian society over the last 200 years. Aboriginal responses to this view are wide-ranging. Some argue that all Aboriginal places of cultural significance ought to be closed to the public and returned entirely to the guardianship of relevant traditional custodians, to the exclusion of the tourism industry. Other argue that heritage sites, while functioning as places of significance to contemporary Aboriginal culture, can also be educational and economic resources.

The latter response invokes a wide socio-economic context. Under this approach, Aboriginal communities may benefit from tourism at their sites, by gaining access to potential sources of revenue, employment, training, and improved relationships between Aboriginal and non-Aboriginal people in Australia. A most frequently expressed opinion concerns the important social role that a change in direction in heritage site management may bring in providing improved opportunities for both the training and employment of Aboriginal people, and the education of non-Aboriginal people about Aboriginal issues and culture. The importance of heritage sites, therefore, is seen within the context of advancing Aboriginal interests within Australian society.

There are, in broad terms, two major influences on the nature and quality of heritage management. Aboriginal involvement within these spheres of influence is regarded as essential by both Aboriginal communities and cultural heritage managers to advance management of Aboriginal heritage. The first influence is the body of legislation and formal policies governing management practice, viewed by many Aboriginal people as being inadequate and requiring change (Fourmile 1992). However, development of suitable legislation policy is complex, often highly politicized and slow, and complicated by the wider legislative policy issue relating to rights of land ownership and Aboriginal authority; in those States and Territories where land rights legislation is lacking or inadequate, attempts are made to use heritage legislation to achieve control of land. The second influence is the presence and activity of the tourism industry. While this economic industry is seen to provide immediate, often short-term, and in many cases detrimental impact on heritage sites, short of removing access to sites there is a growing awareness among those with non-industrial interest in the sites that they must understand the processes by which the tourism industry operates. This enhances control over visitor access and activity by providing opportunity for communities either to work within the industry or to influence the industry in areas such as the marketing of images and provision of information.

On-site management, the most visible part of the management process, appears to be one of the major sources of tension at particular sites. Following the results of poor-quality, non-responsive and inflexible management at many sites, there is an increasingly popular advocacy for more highly organized and developed management structures and practice, including the implementation of forward planning, inbuilt and continuous monitoring, and flexible policies. Central to this approach is the integration of all interested parties at all stages in the process, and thus issues such as communication, correct use of specialist personnel, including Aboriginal people, and increased awareness of different world views (e.g. the Aboriginal versus the archaeological views of the past), are becoming increasingly important, and it is apparent that such issues, if heritage site management is to advance in Australia, need to be aired as constructively as possible.

Beyond policy and planning, on-site management is often most visible in the engineering works and information outlets at such sites, and it is these which play an influential role in developing responses of visitors to a site. Engineering works represent responses to visitor pressure at sites, expressed, for example, in loss of pigment and reduction in image quality at painting sites, in erosion problems, and damage to the surrounding environment. Engineering responses range from complete or partial site closure, controlled site access, using devices such as fencing, boardwalks, pathways, and, in extreme cases, cages around certain sites. Although the engineering aspect of this approach is straightforward, the decision to adopt suitable options is often underrated, since it is an important one, and it reflects the relative values that are placed upon the site. In particular, in many cases, a suitable compromise between the conflicting demands of Aboriginal culture, the tourism market, the tourist, the site manager, and archaeologists is very difficult to make. However, the issue must be considered.

The information presented about sites serves to educate, inform, entertain and protect. Although this information is primarily provided for tourist visitors, it frequently concerns issues of cultural importance to the Aboriginal people in the area, and thus needs to be correct and of as high a quality as possible. This raises issues of intercultural exchange of information, such as the cultural correctness of information, and restrictions upon the permissibility of dissemination of some information, and thus provides an important role for Aboriginal input to site management, tourism development, and advertising. In being able to control the release and transfer of information about their culture, Aboriginal people, therefore, can play a critical role in the development of image and definition of Aboriginal culture for non-Aboriginal people.

Conclusion

For Aboriginal Australian communities, places of significance are perceived as part of a complex system of relationships with the land and the Dreaming (Berndt and Berndt 1988: 135ff.), one in which a person's economic and ritual dependence upon land is matched by obligations toward country; such rights and obligations were transmitted through consanguinity and affinity and, ideally, even with the disruption to traditional life, there should be no place in Australia for which custodial rights and responsibilities could not be defined (Lewis and Rose 1988). These responsibilities with land areas and important places were mediated through ritual by knowledgeable men and women within the various economy-focused bands and the local descent groups through which members were tied to the land mytho-totemically.

For non-Aborigines, such relationships and their geographical foci—Aboriginal heritage sites—cannot have comparable significance, and may be little understood. After much work by Aboriginal mediators, anthropologists and others, such places are now coming under the protection of Australian federal and State law. At the same time, such Aboriginal heritage places, especially where they are tangible (particularly, for example, sites with petroglyphs and painted imagery), are becoming the focus of interest of a new type of tourism and, as a consequence, in need of increased protection. Where such sites are to be accessible to visitors, this protection necessarily involves active management of visitation. Increasingly, Aboriginal people are gaining control of the administration of legislation, are earning professional qualifications in cultural heritage management and joining other professional cultural heritage agencies, and becoming responsible for the management of particular Aboriginal heritage sites and areas. Not only is there the necessity to deal with complex issues of heritage site management and tourism, but also an integration of professional responsibilities with the traditional cultural perceptions of land custodianship and systems of knowledge and its transmission. Today's challenge for Aboriginal heritage and visitor management is to satisfy that necessity.

References

Allen, J. 1983, 'Aborigines and archaeologists in Tasmania, 1983', *Australian Archaeology*, vol. 16, pp. 7–10.

Altman, J. C. 1988, *Aborigines, Tourism, and Development: The Northern Territory Experience*, North Australia Research Unit, Australian National University, Casuarina.

Altman, J. C. 1989, 'Tourism dilemmas for Aboriginal Australians', *Annals of Tourism Research*, vol. 16, pp. 475–6.

Aten, L. E. 1982, 'Planning the preservation of archaeological sites', in *Rescue Archaeology*, eds. R. L. Wilson and G. Loyola, Preservation Press, Washington, pp. 299–343.

Australian National Parks and Wildlife Service 1982, *Uluru (Ayres Rock–Mount Olga) National Park Plan of Management*, Australian National Parks and Wildlife Service, Canberra.

Beacroft, L. 1987, 'Conservation: accommodating Aboriginal interests or the new competitor?', *Aboriginal Law Bulletin*, vol. 26, pp. 3–4.

Berndt, R. M. and Berndt, C. H. 1988, *The World of the First Australians. Aboriginal Traditional Life: Past and Present*, Aboriginal Studies Press, Canberra.

Bogle, S. 1988, 'Confronting the realities of 200,000 visitors each year', *Land Rights News*, vol. 2, no. 9, pp. 38–9.

Boyd, W. E. and Dutton, I. M. (forthcoming), 'An approach to heritage site planning and management: limits of Acceptable Change', in *Proceedings of the AIATSIS/VAS Workshop on Heritage and Tourism, March 1991*, eds. G. K. Ward and

W. E. Boyd, Australian Institute of Aboriginal and Torres Strait Islander Studies, Canberra.

Boyd, W. E., Hall, C. M., and Zeppel, H. (forthcoming), 'Archaeology and tourism: Perspectives from the tourism market', in *Proceedings of the AIATSIS/VAS Workshop on Heritage and Tourism, March 1991*, eds. G. K. Ward and W. E. Boyd, Australian Institute of Aboriginal and Torres Strait Islander Studies, Canberra.

Brady, M. A. 1985, 'The promotion of tourism and its effects on Aborigines', in *Aborigines and Tourism: A Study of the Impact of Tourism on Aborigines in the Kakadu Region, Northern Territory*, ed. K. Palmer, Northern Land Council, Darwin, pp. 10–51.

Charles, A. E. 1984, 'Archaeology and the Native American', in *Ethics and Values in Archaeology*, ed. E. L. Green, Collier Macmillan, London, pp. 236–42.

Creamer, H. 1980, 'Sites of significance to Aborigines', *Australian Social Studies*, pp. 112–15.

Creamer, H. 1983, 'Contacting Aboriginal communities', in *Australian Field Archaeology: A Guide to Techniques*, ed. G. Connah, Australian Institute of Aboriginal Studies, Canberra, pp. 10–17.

Creamer, H. 1986a, 'Modern Aboriginal culture and its relation to sites in New South Wales', in *Planning for Aboriginal Site Management: A Handbook for Local Government Planners*, ed. A. Ross, National Parks and Wildlife Service, Sydney.

Creamer, H. 1986b, 'Cultural resource management and Aboriginal sites', *Australian Ranger Bulletin*, vol. 4, no. 1, pp. 4–5.

Dutton, I. M. and Hall, C. M. 1989, 'Making tourism sustainable: the policy/practice conundrum', in *Proceedings 2nd Environmental Impact Assessment Conference*, Environmental Impact Assessment Conference, Melbourne, pp. 196–206.

Fesl, E. 1983, 'Communication and communicative breakdown', in *Archaeology at ANZAAS 1983*, ed. M. Smith, Western Australian Museum, Perth, pp. 317–21.

Flood, J. 1979, 'Cultural resource management and tourism', in *Who Needs the Past?*, ed. R. Layton, Allen and Unwin, London, pp. 51–6.

Flood, J. 1990, *The Riches of Ancient Australia*, University of Queensland Press, St. Lucia.

Fourmile, H. 1992, 'The politics of managing Aboriginal rock art [Abstract]', in *Second AURU Congress, 30 August – 4 September 1992, Cairns, Congress handbook and abstracts*, ed. R. G. Bednarik, Australian Rock Art Research Association, Melbourne, p. 28.

Gale, G. F. and Jacobs, J. 1987a, *Tourists and the National Estate: Procedures to Protect Australia's Heritage*, Australian Government Publishing Service, Canberra.

Gale, G. F. and Jacobs, J. 1987b, 'Aboriginal art—Australia's neglected heritage', *World Archaeology*, vol. 19, pp. 226–35.

Gartside, C. 1992, 'Aboriginal retouch: a dilemma for site managers', in *Second AURU Congress, 30 August – 4 September 1992, Cairns, Congress handbook and abstracts*, compiler R. G. Bednarik, Australian Rock Art Research Association, Melbourne, p. 28.

Gillespie, D. A. 1988, 'Tourism in Kakadu National Park', in *Northern Australia: Progress and Prospects*, eds. D. Wade-Marshall and P. Loveday, North Australia Research Unit, Australian National University, Darwin, pp. 224–50.

Gordon, P. (forthcoming), 'Tourism at Aboriginal sites in the Newcastle area and a replica painted shelter', in *Proceedings of the AIATSIS/VAS Workshop on Heritage and Tourism, March 1991*, eds. G. K. Ward and W. E. Boyd, Australian Institute of Aboriginal and Torres Strait Islander Studies, Canberra.

Green, E. L. (ed.) 1984, *Ethics and Values in Archaeology*, Collier Macmillan, London.

Hamel, G. and Jones, K. 1982, *Manual of Vegetation Management on New Zealand Archaeological Sites*, New Zealand Historic Places Trust, Wellington.

Hammil, J. and Cruz, R. 1989, 'Statement of American Indians Against Desecration before the World Archaeological Congress', in *Conflict in the Archaeology of Living Traditions*, ed. R. Layton, Unwin Hyman, London, pp. 195–200.

Hubbert, J. 1989, 'A proper place for the dead: A critical review of the "reburial" debate', in *Conflict in the Archaeology of Living Traditions*, ed. R. Layton, Unwin Hyman, London, pp. 131–66.

Johnson, R. W. and Schene, M. G. (eds.) 1987, *Cultural Resources Management*, R. E. Krieger, Malabar, Florida.

Kesteven, S. L. 1987, *Aborigines in the Tourist Industry*, East Kimberley Impact Assessment Project, Australian National University, Canberra.

Lambert, D. 1989, *Conserving Australian Rock Art: A Manual for Site Managers*, G. K. Ward, ed. Aboriginal Studies Press, Canberra.

Langford, R. F. 1983, 'Our heritage—your playground', *Australian Archaeology*, vol. 16, pp. 1–6.

Lawrence, R. 1985, 'The tourist impact and the Aboriginal response', in *Aborigines and Tourism: A Study of the Impact of Tourism on Aborigines in the Kakadu Region, Northern Territory*, ed. K. Palmer, Northern Land Council, Darwin, pp. 52–122.

Layton, R. (ed.) 1989, *Conflict in the Archaeology of Living Traditions*, Unwin Hyman, London.

Lewis, D. and Rose, D. B. 1985, 'Some ethical issues in archaeology: a methodology of consultation in Northern Australia', *Australian Aboriginal Studies*, no. 1, pp. 37–44.

Lewis, D. and Rose, D. B. 1988, *The Shape of the Dreaming: Report on the Cultural Significance of Victoria River Rock Art*, Aboriginal Studies Press, Canberra.

Marcus, J. 1988, 'The journey out to the Centre: the cultural appropriation of Ayers Rock', in *Aboriginal Culture Today*, ed. A. Rutherford, Dangaroo Press, Sydney, pp. 254–74.

Martin, D. 1985, 'Ethics and the anthropological enterprise in Australia', *Australian Anthropological Society Newsletter*, vol. 28, pp. 28–35.

Ministerial Task Force on Aboriginal Heritage and Culture 1988, *Preliminary Report*, New South Wales State Government, Sydney.

Mitchell, B. 1989, *Geography and Resource Analysis*, 2nd. ed., Longmans, London.

Morris, G. 1992, 'Aboriginal perceptions of traditional rock art sites as a means of cultural revival: the needs of conservation versus use', in *Second AURU Congress, 30 August – 4 September 1992, Cairns, Congress handbook and abstracts*, compiler R. G. Bednarik, Australian Rock Art Research Association, Melbourne, p. 28.

Morwood, M. J. 1981, 'The saga of Wild Duck: a recipe for cultural mismanagement', in *Coastal Archaeology in Eastern Australia*, ed. S. Bowdler, Department of Prehistory, Research School of Pacific Studies, The Australian National University, Canberra, pp. 108–13.

Mulvaney, J. 1989, 'Aboriginal Australia; custodianship or ownership; a reflection on the National Estate', *Heritage News*, vol. 11, no. 4, pp. 11–12.

Pearson, C. (ed.) 1978, *Conservation of Rock Art*, Institute for the Conservation of Cultural Material, Sydney.

Pitts, D. 1986, 'Opportunity shift: Development and application of ROS Concepts in Park Management', Unpublished Ph.D. Thesis, Griffith University.

Prott, L. V. and O'Keefe, P. J. 1984, *Law and the Cultural Heritage, Vol. 1, Discovery and Excavation*, Professional Books, Abingdon.

Prott, L. V. and O'Keefe, P. J. 1989, *Law and the Cultural Heritage, Vol. 3, Movement*, Butterworths, London.

Roff, D. 1984, 'Visitor behaviour and management', in *Visitors to Aboriginal Sites: Access, Control and Management*, ed. H. Sullivan, Australian National Parks and Wildlife Service, Canberra/National Parks and Wildlife Service, Sydney, pp. 54–6.

Schiffer, M. B. and Gumerman, J. (eds.) 1977, *Conservation Archaeology: A Guide for Cultural Resource Management Studies*, Academic Press, New York.

Senior, C. 1987, 'Tourism and Aboriginal Heritage with Particular Reference to the Kimberley'. Unpublished typescript held in the Australian Institute of Aboriginal and Torres Strait Islander Studies, Canberra.

Sheppard, D. 1988, 'Parks are for people . . . or are they?', *Australian Parks and Recreation*, vol. 24, no. 2, pp. 11–14.

Smith, L-J. , Clarke, A., and Alcock, A. 1992, 'Teaching cultural tourism: comments from the classroom', *Australian Archaeology*, vol. 34, pp. 43–7.

Sorenson, A. D. and Auster, M. L. 1989, 'Fatal remedies—The sources of ineffectiveness in planning', *Town Planning Review*, vol. 60, no. 1, pp. 29–44.

Sullivan, H. (ed.) 1984, *Visitors to Aboriginal Sites: Access, Control and Management*, Australian National Parks and Wildlife Service, Canberra.

Sullivan, S. 1975, 'Mootwingie: an example of cultural tourism', in *The Preservation of Australia's Aboriginal Heritage*, ed. R. Edwards, Australian Institute of Aboriginal Studies, Canberra, pp. 59–64.

Sullivan, S. 1985, 'Aboriginal site interpretation: some considerations', in *ACT Heritage Seminars*, vol. 3, Heritage Committee, Canberra, pp. 11–22.

Thorne, R. M. 1989, *Intentional Site Burial: A Technique to Protect Against Natural or Mechanical Loss*, U. S. National Park Service, Washington.

Ucko, P. J. 1983, 'Australian academic archaeology: Aboriginal transformation of its aims and practices', *Australian Archaeology*, vol. 16, pp. 11–26.

Ward, G. K. 1983, 'Archaeology and legislation in Australia', in *Australian Field Archaeology: A Guide to Techniques*, ed. G. Connah, Australian Institute of Aboriginal Studies, Canberra, pp. 18–42.

Ward, G. K. 1985, 'The federal Aboriginal Heritage Act and archaeology', *Australian Aboriginal Studies*, no. 2, pp. 47–52.

Ward, G. K. 1991a, 'Preservation of rock imagery', in *Australian Yearbook 1991*, Australian Bureau of Statistics, Canberra, pp. 558–66.

Ward, G. K. 1991b, 'Institute-convened workshop on heritage tourism and Aboriginal sites', *Australian Aboriginal Studies*, no. 1, pp. 85–7.

Ward, G. K. (ed.) 1992, *Retouch: Maintenance and Conservation of Aboriginal Rock Imagery*, Australian Rock Art Research Association, Melbourne.

Ward, G. K. and Boyd, W. E. (eds.) (forthcoming), *Proceedings of the AIATSIS/VAS*

Workshop on Heritage and Tourism, March 1991, eds. G. K. Ward and W. E. Boyd, Australian Institute of Aboriginal and Torres Strait Islander Studies, Canberra.

Witter, D. and Bates, B. (forthcoming), 'A history of ?management at Mootwingie', in *Proceedings of the AIATSIS/VAS Workshop on Heritage and Tourism, March 1991*, eds. G. K. Ward and W. E. Boyd, Australian Institute of Aboriginal and Torres Strait Islander Studies, Canberra.

Wright, R. 1986, 'Changing faces of Australian archaeology: the need to get permission', in *Archaeology at ANZAAS Congress (54th: 1984: Australian National University)*, ANZAAS, Canberra, pp. 241–4.

Zimmerman, L. J. 1989, 'Human bones as symbols of power: Aboriginal American belief systems towards bones and "grave robbing" archaeologists', in *Conflict in the Archaeology of Living Traditions*, ed. R. Layton, Unwin Hyman, London, pp. 211–16.

10

Landscape, Heritage, and Identity
Stories from the West Coast

V. G. Kirby

For the land isn't a static thing that I can happily describe as 'slightly weathered glacial outwash gravel and till, quaternary formation' or 'an area notable for septarian concretions.' (Though those quotations do hold a strange fascination: they say so much—age and structure and process—yet so little about what each place really is) (Hulme 1987a: 1).

The West Coast can't be just a place (John, recorded conversation).

The Heritage Debate

Heritage is a relatively recent addition to the language of resource management in New Zealand. It has come to prominence at a time of intensive and far-reaching economic and organizational restructuring. Pawson and Scott (forthcoming) have recounted how it was assumed that changes which were supposed to be good for the nation's economy would also, by implication, be good for individual communities and places. But people tend to react against the short-term, local effects of such changes and, in the face of uncertainty, they cling to the familiar; to things, places, and memories that are reminders of a known past. The retention of such things removes some of the pain involved in contemplating an unknown, uncertain future. The notion of heritage is particularly powerful in this context.

The Resource Management Act 1991 introduced the concept of heritage into the New Zealand legislature. Although the Act does not contain a definition of the word in the strict sense, its implied meaning includes

> special interest, character, intrinsic or amenity value or visual appeal, or . . . special significance to the tangata whenua [people of the land, or Māori] for spiritual, cultural or historical reasons . . . special interest [means] having special cultural, architectural, historical, scientific, ecological, or other interest (Resource Management Act 1991, section 189).

Here lie, at one and the same time, both the attraction and the danger of the term. It really can mean anything we like. The past is, after all, all that has gone before the brief intensity of the present moment. We may label any part of the past as heritage, and strive to keep it. It therefore becomes important to look at situations where the term is used, in order to try to reveal more precise, meaningful definitions.

The inclusion of heritage in recent legislation follows a growing usage of the word in a land management context. One example was the debate on the then proposed World Heritage Area in South Westland. According to McSweeney (1987):

> In the last 1000 years the arrival of people [in New Zealand] has brought phenomenal changes to the land and its inhabitants. Fire and forest clearance, hunting, the introduction of predators and of browsing mammals have transformed New Zealand. Today much of it resembles European pastureland or North American pine plantations while in places tatty remnants of shrubland begin the slow process of regeneration to native forest.
> What is left today is certainly a shadow of its former glory but it is a *heritage we increasingly recognise and appreciate and cannot afford to lose* [my emphasis] (McSweeney 1987: 15).

To McSweeney the essential heritage of New Zealand is natural. The traces of people on the landscape are significant but are, on the whole, to be regretted. Others (Hulme 1987b; Potton 1987) supported recognition of the cultural significance of South Westland's landscapes, but the eventual designation recognized explicitly only the natural qualities of the land (Department of Conservation [DOC] 1991).

This idea of a national heritage which is common to all New Zealanders, and which is based on the uniqueness of the country's natural features, is valid, but it does not tell the whole story. It becomes increasingly clear that heritage is not a single, unified concept, applicable only in the national context and at a national scale. The things that we choose to keep are strong indicators of our sense of identity. Concentrating on the unique New Zealand biota at a national scale serves us well in demonstrating our identity in relation to other nations. But is also likely that each local community will have its own distinct ideas about heritage, to confirm its own sense of identity and thus, by implication, to separate it from other communities. There are links here with the approach to landscape supported by Hulme (1987b) and Potton (1987)— if landscapes are a complex blend of the natural and cultural, further enriched by the specificity of experience and perception (Jackson 1984), then it is likely that the landscapes that we want to keep will also reflect that complexity.

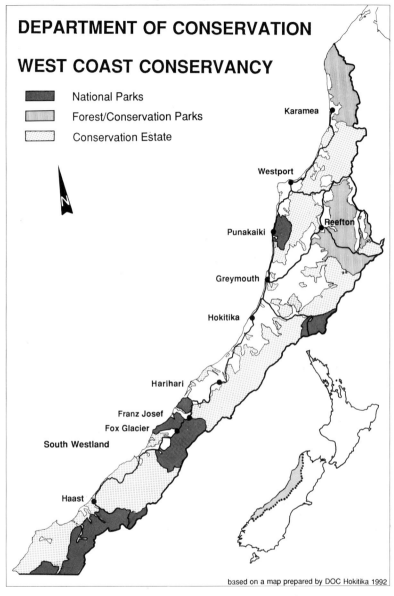

Figure 10.1: Department of Conservation West Coast Conservancy

The West Coast

The West Coast is a distinctive physical area with a number of pasts. It is 'a narrow wedge of land between the Southern Alps and the sea' (Pawson and Scott, forthcoming) (Figure 10.1). It is a place on the margin in the sense used by Shields (1991), one of those regions which are perceived to 'have been "left behind" in the modern race for progress, [and which] evoke both nostalgia and fascination' (Shields 1991: 3).

With its high rainfall, dense bush and difficult terrain, its main attraction to the Māori in the centuries before European colonization was the much-prized pounamu (nephrite jade or greenstone) (Brailsford 1984). Dismissed as a barren, inhospitable land by Cook (Ministry of Works [MoW] 1959) in the 1770s, romanticized as 'Erewhon' by Butler (1873), it was exploited for its gold, coal and timber from the 1860s until the 1990s (MoW 1959). However, most of the land is still heavily forested, and four fifths of the region's total area is managed by DOC as part of the national conservation estate. The population of 35,000 is scattered in small communities along the coastal strip and in valleys such as the Buller and the Grey (Peat 1989).

Although as recently as 1959 the future of the area was still assumed to be in agriculture and industry (MoW 1959), by the late 1980s priorities had changed. In recent years the downturn of the national economy has meant severe retrenchment both in the private and the public sectors.

> Primary produce and raw materials do not have the value they once had and distance to markets limits growth . . . Tourism has been important to Franz Josef and Fox Glacier townships for many years. Other areas are turning to tourism to provide employment and to boost local economies (Coventry 1988: 14).

The West Coast is now being marketed as a destination for tourists, both for its natural and its cultural values. According to Peat 'what were barriers to the explorers of last century are natural and scenic delights to the visitor today' (1989: ix). A marketing strategy prepared for the West Coast Tourism Development Group cited 'The major themes of natural, historic and lifestyle heritage [as being] the very essence of the West Coast tourism product' (Meldrum 1991: 4).

An uncritical reading of such statements might lead to the conclusion that there is general agreement about the nature of the heritage of the Coast and about the role of tourism in the exploitation of that heritage. This is not the case. The hyperbole contained in documents produced specifically for those either involved in, or customers of, the tourism industry, should not hide the intensity of the debate and the depth of feeling concerning heritage. For example, nearly 4000 submissions were received by the Working Party considering the future of State-owned forests in South Westland, prior to the establishment of the World Heritage Area (Ministry for the Environment [MFE] 1988). The Working Party, including representatives from conservation groups, the timber industry, citizens' groups, local and regional authorities, the Mahitahi Māori Committee, and advisers from Government Departments, agreed that 291,000 of the 311,000 hectares of State forest in the study area should be recommended for conservation. Great debate surrounded the remaining 20,000 hectares, with representatives of the local communities and the timber industry wishing to see an exploration into the feasibility of sustained yield logging. This was consistent with their view that it was crucial to retain traditional industries in order to ensure community viability and identity. In contrast the conservation agencies felt that

> any logging would be to the unacceptable detriment of the ecological, botanical, wildlife, landscape, scenic, recreational, and historic qualities of the forests. It was considered that there is considerable potential for tourism to create employment (MFE 1988: 6).

In the event the World Heritage Area that was created in 1990 included all those previously unprotected, predominantly natural parts of South Westland that were adjacent to the existing National Parks. Thus, by implication, the features of the area which distinguished it as significant to ideas of national heritage and identity were presumed to be more important than those features which the local community wished to emphasize. This set of priorities was reflected in proposals for the interpretation programme for the South Westland information centre. Molloy (1990), although acknowledging both 1000 years of Māori occupation and recent colonial history, believed that the major heritage themes for the centre should be those that explored the area's natural characteristics. Similarly, DOC proposed that the three main themes should be forests, water and human endeavour, with the human aspects very much subordinate to the natural (DOC 1990) (See Chapter 5).

The Case Study

Early in 1992 I spent five weeks on the Coast, with the intention of investigating some local interpretations of and feelings for heritage, landscape, and identity. I was interested in exploring what I perceived as a paradoxical situation—a region where most of the land area was managed as part of the nation's conservation estate, primarily for its perceived natural values, and where exploitation of those values by the tourism industry was seen to be a mainstay of the region's economy, but where the people who would be responsible for the day-to-day operation of that industry had a different set of values, deriving their identity from the more immediate past of cultural activity. Such complexities are in fact simply the stuff of the real world, which may have only one physical form but on which a large number of human worlds are based (Harrison and Livingstone 1980; Mercer 1984) and in which there are many versions of reality, each dependent on the particular experience of the participants (Antaki 1988).

I wished to see if West Coasters would be willing and able to put their ideas about heritage into their own words. Therefore I set out to record a series of loosely structured, taped interviews. These would, I hoped, demonstrate the variability of ideas about heritage as related to aspects of the West Coast landscape.

My first tasks were to decide where to go and whom to interview. The sampling strategy used non-probability methods. Both the places and the people were chosen after a process of networking similar to snowball sampling (Burgess 1984). The discussion below summarizes conversations with eighteen people, five from South Westland, seven from Reefton, and six from Hokitika (see Figure 10.1).

South Westland was chosen because it represented an area affected by the recent imposition of a particular interpretation of heritage following World Heritage Area designation. Reefton, in the Grey Valley, was chosen because it contrasted with South Westland in several ways. First, it was an inland town in the northern part of the region rather than a string of small coastal hamlets in the far south. Second, it had a recent history of mineral extraction (coal and gold) as well as the ubiquitous milling of native timber. Third, the process of defining and interpreting heritage as part of the development of the tourism industry was at an earlier stage than in South Westland. The information centre at Haast Junction had been opened in December 1991, whereas DOC was still planning the development of a centre at Reefton, which was due to be started in 1992. Hokitika was chosen because the Department of Conservation had its regional headquarters there, and I wished to include in the schedule of interviews some people who not only lived on the coast, but who also worked for the Department.

My role in each interview was a finely balanced one. Since I was an outsider enquiring into personal feelings about heritage and identity, it was important to establish a relationship with my respondents by giving something of myself to the dialogue (Burgess 1984). On the other hand, it was important not to impose my interpretations of heritage on others, who might then tell me what they thought I wanted to hear. I kept the language of the interviews as free of jargon as possible, concentrating on encouraging people to talk about those aspects of their physical surroundings that contributed most to their sense of identity with and belonging to the Coast.

The Interviews

Many respondents identified with certain aspects of the region as a whole, making particular mention of the physical barrier of the Southern Alps. The Alps isolate the Coast from the rest of the South Island, and are a significant influence on the region's weather. The experience of traversing over one of the passes on the Main Divide was frequently mentioned as marking the beginning of home territory. Ellen's response to my question about where 'home' began, was typical:

> I feel like a sort of dehydrated vegetable if I go out of Haast. When I drive back over, when I get to the top of the pass and the bush starts closing in, I feel as if I've been popped in water and I expand.

Of the eighteen interviews, two were with members of the Māori community. Mary, from South Westland, identified with the Coast in general from Fox Glacier southwards, but also expressed strong feelings for certain places, including a mountain which bore the name of a distant ancestor. She tried to explain the intensity with which Māori people relate to particular areas and features: 'You're bound inextricably to the land, the two can't really be separated, one can't live without the other'.

Although non-Māori interviewees did not express themselves as intensely, there were nevertheless some strong expressions of identity and belonging to certain specific places. Mavis was born in Waiuta, a gold-mining town near Reefton which was abandoned in 1951 when the main shaft collapsed. For her

> Waiuta's home—always will be . . . In the 1970s I got to the stage where I was never going back, it hurt too much to see it overgrown and nobody there . . . [but now] I go up quite a lot with school children . . . as you talk you keep your memories bright.

Mavis's sense of heritage was maintained by consciously activating her memory. Even though Waiuta itself had changed almost beyond recognition in the 40 years since the mine's closure, it remained home.

But for some people feelings of belonging and identity did not relate explicitly to land, but to people. Vera, a miner's widow living in Reefton, felt that home was essentially 'a place which has to have people—a supportive community'.

Heritage Management

Although I was interested in exploring personal senses of heritage, sometimes people raised issues relating to places which were officially labelled as heritage, such as the South Westland World Heritage Area. Such issues implicitly shed some light on their own feelings. Mary's comments reflected the Māori view that people cannot be separated from the land:

> We actually took the trouble of going to UNESCO. We tried to take out an injunction against it [the World Heritage Area] because our request was that it should be made a cultural park . . . You must take into consideration all the cultural values.

The differences between official and personal views on what must be kept were sometimes pointed out with disarming clarity. Bert demonstrated the paradox:

> It's a strange thing. There's so much emphasis at the moment on the environment, you know, you can't do this, you can't do that, because it's going to be out of place in the environment. In the old days the old mines that were established, they paid no attention to the environment at all, but those very things that they did then . . . are the focus for tourism now. And you can go anywhere for a walk through the bush . . . and to me it doesn't really mean a lot, if you've seen one bit of bush you've seen the lot—but if it takes you to some place where there was an old coal mine or a gold mine, still got relics of stuff there . . . it makes quite a difference.

There was considerable interest in Reefton about the new information centre which was at the time of the interviews being planned as a co-operative venture between DOC and the local community. Comments from local people reflected a strong sense of identity with the area's mining past. Geoff talked about

> identifying with our past—pulling a theme out of it, and our theme for the information centre is quartz mining in Reefton, because that's where it started, it was actually called Quartzopolis . . . and so we are identifying something a bit more unique than, say, Westport, that had coal mining, and Greymouth, which had other things.

Steve was also aware of the possible differences between local feeling and official views about the things which should be interpreted as the essential heritage of an area:

> [Reefton people] are obviously going to focus on quartz mining . . . and I think you'll get some opposition within the Department [DOC] . . . I think South Westland is probably the classic example where the focus was going to be on the natural heritage . . . and it caused a tremendous amount of resentment in

the south and we had to fight like hell to get the cultural component incorporated in that interpretation.

What was emerging was a strong sense of the significance of cultural activity and culturally modified landscapes as determinants of heritage at the local level. Mike had strong views on this:

> When I start talking about a river mouth . . . I think of the hydrology, I think of the mokihis, the rafts the Māori built, I think of Brunner when he crossed it in 1846, but I'm in a better position to make decisions about it; it's not just a river mouth, it's a living stretch of water that has been a barrier.

There was also considerable agreement about the importance of acknowledging that although traditionally Māori people identified particularly strongly with their land, people of European extraction felt deeply too, and that what was significant was sense of place, a culturally determined concept:

> I have a deep commitment in sharing power with the tangata whenua . . . There is a spiritual relationship in the way . . . a lot of Europeans relate to the land, and it's reinforced by the Māori, which is much, much stronger, and it adds a whole, another element to the way you perceive a place . . . It needs to be culturally defined. A sense of place is a very important notion (John).

Nevertheless, I did not find unanimity. For some of my respondents the natural features of the West Coast were the most important components. To Peter the heritage of the Coast

> is essentially natural. It contains many of New Zealand's most significant examples of glaciation, alpine and geomorphological processes. It's dissected by a thin ribbon of tarseal which people cluster alongside but other than that it is essentially unspoiled, and unspoiled in that you can't see the effects of human occupation.

Conclusions

The results of this study lend support to the view that, when considering both heritage and landscape, it is essential always to acknowledge a particular spatial and cultural context.

The West Coast is not one landscape, but a whole constellation of landscapes, which overlap, interlock and contrast. To many West Coasters the things that make their local landscapes particularly distinctive derive from personal memories of past cultural activity, although the significance of the overall natural context is also acknowledged by most.

This raises some interesting issues. For example, to what extent should the ideal of the natural dominate land management policies for the eighty per cent of the region which is part of the national conservation estate? Also, what is the proper emphasis of interpretive programmes aimed at the developing tourist industry? Should such programmes portray a landscape whose heritage value derives from those natural features which differentiate the West Coast from other regions and New Zealand from other countries? Or should they seek to interpret local landscapes that are unique blends of the natural and the cultural?

These are obviously heavily loaded questions. It would be easy to jump to the conclusion that a focus on the large scale and the natural is somehow wrong. But that would be giving in to the temptation of wanting to define a single, unified approach to heritage. Ideally the management and interpretation of heritage landscapes should reflect the full spectrum of possible values relevant to each specific context. There will of course be impassioned debate about the nature of these values, much of which will take place at the cutting edge between local communities and government agencies.

There will never be a full and complete resolution of the debate and that is as it should be. What is required on the Coast, and elsewhere, is acknowledgement of the significance of a dynamic, complex series of local, culturally defined heritage landscapes, which are critical components of the sense of identity of each community.

References

Antaki, C. 1988, 'Explanations, communication and social cognition', in *Analysing Everyday Explanation*, ed. C. Antaki, Sage Publications, London, pp.1-14.

Brailsford, B. 1984, *Greenstone Trails*, Reed, Wellington.

Burgess, R.G. 1984, *In the Field: An Introduction to Field Research*, Allen and Unwin, London.

Butler, S. 1873, *Erewhon or Over the Range*, 5th. ed., Trubner, London.

Coventry, N. 1988, *Pacific Asia Travel Association West Coast Task Force Report*, Joint Report of PATA, New Zealand Tourist and Publicity Department and West Coast Tourism Council.

Department of Conservation 1990, *Haast Visitor Centre South Westland*, Department of Conservation, Hokitika.

Department of Conservation 1991, *World Heritage Highway Guide—South Westland and Haast Pass*, West Coast Conservancy, Department of Conservation, Hokitika.

Harrison, R. T. and Livingstone, D. N. 1980, 'Philosophy and problems with human geography: a presuppositional approach', *Area*, vol. 12, pp. 25-31.

Hulme, K. 1987a, 'Okarito and Moeraki.' in *Te whenua, te iwi: The Land and the People*, ed. J. Phillips, Allen and Unwin, Port Nicholson Press, Wellington, pp. 1–9.

Hulme, K. 1987b, 'Te Whenua Whai-Taoka,' in *Forests, Fiords and Glaciers—the Case for a South West New Zealand World Heritage Site*, eds. G. Hutching and C. Potton, Royal Forest and Bird Protection Society, Wellington, pp. 77–83.

Jackson, J. B. 1984, *Discovering the Vernacular Landscape*, Yale University Press, New Haven.

McSweeney, G. 1987, 'Our global heritage in trust for humankind', in *Forests, Fiords and Glaciers—the Case for a South West New Zealand World Heritage Site*, eds. G. Hutching and C. Potton, Royal Forest and Bird Protection Society, Wellington, pp. 15–27.

Meldrum, D. 1991, 'Marketing guidelines for the West Coast', unpublished consultant's report, June 1991.

Mercer, D. 1984, *Reading the Book of Nature: Physical and Human Geography and the Limits of Science*, Monash University, Department of Geography Working Paper No. 18.

Ministry for the Environment 1988, *South Westland South of the Cook River: Resource Management Study*, Ministry for the Environment, Wellington.

Ministry of Works 1959, *West Coast Region*, Government Printer, Wellington.

Molloy, L. F. 1990, 'Te Wahipounamu—an approach to the interpretation of world heritage wilderness', Department of Conservation, unpublished report.

Pawson, E. and Scott, G. (forthcoming), 'The regional consequences of economic restructuring: the West Coast, New Zealand, 1984-1991', in *Journal of Rural Studies*.

Peat, N. 1989, *The West Coast, South Island*, GP Books, Wellington.

Potton, C. 1987, 'From exploitation to appreciation—200 years of European settlement', in *Forests, Fiords and Glaciers—the Case for a South West New Zealand World Heritage Site*, eds. G. Hutching and C. Potton, Royal Forest and Bird Protection Society, Wellington, pp. 85–9.

Shields, R. 1991, *Places on the Margin: Alternative Geographies of Modernity*, Routledge, London.

11

Marketing a Sense of Place

Graham Brown

Introduction

It has been suggested that 'people demonstrate a sense of place when they apply their moral and aesthetic discernment to sites and locations' (Tuan 1974). The outcome of such an assessment may be a feeling of attachment; a belief that a place is, in some way, personally meaningful (see Chapter 10).

Expressions of favourable attitudes toward a particular place appear frequently in the popular media; in newspapers and magazines. Under the heading 'Places in the Heart', the *Weekend Australian* asked 'five famous Australians' to 'let their minds wander to the one perfect, private location where they recharge their batteries' (Fox 1991: 32) and *Travel and Leisure* included an article in each issue entitled 'Special Places', before publishing *Favorite Places*, a book in which the magazine's columnists and writers described 'a place that, for whatever reason, meant more to him or her than any other' (Fiori 1989: 13).

An endorsement of the kind provided in these articles represents excellent publicity for a tourism destination. If a destination commands a more widely held belief that it has a unique sense of place, it is able to readily achieve product differentiation, gaining advantage from competitors which are perceived to have few distinctive characteristics.

This paper will be in two parts. The first will explore the relationship between personal identity and place, focusing on the importance of environmental symbolism. Reference to interactions with destinations visited as a tourist will represent an integrative thread throughout the discussion. The second part will describe a particular interpretation of how to create a sense of place and will attempt to apply the suggestions to the benefit of destination marketing. Attention will be directed toward the implications for heritage management at appropriate points in the discussion and in the conclusion.

Symbolism, Identity, and Sense of Place

The study of psychological bonds with tangible surroundings has been dominated by an interest in the home environment (Fried 1963; Cooper 1976; Relph 1976; Seamon 1979; Buttimer 1980). It has been proposed that these bonds are developed following long-term involvement, as illustrated by the belief that 'it takes time to get to know a place' (Tuan 1977: 179). Through the routines of daily life, the home environment becomes a place of familiar and predictable activities, comprising experiences which are, most often, unconscious or taken for granted. The process of attending to and providing interpretations of the home environment means that people not only come to know and have feelings about these places, they also come to know and have feelings about themselves.

An alternative conceptualization has contended that 'place-identity is construed from epistemic acts directed toward locating oneself in the geographical ecology' (Sarbin 1983: 338). To Sarbin, this perspective represented an action-oriented framework, in which people 'fashion their place-identities' (1983: 339). It was adopted in a model by Korpela (1989) which proposed that a range of physical settings can be used to support one's self-conceptions. Thus, it is particularly relevant to heritage tourism and visitor management. An emotional attachment to place is a central feature of her model and, once again, attention was directed to the symbolic significance of environments.

It may be argued that increased mobility has been accompanied by a reduction in identification with the home and its surrounding community as more individualistic lifestyles find expression in a dispersed pattern of socio-spatial activities. According to Ericksen (1980), spatial identification may no longer be related to place of residence but to the question 'Have you been there?' Interactions with the environment by tourists may become increasingly important as people 'attempt to establish some degree of symmetry between self and external behavior in space' (Wilson 1980: 145) and a tourism destination may become the setting for an experience that renders that particular place 'a discrete, temporally and perceptually bounded unit of psychologically meaningful space' (Godkin 1980: 73). It may therefore be perceived as having a unique sense of place.

The emergence of meaning and of meaningful experiences, as a product of person–environment encounter, is consistent with a symbolic interactionist perspective. Such a perspective would also conceive the tourist as an individual who uses information about the environment to define situations prior to behaviour and the ability to define situations would be enhanced if a destination embodies shared meanings as a symbol endowed with cultural significance. The relationship between a tourist and the environment would therefore be mediated by the perception of destinations as features within a symbolic landscape.

According to Meinig (1979: 164) 'every mature nation has its symbolic landscapes. They are part of the iconography of nationhood, part of the shared set of ideas and memories and feelings which bind a people together'. Rowntree and Conkey (1980: 461) have suggested that 'the cultural landscape in part functions as a narrative, a symbolic legacy' and Relph (1976) has nominated Red Square, Niagara Falls and the Acropolis as national symbols of common experience which foster a sense of national unity and pride. Few people would deny according Uluru, the Sydney Opera House and Milford Sound a similar status.

Although it is unlikely that people would make an unprompted reference to the symbolic quality of a place, a recent survey revealed that seven per cent of residents in Byron Shire cited the area's location as the most easterly point in Australia as one of the main features which they believe attracts tourists to the area. A further twenty-two per cent specifically mentioned the power of the lighthouse as an attraction. The role of the lighthouse as a symbol for the area is apparent by its prominence on postcards and the behaviour of camera-clicking tourists. The same study also sought information on resident attitudes and, significantly, fifty-six per cent of people living in Byron Bay, strongly agreed that 'Byron Bay has a unique sense of place which cannot be found anywhere else in Australia'. A further thirty-five per cent agreed with the statement (Brown 1992).

An analysis of attractions as sacred places by Sears (1989) was based on the premise that tourism played a powerful role in America's invention of itself as a culture. Americans sought their identity in their relationship to the land they settled and because the cultural identity was not given by tradition, it had to be created. Tourist attractions such as Niagara Falls, Yosemite, and Yellowstone played an especially important role in this process. 'Tourism provided a means of defining America and taking special pride in the features of its landscape' (Sears 1989: 5). Relating this form of interpretation to self-reflection, tourism can be seen as 'a significant means by which modern people assess their world, defining their own sense of identity in the process' (Jakle 1985: xi).

Attempts to achieve a sense of place frequently involve the promotion of historic preservation and it is generally agreed that the conservation of the built environment has helped retain the special character of cities such as Bath and Chester in England (Ford 1974). A similar rationale accounts for the current planning policies in Adelaide which are part of an attempt to 'make

South Australia special'. However, it has been suggested that preservation can be antithetical to the development of a sense of place. Lewis (1975) observed that although the physical legacy of the past has been saved in New Orleans, other elements of the area's tradition relating to function and social character have been destroyed. The same argument could be made about the many areas, such as the Rocks in Sydney, where buildings with hollow shells are transformed into tourist attractions. This form of preservation has been referred to as 'museumification' or 'disneyfication' (Relph 1976).

The creation of homogeneous landscapes by tourism developers has long been recognized (Gunn 1972; Rosenow and Pulsipher 1979) and the term 'identikit resorts' has become an accepted part of our vocabulary. It has been claimed that uniform planning and environmental design, by doing away with localism, has meant that man has no sense of the deep and symbolic significance of places, and no appreciation of the role of places in his own identity (Relph 1976).

Creating a Sense of Place: Marketing Implications

In an article entitled 'Rootedness versus sense of place', Tuan (1980: 6) argued that:

> Words have great power in creating place . . . Australian Aborigines maintain their awareness of place not so much with their material fabrications as with words and gestures—with the stories they tell and the rituals they perform . . . City people are constantly 'making' and 'unmaking' places by talking about them . . . in a sense, a place is its reputation.
>
> Gestures, either alone or in association with speech and the making of things, create place. For example, when an explorer names a mountain he may at the same time put a cross on it: the ritual words for place-making are reinforced by a ritual gesture . . . a meadow becomes a sacred place in the duration that an open-air mass is being celebrated there: the holy rites alone give an otherwise ordinary meadow its special significance.
>
> Words and gestures are ephemeral compared with objects.
>
> In the most literal sense, we create places with sticks and stones. A built object organizes space, transforming it into place . . . The object may be an ordinary house or a monument such as the Eiffel Tower, a warehouse or a striking office building . . . in the course of time, the Eiffel Tower is not only accepted by Parisians but has become a proud symbol of their city.

Tuan has suggested that words, gestures translated into ritual practices, and physical objects are the building blocks for the creation of place. This insight can be used by marketers to direct planning and management decisions. The following points illustrate how attempts can be made to establish an environment which supports the development of a sense of place:

The creation of place is a dynamic process, continually reinforced or reshaped by what people say, by its subsequent reputation. The foundation for the process must therefore be based within the host community. It is important for local residents to believe that they live in a special place for this will be the message that they pass to visitors in the course of the everyday interaction between host and guest. Marketers must acknowledge the power of this process by making 'internal marketing' a prerequisite for all other activities. This would involve communicating with local groups to gain their support rather than projecting an image to an external audience which is inconsistent with local attitudes and beliefs.

Interpretation can be one of the tangible 'gestures' which help create a place. The attributes of an area, its culture and physical qualities, need to be communicated with appropriate forms of interpretation. This is critical if there is a desire to enhance opportunities for the emergence of meaning on the part of visitors.

Festivals are staged as an attraction in many tourism destinations. They represent a useful marketing tool and those which are rooted in the local culture can enhance the 'special significance' of a place. A similar outcome is achieved in many country areas such as northern New South Wales when car parks and fields become the site of local markets. Once a month the sites are redefined as the markets add a ritual dimension to the way of life.

An experience of word, gesture, and ritual may be 'ephemeral' but a sense of attachment may be extended if objects which encapsulate the essence of a place are retained. This demonstrates the value of making items which have a direct association with the destination available to tourists as souvenirs. It is suggested that an appropriate association may be the result of local manufacture, the use of local materials or a design which is clearly identified with the place. The development of a locally based art and craft industry would clearly meet these criteria.

Place may be defined at a range of different scales. This was confirmed when places ranging from a bridge to a large geographical region were nominated in a study which asked people to list 'places that have been particularly meaningful for you in your life' (Brown 1990). Thus, the task of promoting a destination demands an appreciation of the range and nature of environmental responses experienced by tourists and hence the need for research. Insight related to place experiences may be revealed more readily by using qualitative research techniques (Brown 1991).

Conclusion

This discussion has demonstrated that destination marketing involves more than providing a series of advertisements which present an image designed to appeal to a target market at a particular point in time. It involves working with local people, attempting to understand the way the local environment may be perceived and interpreting that environment to promote meaningful experiences at places within that environment for both hosts and guests.

It is necessary to establish a genuine dialogue with local people, to provide information which is sensitive to the needs of visitors and to manage space in a way which permits the staging of communal events and encourages a form of design which reflects the area's heritage. All of these activities must be underpinned by appropriate planning and it is fitting to conclude this assessment of place by quoting from a current tourism strategy which states one of its main objectives to be 'to encourage authenticity in tourism which gives visitors an understanding and appreciation of places visited' (Tourism South Australia 1989).

References

Brown, G. P. 1990, 'Tourism and place-identity', Unpublished PhD thesis, Texas A & M University.

Brown, G. P. 1991, 'The meaning of tourist experiences', Paper presented to the 3rd Global Congress of Heritage Interpretation International, Honolulu, Hawaii, 3–8 Nov.

Brown, G. P. 1992, 'Tourism in Byron Shire', Report prepared for Byron Shire Council, Byron Bay.

Buttimer, A. 1980, 'Home, reach and the sense of place', in *The Human Experience of Space and Place*, eds. A. Buttimer and D. Seamon, St. Martins Press, New York.

Cooper, C. 1976, 'The house as a symbol of self', in *Environmental Psychology: People and their Physical Settings*, eds. H. M. Proshansky, W. H. Ittelson, and L. G. Rivlin, Holt, Rinehart and Winston, New York.

Ericksen, E. G. 1980, *The Territorial Experience*, University of Texas Press, Austin, Texas.

Fiori, P. 1989, 'Favorite places. Announcing the birth of Travel and Leisure's first book', *Travel and Leisure*, Jan., p. 13.

Ford, L. R. 1974, 'Historic preservation and the sense of place', *Growth and Change*, vol. 5, pp. 33–7.

Fox, P. 1991, 'Places in the heart', *Weekend Australian*, 27–28 April, pp. 32–7.

Fried, M. 1963, 'Grieving for a lost home', in *The Urban Condition*, ed L. Duhl, Basic Books, New York.
Godkin, M. A. 1980, 'Identity and place: clinical applications based on notions of rootedness and uprootedness', in *The Human Experience of Space and Place*, eds. A. Buttimer and D. Seamon, St. Martins Press, New York.
Gunn, C. A. 1972, *Vacationscape*, University of Texas, Austin, Texas.
Jakle, J. A. 1985, *The Tourist: Travel in Twentieth-Century North America*, University of Nebraska Press, Lincoln, Nebraska.
Korpela, K. M. 1989, 'Place-identity as a product of environmental self-regulation', *Journal of Environmental Psychology*, vol. 9, pp. 241–56.
Lewis, P. E. 1975, 'The future of the past: our clouded vision of historic preservation', *Pioneer America*, vol. 7, pp. 1–20.
Meinig, D. W. 1979, 'Symbolic landscapes', in *The Interpretation of Ordinary Landscapes: Geographical Essays*, ed. D. W. Meinig, Oxford University Press, New York.
Relph, E. 1976, *Place and Placelessness*, Pion, London.
Rosenow J. G. and Pulsipher, G. L. 1979, *Tourism: the Good, the Bad and the Ugly*, Century Three Press, Lincoln, Nebraska.
Rowntree, L. B. and Conkey, M. W. 1980, 'Symbols and the cultural landscape', *Annals of the Association of American Geographers*, vol. 70, pp. 459–74.
Sarbin, T. R. 1983, 'Place identity as a component of the self: an addendum', *Journal of Environmental Psychology*, vol. 3, pp. 337–42.
Seamon, D. 1979, *A Geography of the Lifeworld*, St. Martins Press, New York.
Sears, J. F. 1989, *Sacred Places: American Tourist Attractions in the Nineteenth Century*, Oxford University Press, New York.
Tourism South Australia 1989, *The Tourism Product Strategy*, Tourism South Australia, Adelaide.
Tuan, Y. F. 1974, 'Space and place: humanistic perspective', *Progress in Geography*, vol. 6, pp. 221–52.
Tuan, Y. F. 1977, *Space and Place: The Perspective of Experience*, University of Minnesota, Minneapolis, Minnesota.
Tuan, Y. F. 1980, 'Rootedness versus sense of place', *Landscape*, vol. 24, pp. 3–8.
Wilson, B. M. 1980, 'Social space and symbolic interaction', in *The Human Experience of Space and Place*, eds. A. Buttimer and D. Seamon, St. Martins Press, New York.

12

Marketing Indigenous Heritage
A Case Study of Uluru National Park

Josette Wells

The satisfaction of tourism requirements must not be prejudicial to the social and economic interests of the population in tourist areas, to the environment, or above all, to the natural resources, which are the fundamental attraction of tourism and historical and cultural sites (Manila Declaration, Paragraph 18, in World Tourism Organization 1985).

Introduction

The tourism industry has observed increasing interest in the Aboriginal arts and culture on the part of international visitors to Australia. Hall (1991) reported that half of the visitors to Australia were interested in seeing and learning about Aboriginal arts and crafts. Similarly, there is the trend for Aboriginal people to become more involved in management of tourism to areas where communities have direct involvement (see Chapter 9). Many of these areas such as Uluru and Kakadu already have international appeal. However, indigenous people have no control over the marketing of their destination. Therefore, marketing of indigenous heritage requires a strategic approach, whereby the aspirations of tourists can be met and those of the host community can also be satisfied over a longer period of time (see Chapter 3).

The marketing of indigenous heritage presents a great challenge. Contemporary marketing is essentially concerned with satisfying the needs and wants of visitors (consumer orientation). However, tourism marketing needs to consider not only the satisfaction of demands, which may in the extreme represent an insatiable desire to experience the cultural resources of a destination, but also assess the sustainability of a region and its capacity to absorb tourists. Therefore, marketing in this context is a primary tool for managing the indigenous cultural resources of a nation, or a region or a community.

Defining Indigenous Heritage

Australia's indigenous cultures are an integral part of the national heritage and offer significant tourism potential, not on the basis of indiscriminate marketing, but on the basis of planned and sustainable tourism where the wishes of the indigenous community are sought and incorporated into an overall plan for development. The Australian Heritage Commission (1991: 7) defines heritage as 'those components of the natural environment of Australia or the cultural environment of Australia that have aesthetic, historic or social significance or other special value for future generations, as well as the present community.' Aboriginal sites in the Register of the National Estate at June 1988 were categorized into different types of sites, the most significant being those sites of anthropological significance (Prehistory/Occupation), including shell midden sites, and those of aesthetic value (Art and Creative activities) including rock painting sites, rock engraving sites, and painting and engraving sites.

Indigenous heritage essentially involves the sociocultural structures of indigenous peoples. 'This will involve a set of beliefs, values and attitudes and forms of behaviour that are shared by people and handed on from generation to generation or specifically everything which is learned and shared by the members of society including material and non-material components' (Loudon and Della Bitta 1984: 170). Such an interpretation is endorsed by defining culture in a more comprehensive sense so that 'all cultures form part of the heritage of mankind' (World Tourism Organization 1985: 9), a definition which highlights the need for integrity and respect for all cultures, particularly those that are vulnerable to change and domination by more influential Western values and life-styles. 'All this points to the need for cultural policies that will protect, stimulate and enrich each people, respect identity and cultural heritage and establish absolute respect for an appreciation of cultural minorities and other cultures of the world' (World Tourism Organization 1985: 9).

Towards Strategic Marketing in Tourism

The marketing of indigenous heritage for tourism needs to be concerned with the long-term implications of tourism development. Proactive strategies, which attempt to influence the environment rather than react to negative situations such as indigenous dissatisfaction with tourists and deterioration of heritage sites, will be required to accommodate the increasing interest in all manifestations of heritage.

Current tourism marketing practices both at national, regional, and local level often display a disregard for sociocultural and environmental resources, often exposing the sometimes fragile nature of material and non-material indigenous culture to overly rapid tourism development (Getz 1986). Strategic marketing practice should be the *sine qua non* of tourism marketing management and presents the approach to management which provides for the longevity of the destination, the support of the host community, and the consistent satisfaction of customers. By defining the needs of each market segment and translating these needs into elements of the touristic experience, we can prevent those forms of development that incorporate in their very design the decline of the attraction.

> To be successful, tourism development must correspond to the inherent characteristics and needs of the region, its society and consumers sought . . . the long lived, carefully conceived development does not force the whims and aspirations of a multitude of strangers on a region, it uses the indigenous qualities of a region, whether social or natural to satisfy the expressed needs of a selective clientele (Reime and Hawkins 1979: 74).

Strategic marketing management or market management represents the best response to indigenous heritage management and involves comprehensive research and analysis into key components of the tourism system:

The market (demand component): Its present and potential consumers, segments and their characteristics which include motivations, travel patterns, and unmet needs; competition; market analysis such as size and projected growth and environmental analysis, or environmental scanning of economic, environmental, governmental, cultural and technological trends.

Resources (supply component): The physical and social carrying capacity of the region based on existing and potential land use and tenure patterns, environmental qualities and characteristics, sociocultural patterns and trends, government legislation and regulations, existing government and private sector tourism organizations, and present investment policies and availability of capital.

Transportation and communication (linking component): Existing and potential access and transport links. Communication methods such as promotion and distribution may be assessed as a separate exercise rather than included in either demand or supply analysis.

The essential point about marketing indigenous heritage to provide for visitor satisfaction and community goodwill is that it involves a commitment to research, analysis and synthesis as prerequisites to effective planning for any destination area. This means adopting a proactive approach to influencing events in the environment rather than simply reacting to environmental forces as they occur (Aaker 1992: 13). Prevention of negative tourism impacts should be a proactive consideration not a reactive one. Proactive strategies intervene to prevent negative situations such as indigenous dissatisfaction with tourists or the irrevocable deterioration of heritage sites. All too often, marketing approaches at national and state levels in Australia rely on advertising at the expense of research and strategic marketing (*Australian Financial Review* 1991). The aim of strategic marketing with regard to indigenous heritage should be to achieve a balance between product (that is, the cultural characteristics of communities and groups) and identified market segments so that an optimal outcome for the destination is achieved. Market growth and market share need to be considered in terms of regional sustainability. Therefore, tourism marketing goals need to balance visitors with environmental considerations and also with the sociocultural structures and values of indigenous groups.

Case Study—Uluru National Park

A study of Uluru National Park (Ayers Rock) in terms of the marketing of indigenous heritage provides an interesting perspective on the marketing of heritage. The views of the indigenous community towards tourism and tourists are difficult to realize because of the separation of interests which exists between the Northern Territory, which markets Uluru National Park, and the Federal Government which administers the Park through a leasing arrangement from the original owners, the Uluru-Katajuta Aboriginal Land Trust. Altman (1987) noted that although the Uluru-Katajuta Land Trust received the most comprehensive park rental payments ever received by Aboriginal interests in Australia (although minimal in comparison to mining royalties) before Aboriginal land rights were proclaimed under Commonwealth legislation in September 1985, Aboriginal interests had little control over the number of tourists who entered the park.

The problem of protecting Aboriginal interests and ensuring a more active role in development of the region was compounded by the development of the Yulara Tourist Village, a $200 million development with two hotels, a motel, lodge and camping grounds and shopping centre. The village had a capacity to accommodate 5000 tourists. During a recent visitor survey, the maximum number of visits to the park in one day was 4228. It is estimated that this will rise to 6200 daily visits by the year 2000 (Australian National Parks and Wildlife Service 1990). Under the terms of development, the Northern Territory Government subsidizes any shortfall in occupancy rate of the principal hotel.

Uluru National Park, which covers approximately 1325 km^2 of arid landscape, is one of Australia's most important destinations for overseas visitors and also for increasing numbers of domestic tourists. The Park has consistently attracted more visitors than any other park in the Northern Territory. Provisional numbers for 1992 estimate the number of visitors to be about 250,000, an increase since 1985 of 80,000 visitors per annum. In 1987 Uluru National Park was inscribed on the World Heritage List established by the convention concerning the Protection of the World Cultural and Natural Heritage (Hall 1992).

Community Planning and Conservation
Uluru National Park is administered by a Board of Management which comprises six members nominated by the traditional Aboriginal owners, one member nominated by the Federal Minister responsible for tourism, one member nominated by the Federal Minister for the environment, one scientist, and the Director of the Australian National Parks and Wildlife Service (ANPWS). The functions of the Board allow for the five-yearly preparation of plans of management in respect to the park or reserve and allow for public comment during the preparation of the plan. The Board is empowered to make decisions that are consistent with the plan of management and monitor the management of the park in conjunction with the Director. The Board of Management also gives advice to the Director and the relevant Minister on all aspects of the future development of the park.

The present nature of community involvement can be regarded as enlightened by Australian standards. The current plan of management identifies four sets of values which are accorded protection and management, the most significant being the protection of the cultural and religious significance of the park to the Aboriginal people. However, the values of members of the Board of Management may sometimes be in conflict. For example, in 1992, a rally which had been promoted by the Northern Territory Commission was refused access to the Park by the Director of the ANPWS on the grounds of previous abuse of religious sites by some of the participants.

Implications for Park Management
A recent survey which documented the characteristics and origins of visitors and their patterns of park use noted that there was no evidence that visitor enjoyment or satisfaction is being significantly affected by current use

densities. There are perceptions of crowding at some sites and issues of carrying capacity, but this does not yet appear to have reached a point where satisfactions are affected (ANPWS 1990). Nevertheless, it has been argued that the park will reach environmental limits within fifteen years and management should not be complacent about the potential risk of increasing use adversely affecting visitor satisfaction (ANPWS 1990: 70). The major needs expressed by visitors were for information and interpretive services particularly in relation to Aboriginal culture, geology and vegetation. Therefore park management needs to consider marketing strategies which will provide for continued visitor satisfaction, and a reorientation of the product to provide for increasing Aboriginal participation.

Market Characteristics
The number of visitors to Uluru National Park is higher than any other area in the Northern Territory; however, visitor nights compare less favourably than Darwin. Thirty-seven per cent of visitors to Uluru are from overseas, compared to nineteen per cent of all visitors to the Northern Territory. Visitors from the United Kingdom and other European countries account for nearly sixty per cent of overseas visitors to the park. Most overseas visitors stay one or two nights (ANPWS 1990), with the majority in the 20–34 age group and with females slightly outnumbering males (52/48 per cent) (Northern Territory Tourist Commission 1991).

The primary tourist motivation for visiting Uluru National Park is overwhelmingly to see the monolith (Ayers Rock), arguably the most distinctive landscape symbol of Australia and ubiquitously used in international promotional campaigns (Altman 1987; Hall 1991). The next highest ranking reason for visiting Uluru is to climb Uluru, while in third place is to visit the Kata Juta, the Olgas. Experiencing the outback ranks fourth, whilst seeing the wildlife ranks ahead of learning about Aboriginal culture in the area. Anangu perceptions of tourists similarly confirm these trends. Apart from believing that too many tourists come to the Uluru, over three-quarters saw this as the main reason for the visit: 'Tourists were "ants", hungry for this Puli, this rock' (Institute for Aboriginal Development 1991). Although three-quarters of the Anangu thought tourism was good, only one-sixth believed that tourists were motivated by an interest in some aspect of Aboriginal culture and over two-thirds thought they should learn about Anangu. These opinions substantiate the view that the community does not see tourists as necessarily sharing in Aboriginal expectations from tourism.

Marketing Strategy and Indigenous Peoples
Sensitive environments cannot host mass tourism if the nature of the

experience is to be preserved. Arguably, with respect to indigenous peoples, marketing strategy needs to strive for a better match between the host and visiting cultures. Anangu have a traditional culture predicated on limited material accumulation whereas visitors are primarily affluent and materialistic (Altman 1987). Similarly, Altman regarded tourism pressure as being too high, while seventy per cent of Anangu interviewed felt that there were too many tourists. Even 'eco-tourists' will have negative impacts on the environment unless Aboriginals are more proactive and informed about providing particular Aboriginal Tourist Experiences (ATE) for groups of tourists (Burchett 1992).

Any assessment of marketing strategy needs to take account of the Anangu perceptions of tourists and tourism which have been articulated in certain research. The needs of the Anangu and the values predicated by the Board of Management need a higher priority. For example, Anangu want to control tourist numbers and product development, and encourage tourists to learn about their culture (Institute for Aboriginal Development 1991). Therefore, target marketing by national and state organizations needs to consider alternative marketing strategies for Uluru which focus on attracting clientele better suited to the values of the local community who are motivated to learn about Aboriginal culture. In other words, Uluru becomes a secondary, but integral, focus for the culture and traditions of the Aboriginal groups. Such an approach indicates the need to determine thoroughly the visitor motivations so that Aboriginal groups and operators are able to develop a number of products which ultimately mean more direct participation for Aboriginals in the industry, ranging from soft exposure to the 60,000 year old culture (through its arts and crafts) to rugged 'hands on' participative adventure (Burchett 1992).

Marketing mix variables, the set of variables which are used by the marketer to satisfy the needs and wants of the target group, need also to be formulated with the desired outcome for the destination and the community as a central marketing objective. The variables include the traditional four P's (product, price, place, and promotion), and in order to give greater effectiveness to the ATE, a fifth 'P' (people) needs to be incorporated as an integral element of the product.

The result should be a better product–market match and a better understanding between the stakeholders about each other's expectations and needs. For example, a prime consideration for Aboriginal groups is to understand what participation in the tourism industry entails, such as extensive time commitment and customer relationships with tourists, and what the potential is for disruption and impacts on their social and cultural obligations. Perceptions of the visitors by the Aboriginal operator tend also to be stereotyped and there tends to be a limited appreciation of or interest in the visitors' own backgrounds (Burchett 1992).

In order to achieve a more effective product–market match, interpretation becomes a key tool which transforms the visit into a mutually rewarding experience for both host and guest (see Chapter 2). As the industry matures and consumers become more sophisticated in their demands at the destination, interpretation becomes a potent technique with which to offer an enhanced experience such as developing an awareness and appreciation of Aboriginal culture (Cooper 1991). At the same time, interpretation offers a management tool to help inform visitors about potential impacts and thus enable tourists to be steered away from sensitive areas.

The product, therefore, can become considerably augmented as interpretive features are added to the visitor experience. Authenticity is one of the key motivational forces for those travellers with an interest in foreign cultures and destinations (Hall 1991). Community input into the product at the planning stage and the desire of visitors to learn about interpretive features of Aboriginal culture provide a useful starting point. The concept of 'a sense of place' and the strong spirituality and identity with which Aboriginal people relate to their land and traditional culture cannot easily be conveyed to visitor audiences on a large scale, and there is a risk that the concept may become devalued. Therefore, interpretation becomes a key planning issue so that visitors may have enriching and meaningful experiences. Thus, close co-operation at community level will be necessary. Discussions with Aboriginal people should include all aspects of site interpretation—the sustainability of a site for public visitation, the site's significance, and how this may most effectively be interpreted to the public (Upitis 1989: 54)

Pricing is traditionally linked to target markets and their ability to pay; however, other objectives used by park managers may include rationing, such as controlling either time or geographic overcrowding, or encouraging positive user attitudes (see Chapters 2 and 21). Price, whether it be admission to the Park or access to certain amenities and facilities, may be based on a user-pays principle. Other aspects of price, particularly the tour package, including Aboriginal involvement, would be set at a level which the target market would be willing to pay after consideration of competition for similar products.

Other marketing mix variables may also need refocusing if the target market is to be compatible to the community's ability to cope with tourism in the short and long term. Channels of distribution, those points of sale which are identified with the target market, should be used more than expensive advertising and promotional campaigns. Publicity in the form of articles in journals which are read and appraised by target groups, and brochures and packages designed to attract ecologically sensitive groups, will be more effective. Indigenous peoples are an integral part of the product and form a vital part of the tourist experience; however, it is doubtful if their participative role in interpretation can be sustained unless they are able to determine the appropriate growth rate for visitation.

Conclusion

Target marketing provides the link in the planning for development. The development of the indigenous product requires a comprehensive knowledge and understanding of the relationship between markets and the resources of the destination. The traditional concern of tourism commissions at national and state levels is to increase the number of visitors as a measure of the economic contribution that tourism makes to the nation and the region (Hall 1991). However, without community input to the planning process and consideration of the nature of the tourism development which can be sustained, the visitor experience and the sustainability of tourism will be compromised. In order to establish a sustainable formula for development, tourism plans must provide procedures for community consultation before any marketing strategy is created and must help ensure that tourism will be economically beneficial and culturally viable. Therefore, a reorientation in marketing practice by national and state tourism commissions towards indigenous communities will be required. Community consultation, market research to evaluate demand and supply, a more sophisticated application of segmentation procedures, and matching of the mix to the market should be the role of marketers with regard to indigenous heritage. Appropriate tourism marketing needs to think small, and for tourism commissions with objectives which are expansionary, a conundrum now presents itself. Indeed, tourism marketing objectives at national and state marketing level should integrate sustainable development and community consultation procedures as a key component of the marketing strategy. Greater emphasis needs to be placed on one of the principal objectives stated in the Australian Tourism Commission Act 1987, which is to ensure that Australia is protected from adverse environmental and social impacts of international tourism (Australian Tourist Commission 1990). Tourism development cannot be sustained unless a greater emphasis and attention is directed to product–market match. For sustainable development to occur, strategic marketing, in the sense of a thorough assessment of matching demand to supply, must be incorporated into tourism planning and should be an integral part of the tourism marketing process at international and State levels.

References

Aaker, D. A. 1992, *Strategic Market Management*, John Wiley and Sons, New York.

Altman, J. C. 1987, *The Economic Impact of Tourism on the Mutitjulu Community, Uluru (Ayers Rock–Mount Olga National Park)*, Research School of Pacific Studies, Australian National University, Canberra.

Australian Financial Review 1991, 'Tourism Bureau hits at "ad fundamentalism"', *Australian Financial Review*, November.

Australian Heritage Commission 1991, *Annual Report 1990–1991*, Australian Government Publishing Service, Canberra.

Australian National Parks and Wildlife Service 1990, *Uluru, Visitor Survey Report (Draft)*, Australian National Parks and Wildlife Service, Canberra.

Australian Tourism Commission 1990, *Corporate Plan 1990/91–1994/95*, Australian Tourism Commission, Canberra.

Cooper, C. 1991, 'The technique of tourism interpretation', in *Managing Tourism*, ed. S. Medlik, Butterworth-Heinemann, London.

Getz, D. 1986, 'Models in tourism planning: towards integration of theory and practice', *Tourism Management*, vol. 7, no. 1, pp. 21–32.

Hall, C. M. 1991, *Introduction to Tourism in Australia: Impacts, Planning, and Development*, Longman-Cheshire, South Melbourne.

Hall, C. M. 1992, *Wasteland to World Heritage: Preserving Australia's Wilderness*, Melbourne University Press, Carlton.

Institute for Aboriginal Development 1991, *Sharing the Park: Anangu Initiatives at Ayers Rock*, Australian National Parks and Wildlife Service, Canberra.

Loudon, D. and Della Bitta, A. J. 1984, *Consumer Behaviour*, McGraw-Hill, New York.

Northern Territory Tourist Commission 1991, *Selected Tourism Data, 1990–1991*, Northern Territory Tourist Commission, Darwin.

Reime, M. and Hawkins, D. 1979, 'Tourism development: a model for growth', *Cornell Hotel and Restaurant Quarterly*, vol. 20, no. 1, pp. 67–74.

Upitis, A. 1989, 'Interpreting cross-cultural sites', in *Heritage Interpretation, Vol. 1, The Natural and Built Environment*, ed. D. Uzzell, Belhaven Press, London, pp. 153–60.

World Tourism Organization 1985, *The State's Role in Protecting and Promoting Culture as a Factor of Tourism Development and the Proper Use and Exploitation of the National Cultural Heritage Sites and Monuments for Tourism*, World Tourism Organization, Madrid.

13

Presenting History *in situ*

Historic Site Management on Public Land in Victoria

Jane Lennon

Definition and Administration of Historic Sites in Victoria

Just over a third of Victoria is public land managed by the Department of Conservation and Natural Resources. The land may be reserved as national park, state forest, coast reserve, garden or public park, or for a host of urban public purposes or 'conservation of a feature or site of historic interest' (Lennon 1992).

Not all identified historic relics, features or sites have been specifically reserved for conservation of their historic values. The range of historic places under the control of the Department varies greatly in type and size. The term 'historic place' has been used, in accordance with the terminology of ICOMOS (the International Council for Monuments and Sites) whereby it means a 'site, area, building or other work, group of buildings or other works together with pertinent contents and surroundings' (Australia ICOMOS 1988). It includes structures, ruins, archaeological sites and areas.

Historic places on public land are managed either directly by the Department or indirectly by committees of management, trustees, or lessees. Sites, structures and buildings on public land can be protected and managed under a set of Acts directing management, including:
- Crown Lands (Reserves) Act 1978: Section 4 provides for the reservation of small areas of public land for public purposes, including 'conservation of an area of historic interest', and has been used for sites ranging from Werribee Park mansion and Gulf Station farm complex to the Central Deborah mine and a suite of former courthouses. Where land is not reserved forest or under the schedules of the National Parks Act, this Act provides the most convenient and flexible way to reserve public land.

- Forests Act 1958: Section 50 (as amended by the Conservation, Forests and Lands Act 1987) provides for the protection of sites and structures in reserved forest, for example the Lal Lal Blast Furnace in Bungal Forest and Guggenheim's cottage at Blackwood.
- National Parks Act 1975: Sections 17 and 18 provide that features of historic interest in national and other parks shall be controlled and managed to preserve and protect them. Section 22 of the Act provides for the proclamation of zones within parks and may be used to protect historic features.
- The Historic Buildings Act 1981 (as amended 1990) cuts across the above described Acts in that if a site, structure or building is listed on the Historic Buildings Register then the site manager must obtain a statutory permit to alter any registered place. For example, Woodlands homestead complex in Gellibrand Hill Park or Mt Buffalo Chalet in Mt Buffalo National Park must have any alterations to the structure and designated surroundings approved in accordance with the provisions of the Historic Buildings Act.

Assessment of Cultural Significance

Where places have been identified as having historic value, we need some means of evaluating those areas which are more culturally important than others and identifying the specific nature of their importance. This is done by assessing their cultural significance. In the Australia ICOMOS Charter for the Conservation of Places of Cultural Significance (the Burra Charter) (1988) the term 'cultural significance' means 'aesthetic, historic, scientific or social value for past, present or future generations'. It should be noted that the terms are not mutually exclusive.

The categorization into aesthetic, historic, scientific and social values is one approach to understanding the concept of cultural significance. More appropriate categories may be developed as understanding of a particular place increases.

Places that are likely to be of cultural significance are those which help an understanding of the past, enrich the present, and which we believe will be of value to future generations. They tell their human story and locate them in their past social and geographical context. The place presents a sequence of historic evidence of past occupation and changing use and is not just 'old'.

The most obvious historic places on public land are the seventy-four recommended by the Land Conservation Council as Historic Areas and Reserves for its Melbourne, North Central, Ballarat, North East, Alpine, Mallee, and East Gippsland Study Areas. The Land Conservation Council defined Historic Areas as 'relatively large areas of land that contain historical relics covering a range of historical themes. They are large enough to permit the development of interpretive centres and recreational facilities such as picnic areas and walking tracks'. Historic Reserves are usually smaller and will 'generally preclude the development of recreational facilities, although some aids to interpretation could be provided'. The following case studies examine a variety of management techniques for historic sites in parks and reserves in Victoria.

Point Nepean National Park

Point Nepean National Park is located on the eastern entrance to Port Phillip Bay and was opened to the public in late 1988 as part of Australia's Bicentennial celebrations (Department of Conservation, Forests and Lands 1989). Because of its remote location from Melbourne, its rugged coastal topography and limited access from the bay, Point Nepean was developed as a quarantine station from 1852 by the colonial government. Military occupation of the area dates from 1881 and the School of Army Health still occupies the quarantine station, while the cemetery and coastal forts are located in the park separated by several kilometres of military training land from the park entrance gate.

On arrival visitors must pay an entry fee and pass through the orientation centre. They can either travel on the transporter which seats fifty persons per trip, or walk or ride bicycles to the forts. The entry fee covers travel on the transporter. Public access and numbers have to be strictly controlled (a maximum of 600 visitors at any time) because of the following constraints:
- The very sensitive and erosion-prone nature of much of the coastal land;
- Five designated areas containing unexploded ordnance;
- Continued Army use of four weapons ranges and designated training areas;
- Natural hazards, particularly the strong currents and rips occurring on both the ocean and bay beaches; and
- The small size of the area (338 ha including 83 ha intertidal zone) acquired for park purposes.

The transporter stops at key points along Defence Road, the single lane sealed road along the spine of the park. These are the Cemetery, Cheviot Hill, Observatory Point and The Bend and Fort Nepean. Walkers must keep to the road and designated tracks because of the dangers from unexploded ordnance.

The present Cemetery was established in 1854 and although its records are incomplete, up to 300 people are believed to have been buried in it, but many graves are unmarked. However, the Cemetery does contain the stories of some immigrants, seamen, and others whose deaths might otherwise be unrecorded, and reflects Victoria's migration history—the lives and deaths of people who crossed the oceans to a new land. The Cemetery has been refenced and an interpretive sign erected.

A new walking track has been built to the top of Cheviot Hill, which at 54 metres above sea level is one of the highest spots in the park and affords panoramic views of both the high-energy ocean coast and the low-energy bay coast. Along the track, informative signs identify the landscape features that can be seen, and introduce Point Nepean's Aboriginal history, natural vegetation and defence significance. Cheviot Beach, where the steamship *Cheviot* was wrecked in 1887 and where Prime Minister Harold Holt disappeared while swimming in 1967, can be seen from the summit. The rough benches that were constructed for mourners at the memorial service for Harold Holt on the summit have also been retained. The road then passes two additional fortified areas (Eagle's Nest and Fort Pearce) before reaching Fort Nepean.

Fort Nepean was part of a defence complex commenced in 1881, which was to comprise defences at Queenscliff, Point Nepean, Swan Island, South Channel Fort, Fort Franklin (Portsea) and Pope's Eye. Built in response to fear of attack by Russia or other possible enemies, the defence system was devised by British army officers, Colonel Sir Peter Scratchley and Lieutenant General Sir William Jervois, for the wealthy but vulnerable colony of Victoria. Over £1,500,000 was spent in constructing the complex, one of the biggest engineering projects undertaken by the colonial government. The Fort was divided into different levels for the gun emplacements, the service levels (where ammunition was moved around) and at the lowest level, the magazines. The barracks were adjacent and above ground on a levelled area. They were weatherboard buildings with corrugated iron roofs and were demolished in the early 1950s.

A self-guiding walk through Fort Nepean has been developed by the Department of Conservation and Natural Resources and a booklet is available. The walk follows black and white painted lines and arrows through the Fort and defined paths outside. The painted lines were used when the Fort was in operation. The first part of the walk is accessible for people with disabilities. The second part (from gun emplacement no. 5 and down to beach level) involves steps and steep tracks, and is less accessible.

In the four years since the park has opened it has been visited by just over 200,000 people (with a peak of 50,370 in 1989–90), contributing $792,000 to park revenue. The park offers a most comprehensive interpretation of Victoria's quarantine and defence history as well as allowing public access to what was previously a prohibited area for 135 years.

The controlled access approach to managing public use in a fragile environment has been very successful. Complaints are restricted to summer months when there are more visitors than seats available on the transporter. Park staff also worry that the approach is too successful in that the ride becomes the experience rather than a means to visit fragile sites. The transporter system is costly to operate and maintain and inflexible in that it must keep to a timetable, but the approach has public support and is environmentally friendly.

Maldon Historic Reserve

Maldon is one of a handful of Victorian towns that was born with the great alluvial gold rushes of the 1850s and continued as a deep quartz reef mining centre into the 1920s. The Maldon Historic Reserve covering 2250 ha illustrates the evolution of the Victorian gold mining industry from primitive, shallow alluvial diggings through to capital intensive gold extraction and treatment processes (Department of Conservation, Forests and Lands 1988a). It retains evidence of a wide range of mining activities, technologies and gold processing methods used by European and Chinese miners. Examples of the entire range of gold mining activities, except deep lead mining, can be seen. In many instances, the historic features which remain are among the most intact or most important examples of their type in Victoria.

The North British Mine site on Parkins Reef, at Maldon, displays one of the most intact collections of evidence in Victoria of the evolution of the technology of gold extraction. The site contains a shaft (509 metres deep), mine dams, mullock heaps, sand heaps and a pump bob pit, as well as the foundations of a steam engine, winder and winder engine, battery, boiler house, compressor, quartz roasting kilns, jaw crusher, chlorination plant, blacksmith's shop and engineering shop. Such an extraordinary range of features on one mine site is an indication of the enthusiasm with which its owners kept up with the latest technology until closure in 1929.

The Beehive Mine (1854 to 1900s) in Maldon is distinguished by the tall brick chimney remaining. Quartz roasting kilns are also a notable feature of the Maldon Reserve—the largest were at the Union Hill mine; others occur at the North British Mine. An on-site interpretive walk has been developed around the surviving footings, features and mullock heaps of the North British Mine at Parkins Reef, which was first opened for alluvial mining in 1857.

Robert Dent Oswald registered the North British Quartz Mining and Crushing Company in 1864. By 1865 three of the existing kilns at the North British Mine were in place and capable of roasting 100 tons of quartz at a time, to remove arsenical, iron, and copper pyrites impurities. After burning in the kilns, the quartz was transported to the twenty head of stamps and the

Plate 13.1: Interpretive signs and fencing at Maldon Historic Reserve, Victoria

chilean wheel for crushing. The tailings were then treated with mercury and the amalgam formed was smelted to produce gold bullion. In 1877 Oswald refurbished the mine with the installation of a head frame above the shaft and a steam winder. Compressed air rock drills were introduced and in 1885 a new battery was erected, with 50,000 ounces of gold being produced between 1885 and 1889. Then disaster struck in December 1890, when fire destroyed the winding and pumping machinery and 100 men were laid off until the mine machinery was replaced. Oswald installed a chlorination plant to treat tailings but he died in November 1891, before he could realize on his investment in this new plant. His trustees operated the mine until 1913 when it was floated as a public company and continued employing labour until 1928.

Stabilization of brick footings, restoration of stone arches around the kilns, fencing, and defined access have been undertaken and interpretive signs installed at key points along the walk, including the former lamp room, mine shaft, boiler beds, and kilns (Plate 13.1). This has transformed the site from a derelict eyesore, where materials were 'cannibalized' for new constructions and rubbish dumped, to a tourist destination. Toilets, a carpark, picnic area, and interpretive shelter all assist the visitor to this historic site.

Presenting History *in situ*

Walhalla Historic Area

The Walhalla Historic Area lies to the north of the Latrobe Valley in steeply dissected mountain country. The township now consists of about 72 ha, while the surrounding historic area comprises 2500 ha. It was gazetted as an Historic Area by the Governor in Council in 1983. Gold was mined here between 1863 and 1915. Today Walhalla has a dozen permanent residents. It has no mains electricity and few of the amenities associated with small towns. However, there are many part-time residents occupying holiday houses and thousands of visitors annually. The Walhalla Historic Area contains a large number of historic places of regional or State significance (Department of Conservation, Forests and Lands 1988b). Owing to the lack of development it has an atmosphere of untouched charm. In recent years some of the abandoned gold mines have been reopened for exploration.

The Walhalla Historic Area is managed by the Shire of Narracan and the Department of Conservation and Natural Resources both directly and by delegation to committees of management for the Long Tunnel Extended tourist mine, the former Post Office and the cemetery. Planning and management have been co-ordinated through the Walhalla Historic Area Advisory Committee, which meets every two months to advise on planning permit applications and other proposed works.

One of the most remarkable aspects of Walhalla is the extraordinary photographic record which exists almost from the beginning, clearly documenting the growth of the town, the effect of fire and flood, the boom time, the mass exodus, and finally the drift into quiet isolation. These photographs serve to enhance the cultural significance of Walhalla in that they vividly illustrate so many aspects of life in one of Victoria's most inaccessible yet highly productive mining towns.

Aesthetically, Walhalla no longer has the stripped hillsides of the early photographs nor the many shops and houses of the busy township. Nonetheless, the past lives on in the familiar landscape and the man-made reminders for future generations of a golden time in Victoria's history. Historically, Walhalla offers an important opportunity to examine the physical evidence of both mining methods and living conditions in a location that was so inhospitable the noted English novelist Anthony Trollope wrote: 'I could not have believed there had been so much traffic across the mountains and through the forests had I not afterwards seen the things at Walhalla'.

Individually the various historic sites and places within the Walhalla Historic Area are crucial to a scientific evaluation of the gold-mining period. Of added interest is the ingenuity displayed in Walhalla by the residents in overcoming the steepness of the hillsides enclosing the town. The way houses, buildings, mines, the cricket ground and even the cemetery were constructed says a great deal about the people who lived, worked and died in the valley. Socially, the value of Walhalla is almost impossible to assess. Nowhere else in Victoria combines an atmosphere of historical integrity with a setting of such outstanding natural beauty. In 1910 the town was frequently referred to by locals and visitors alike as 'the Switzerland of Australia'. However, the failure of the mines and the lack of work in the town has taken a heavy toll on what remains. Management today seeks to balance the needs of conservation, the demands of tourism and the expectations of the permanent and weekend residents without losing anything of the special atmosphere which makes it one of the treasures of our past.

Walhalla presents a very difficult management problem to the relevant managing authorities, the community and concerned Government bodies. These problems arise from a number of causes including the historical development of the town, tourism, mining and land tenure issues, and the many groups interested and involved with the town. Before the establishment of the Walhalla Historic Area Advisory Committee, there was a considerable lack of direction and co-ordination between these different agencies. This, combined with a lack of research prior to works being carried out, contributed to the deterioration of Walhalla. With regard to all works, development and planning, the overriding consideration is the necessity to protect the historical nature of the town.

In 1988, following extensive consultation, a management plan covering both private and public land in this historic area was adopted. Mining was permitted subject to stringent conditions, which also enabled visitors to continue using the historic tramways which gave access to the mines. The historic town centre has many gaps in its building streetscape due to fire, flood, demolition, and removals. The plan specified that any new buildings permitted should be replicas of the former buildings on the site in Walhalla's heyday. This policy was adopted because the local population wanted replicas and so that private property owners would be able to present tourists with an image of the physical shape and density of Walhalla at its peak of development.

Intensive mining exploration was conducted in Walhalla during the 1980s and the management plan permitted its continuation subject to conditions, such as continued tourist access to the underground machinery chamber of the Long Tunnel Extended mine. However the cost of extraction led to cessation of the mining activity and mining history is now the attraction for visitors.

The management of Walhalla as an historic area offers a unique combination of private property owners, delegated committees of management for key historic sites, and government departments providing ranger patrol, forest management, rubbish removal, and road, track and picnic area maintenance. All these activities are co-ordinated by an advisory committee and the management objectives of conservation of an area of historic interest are being well realized by total community and specialist interest involvement.

Woodlands Homestead, Gellibrand Hill Park

The Woodlands homestead complex is situated within Woodlands station of 671 acres near present-day Tullamarine Airport. It was purchased for £1 per acre by Captain William Pomeroy Greene in March 1843. An imported prefabricated timber house was soon erected and a dairying business commenced. By 1848 the property had doubled in size. In 1977 the Woodlands property was acquired by the State Government as Stage 1 of the Gellibrand Hill Park, which now totals 646 ha. Following extensive research, the homestead and outbuildings have been restored and an interpretive display within the homestead explains the Greenes' pastoral activities and the architectural significance of one of the oldest remaining pastoral homesteads in Victoria (Lennon 1992).

The house is not furnished in period style as the policy for the prefabricated west wing is to reveal evidence of its construction techniques. Room 1 combines architectural models and wall panels which illustrate the sequence of construction of the complex. In Room 2 wall panels and openings in the structure explain the building details and construction methods. In Rooms 3 a video explains the process of revealing the 1849 wall painting scheme. Sections of wall have been left in varying stages of exposure so that visitors can see the effect of work in progress. Room 4 is the showpiece where all the 1849 decoration details have been revealed. Room 5, the reading room, contains resource documents as well as free-standing easels depicting the social history of the owners of *Woodlands*. However, visitors arrive at historic houses with preconceptions about furnishing and presentation. The visitors' book contains comments which show that they hope we get the funds to furnish the house and finish the restoration. They have failed to read our introductory panels which tell them why this house is different and not furnished. The 1847 paint scheme revealed in one room had been criticized as 'too dull', visitors having become accustomed to the new, bright heritage colours replicated by leading paint companies and applied to other unrevealed sections of walls in other rooms.

The original property was named *Woodlands* in 1843 because of its landscape setting. The conservation policy for the landscape setting of the homestead complex aims to retain this open, rolling woodland scene when viewed from the surrounding main roads. Pastoral grazing is a compatible use but new fencing and landscape intrusions, such as car parking areas, should be kept to a minimum. Other sections of the property, now incorporated into the park, are managed as far as possible to illustrate a landscape of the 1840s—woodland overstorey covers the native grassland understorey.

Conclusions

The preceding case studies illustrate a range of techniques used in the management and presentation of historic places on public land in Victoria. The usual approach is one of on-site interpretation either by a numbered trail with a trail brochure or a trail with interpretive plaques at key points as at the North British Mine. The Point Nepean example illustrates a total approach to visitor management by controlling access which then enables information and interpretation to be provided at the entry orientation centre, on the transporter and at the stops along the route. Woodlands Homestead provides a thought-provoking approach to understanding the construction and evolution of the buildings on site. However, it is too subtle for some visitors, and the employment of some persons to act as guides would probably enhance the experience of the homestead and its woodland setting for most visitors. Walhalla offers an integrated approach to historic place management and interpretation by involving both public and private sectors and is a useful example for other communities. Each case study highlights a solution tailored to that specific place and its visitors.

References

Australia ICOMOS 1988, *The Australia ICOMOS Charter for the Conservation of Places of Cultural Significance (The Burra Charter)*, Australia ICOMOS, Sydney.
Department of Conservation, Forests and Lands 1988a, *Maldon Historic Reserve Management Plan*, Department of Conservation, Forests and Lands, Melbourne.
Department of Conservation, Forests and Lands 1988b, *Walhalla Historic Area Management Plan*, Department of Conservation, Forests and Lands, Melbourne.
Department of Conservation, Forests and Lands 1989, *Discovering Historic Point Nepean*, Melbourne.
Lennon, J. 1992, *Our Inheritance—Historic Places on Public Land in Victoria*, Department of Conservation and Environment, Melbourne.

14

Waldheim Chalet

A Link Between Tasmania's Cultural and Natural Heritage

R. E. Saunders

Introduction

The meanings visitors perceive in heritage are greatly influenced by the way managers relate to its value and significance. Appropriate interpretation can play a major role in elucidating heritage objects, events, and settings. However, inappropriate management action or inaction can contradict claims of value and significance. This case study explores the history of one of Tasmania's icons of cultural heritage, the Waldheim Chalet near Cradle Mountain. It demonstrates how incremental management can lead to loss of meaning, but it also shows how community awareness and co-ordinated planning for cultural tourism can at least partially redress the mistakes of the past.

Waldheim is a link between Tasmania's natural and cultural heritage. Its full meaning can only be found in the interplay between environment and people. From being the birthplace of a national park, it has evolved to find new meaning at a time when community attitudes to the natural environment were undergoing radical change.

Weindorfer's Vision

Standing with arms outstretched on the summit of Tasmania's Cradle Mountain in January 1910, Gustav Weindorfer outlined his vision for the future of this then remote area:

> This must be a National Park for the people for all time. It is magnificent, and people must know about it and enjoy it . . . We must build a Chalet and get a road and then people will come from everywhere to see this place . . . We will build a house ourselves and then when the people start coming the Government will make a road and the house can be made bigger . . . (Smith 1937).

Weindorfer built his 'Chalet' in the manner of the prospectors and snarers of the time, cutting and splitting the local King Billy pine on site. Enhancing the basically rectangular building with a distinctive porch evocative of alpine huts in his native Austria, he called the chalet Waldheim, meaning 'forest home'. After the death of his wife Kate in 1916, Gustav made Waldheim his permanent home.

Weindorfer was a charismatic figure. With his charming European manner, pioneering independence and deep knowledge of natural history, he entertained and delighted visitors from near and far. After World War I, during which many locals began to consider him a hermit and rumours circulated that he was a German spy, Weindorfer began to take on an almost legendary status. During the 1920s Waldheim became a favoured haunt of the cognoscenti (Giordano 1987: 97). Indeed, it was largely through Weindorfer's efforts and the active support of influential people who stayed at Waldheim and walked in the mountains under his guidance that the area from Cradle Mountain to Lake St Clair was proclaimed a Scenic Reserve and Wildlife Sanctuary in 1922. But it was well after Weindorfer's death in 1932 that the road to Waldheim was finally completed and many years later that national park status was achieved. It is now an integral part of the Tasmania Wilderness World Heritage Area.

Waldheim was also enlarged in response to growing demand, just as Weindorfer had intended. After his death it gradually became a sprawling, ramshackle building with new rooms added and the porch enclosed, changing its form and character. Cradle Mountain became more popular than ever after World War II. The Overland track was established from Waldheim to Lake St Clair and soon became Australia's premier hiking trail. Meanwhile Waldheim deteriorated under the cumbersome management regime of the Scenery Preservation Board. Even the creation of a new agency to manage Tasmania's parks and reserves in the early 1970s did little to resolve Waldheim's predicament. The chalet was judged to be structurally unsound and inadequate to meet the changing demands of tourism (Minutes of Cradle Mountain–Lake St Clair Board meetings). Eventually, fearful for public safety, the then National Parks and Wildlife Service demolished the original building in 1976.

Reconstruction

Amid public disbelief and outcry (Giordano 1987: 115), the National Park Service built a reconstruction, stripped back to match the appearance of the Chalet during Weindorfer's lifetime. The new Waldheim included some materials salvaged from the original and used what was known of original techniques and design. But it would no longer be used for accommodation. By the mid-1980s the idea was to make it into a museum (Giordano 1987: 116).

The fate of Waldheim contravenes the principles of the Australia ICOMOS Charter for the Conservation of Places of Cultural Significance which was drawn up in 1979, three years after the original Chalet's demolition (Australia ICOMOS 1988). Nevertheless, in his Conservation Plan for the area, Bannear (1990: 23) considered the reconstructed Chalet to have inherited the cultural significance of the original. Bannear saw value in its new role as a museum and recognized the vision of the people who had opposed its demolition and forced its reconstruction.

Interpreting the Significance of Waldheim

Despite the intentions of the managing agency the Waldheim replica remained empty for many years. It was not until 1990 that proposals for interpretation were funded (Saunders 1990a).

For much of the 1980s, developments at the entrance to the park, five kilometres away, took precedence. Comfortable commercial accommodation, cabins and campgrounds were built, a large new visitor centre was opened and new road links finally ended any semblance of isolation. Visitor numbers increased from about 55,000 in 1984/85 through 81,000 in 1987/88 to more than 160,000 in 1990/91 (Department of Parks, Wildlife and Heritage 1992: 21). In many ways the Cradle Mountain area retains the values that first attracted visitors from the Australian mainland and other countries during the Weindorfer era. The view from the summit has barely altered and the flora, fauna and landscape are remarkably intact. However, the visitor experience has changed beyond recognition.

In Weindorfer's day it was an adventure just getting to Waldheim. Horse-drawn wagons took an entire day to haul passengers the 30 miles (48 km) from the nearest town, and even then stopped one mile short of the Chalet (Giordano 1987: 60). Few people now remember those days, but many present-day visitors recall the original Waldheim between the 1940s and the early 1970s when it was still an outpost of warmth and civilization on the edge of the wilderness. Nowadays this wilderness has been tamed. The Overland track presents little challenge to the experienced walker and Cradle Valley is visited by more people in one day than Weindorfer saw in a year.

Presenting the full history and significance of Waldheim to visitors has been made more difficult by its reconstruction to an 'original' form. But its

Plate 14.1: The conflict between tourism and conservation at the Waldheim Chalet, Cradle Mountain, Tasmania

meaning has also been compromised by far-reaching if less tangible changes to the whole cultural context of the area. This is not a unique problem. As Horne (1986) has observed, the past is frequently presented out of context to tourists, who often lack the skills and knowledge to reconstruct the original meanings of the monuments and sites they visit.

Years of incremental improvement in the accessibility of Cradle Valley have led to the development of a large and unsightly car park that dominates the approach to Waldheim. In summer it is often overcrowded by visitors attracted by the resident wallabies and other wildlife. Even the visionary Weindorfer had not foreseen the potential conflict between tourism and conservation (See Plate 14.1)

In interpreting the Waldheim replica it was clearly important to avoid any pretence that this is Weindorfer's Waldheim somehow magically preserved, frozen in time. This would simply deny fifty years of history and further manufacture the past, giving the impression that change is not occurring. Bannear (1990: 24) specifically warned against further replication of the 1932 appearance of the chalet and argued instead for using the replica to tell the story of the building's evolution, including its demolition and reconstruction. In essence, the reconstruction represents a further stage in the evolution of the building and reflects a major change in community values and motives: conservation has replaced development as the major management objective

(Bannear 1990: 21). In this regard it is perhaps significant that the demolition and reconstruction of Waldheim took place between the two seminal conservation issues in Tasmania's recent history: the flooding of Lake Pedder and the historic intervention of the Australian Government to prevent the flooding of the State's last wild river, the Franklin (Hall 1992).

In interpreting Waldheim it was also vital to actively involve the local community of northern Tasmania which, through the 'Weindorfer Memorial Service Committee' commemorates his life and contribution in a simple ceremony at the graveside near Waldheim each New Years Day. Weindorfer's sister first sent the traditional edelweiss and candles from Austria after his death and, except for a break caused by World War II, this custom has been continued by family friends ever since. It was also important to avoid further romanticizing Weindorfer or interpreting his actions and philosophies in the context of current attitudes to the environment. Wider reading also suggested that greater recognition was needed of the role of other key players in the story, especially that of Kate Weindorfer (Bergman 1959).

Site Planning

Planning for the interpretation of Waldheim was influenced not only by the Conservation Plan (Bannear 1990) for the Chalet area but also by discussions and decisions leading to the development of the Draft Site Plan for Cradle Valley (Department of Parks, Wildlife and Heritage 1992). Because these plans were being developed concurrently, specific interpretive proposals were able to be assessed in the Conservation Plan and interpretation considerations were also able to influence site design in the Waldheim precinct. However, it is surprising how rarely, in the Australian park management scene, planning for interpretation proceeds in parallel with related considerations, despite the obvious advantages. Perhaps, as interpretation becomes more widely accepted as a professional discipline, this will occur more routinely.

The basis of the interpretation plan, proposed in a discussion paper (Saunders 1990b) distributed to historical and archaeological specialists in the Department of Parks, Wildlife and Heritage as well as the Weindorfer Memorial Service Committee, was the integration of three existing but separate features into a meaningful sequence. The concept was to encourage visitors to walk from the existing carpark into the Waldheim replica and from there to complete a circuit through 'Weindorfer's Forest' to return via Weindorfer's grave. This involved the reconstruction of a footbridge across the creek beneath the bath-house behind Waldheim and the re-routing of the entry and exit sections of the nature trail through the forest. Historical photographs were used to ensure the accurate location and form of the footbridge.

Interpretation Planning

Input from the Conservation Plan highlighted the crucial importance of telling the entire story of Waldheim's evolution. This was achieved using display boards in one bedroom, with headings based around a series of statements taken from Weindorfer's speech on the summit (Smith 1937). Signs along the forest trail complement and reinforce the story presented inside the building.

The Weindorfer Memorial Service Committee suggested the development of a diorama of the key players involved during the Weindorfer era. Although this involved the installation of a viewing window in a wall between two of the bedrooms, it was recommended in the Conservation Plan (Bannear 1990: 26) because it was seen as aiding the interpretation without altering the external form of the building. There is some irony in the fact that the (now inappropriate) dismantling of the original fabric of Waldheim has enhanced the freedom and flexibility of interpretation. Members of the Committee were also highly supportive of the idea, suggested in the discussion paper, of bringing the story of Kate and Gustav Weindorfer to life using a sound system. A visitor-operated, auto-stop 12 volt system was developed for this application (Saunders 1991.) and a narrated play was scripted and produced.

Signage throughout the sequence of experiences both inside and outside the Chalet was used with discretion. Direct quotations from Weindorfer, his contemporaries, and visitors were used to highlight the human context of the times through the immediacy of personal experiences (Figure 14.1).

Planning for further redevelopment of the Waldheim precinct is now at an advanced stage. The currently intrusive car park will be reduced in size and redesigned so as not to impinge upon the view of Waldheim from Weindorfer's grave. The progressive introduction of a public transport system is also proposed to resolve growing parking problems. Redundant buildings with low cultural value will be removed and picnic tables will be provided in sunny spots giving views over Cradle Valley.

The consolidation of the Waldheim area as an historic precinct is an appropriate and forward-looking concept. Waldheim remains a node for several walking trails including the original starting point of the Overland track, itself now an historic feature. With the pedestrian character and human scale of this precinct restored, the Waldheim area is destined to become an attractive and appropriately managed feature of the World Heritage Area.

On meeting Weindorfer

Every New Years Day, a memorial service for Gustav Weindorfer is held in Cradle Valley. For the 1982 service — 50 years after Weindorfer's death — Bill Perkins prepared a moving address. In this brief extract, he captures some of the essence of the man and his times:

> "February 26th, 1930 was one of the most important days in my life. On that day, at age 19½, I first climbed to the summit of Cradle and later in the day met Gustav Weindorfer. All this and heaven too!
>
> "... My first impression, which has not faded in 52 years, was of a tall, bearded, handsome, charismatic, genial, jovial man who warmly greeted his 'little friend Woolstoncroft' [Perkins' smallish travelling companion from Melbourne] and welcomed me as a big new friend. Realising that we were both very hungry, he quickly prepared for us a Dorfer special — three large brimming plates of his famous 'badger' (wombat) stew lavishly laced with garlic — a mixture that today would kill me in five minutes but then was perfect for my youthful ravenous appetite.
>
> "... All this while our busy, distinguished host regaled us with scurrilous jokes and humorous anecdotes, but above all a vituperative tirade against the government of the day for the failure to provide a suitable access road into his beloved Waldheim. The whole of this, like his stew, liberally spiced with his most attractive accent, with a generous sprinkling of the great Australian adjective, the local and irrational grammar of which he had mastered to perfection."

Figure 14.1: Interpretation at Waldheim: 'On meeting Weindorfer'

Conclusion

Managers of natural and cultural heritage face many challenges, not the least of which is the impact of large numbers of visitors on these resources. The history of Waldheim illustrates how attitudes to heritage and to tourism have changed and management has responded, not always appropriately. Weindorfer's vision that Cradle Mountain 'must be a National Park for the people for all time' and his insistence that 'people must know about it and enjoy it' (Smith 1937) reflects the attitudes of a time when nature seemed limitless and human impact minute and temporary.

In response to increasing pressure of use, heritage managers during the last 60 years have commonly chosen to streamline access, increase accommodation, and generally encourage the commodification of heritage. It is only in recent times that this approach has been questioned and the benefits of an entirely different style of tourism considered. While it is perhaps a little optimistic to expect that appropriate management will attract only appropriate use, there is no doubt that inappropriate management attracts inappropriate use.

Cultural and heritage tourism emphasizes the quality and meaning of visitor experiences (see Chapter 1). It 'is increasingly the preferred type of tourism as promoters and consumers alike recognize its particular popularity and benefit to contemporary and future societies' (Koster in Canadian ICOMOS 1990: 6). The essence of cultural tourism is to interpret and present cultural heritage in ways which enable visitors to 'draw personal as well as universal conclusions from the encounter' (Moulin in Canadian ICOMOS 1990: 6). A visit to Waldheim Chalet will continue to be part of the Cradle Mountain experience for future generations of visitors. Let us hope many find meaning in Weindorfer's motto:

> This is Waldheim, where there is no time and nothing matters (Giordano 1987: 69).

References

Australia ICOMOS 1988, *The Australia ICOMOS Charter for the Conservation of Places of Cultural Significance (The Burra Charter)*, Australia ICOMOS, Sydney.
Bannear, D. 1990, *Conservation Plan for Waldheim Chalet Area, Cradle Mountain–Lake St Clair National Park*, Department of Parks, Wildlife and Heritage, Hobart.
Bergman, G. F. J. 1959, *Gustav Weindorfer of Cradle Mountain*, Tasmania.
Canadian ICOMOS 1990, *Newsletter, National Committee on Cultural Tourism*, ICOMOS National Committee on Cultural Tourism, Ottawa.
Cradle Mountain–Lake St Clair Board n.d., 'Minutes of Cradle Mountain–Lake St Clair Board meetings', in *AA580/1, Box 1 (Files, General)*, Tasmanian State Archives, Hobart.

Department of Parks, Wildlife and Heritage 1992, *Draft Site Plan for Cradle Valley*, Department of Parks, Wildlife and Heritage, Hobart.

Giordano, M. 1987, *A Man and a Mountain, The Story of Gustav Weindorfer*, Launceston, Tasmania.

Hall, C. M. 1992, *Wasteland to World Heritage: Preserving Australia's Wilderness*, Melbourne University Press, Carlton.

Horne, D. 1986, *The Great Museum: The Representation of History*, Pluto Press, London.

Saunders, R. E. 1990a, 'Presenting Tasmania's World Heritage Area: A Strategy for Interpretation'. Unpublished report, Department of Parks, Wildlife and Heritage, Hobart.

Saunders, R. E. 1990b, 'Your chance to say something about Waldheim Chalet Interpretation'. Unpublished report, Department of Parks, Wildlife and Heritage, Hobart.

Saunders, R. E. 1991, 'Auto-stop 12 volt sound system for interpretation at remote locations', *Australian Ranger Bulletin*, vol. 6, no. 2.

Smith, R. E. 1937, 'Cradle Mountain, with notes on wildlife and climate by Gustav Weindorfer'. Unpublished manuscript in Department of Parks, Wildlife and Heritage Library, containing copies of articles from Tasmanian newspapers dated 1935–37 (newspaper sources not credited).

Cultural Perspectives
European Culture and the Built Environment

Introduction

The six chapters in this section examine issues of managing European culture and the built environment over a number of scales. Chapter 15 by Butts provides an account of the institutional framework with which heritage is managed and protected in New Zealand. In particular, Butts stresses the critical role that government plays in heritage management not only through the legal environment but also through policy-making and administrative structures. Indeed, the significance of central and local government is one of the themes that runs through all the papers in this section. The institutional arrangements set the broad framework within which heritage is managed. The following chapters in this section examine heritage management at regional and local levels.

Chapter 16 by Davies discusses the protection and management of built European heritage within an Australian context, and stresses the difficulties encountered by managers in reconciling authenticity with the range of values that exist at a heritage site.

Chapter 17 by Kearsley discusses the significance of European heritage for tourism in Otago and the positive imaging of the region. However, he also notes the very important links between the cultural and natural landscape and the complementary relationship that exists between them in attracting tourists to the region. Similarly, the role of tourism as a justification for heritage protection and maintenance is a significant issue in the studies by McGregor of the Art Deco city of Napier (Chapter 18), Page on the Wellington Waterfront and the new National Museum of New Zealand (Chapter 19), and Wilson on the Hobson Wharf Auckland Maritime Museum development (Chapter 20).

15

Institutional Arrangements for Cultural Heritage Management in New Zealand

Legislation, Management, and Protection

David J. Butts

Introduction

Eastern Polynesians settled Aotearoa/New Zealand about 1000 years ago and evolved into the iwi (tribes) now collectively called Māori (Davidson 1984: 219–25). European settlement expanded rapidly after the signing of the Treaty of Waitangi between iwi Māori (Māori tribes) and the British Crown which facilitated the development of colonial government (Dalziel 1981). During the late nineteenth and twentieth centuries significant numbers of Asian and Polynesian peoples have settled and continue to settle in Aotearoa/New Zealand (Thomson and Trlin 1970).

Governments throughout the world recognize the responsibility of each nation to ensure the protection and management of the cultural heritage of their peoples through the implementation of a variety of forms of legislation (O'Keefe and Prott 1984, 1989). This chapter outlines both the current Aotearoa/New Zealand heritage protection and management legislation and examines proposed new legislation and the reasons for the proposed changes. Such an analysis provides a means of evaluating changing needs and attitudes to the protection and management of material cultural heritage resources in Aotearoa/New Zealand. Of necessity such an analysis reflects these needs as perceived at a national level and will not reflect the full range of needs and attitudes at a local level amongst the peoples of Aotearoa/New Zealand.

Reference to the 'peoples' of Aotearoa/New Zealand acknowledges the cultural diversity of our society and the right of each cultural group to determine the most appropriate means of protecting and managing their cultural heritage. Such rights are guaranteed to iwi Māori under Article Two of the Treaty of Waitangi (O'Regan 1990). As Aotearoa/New Zealand becomes increasingly multicultural, legislators should be cognizant of the need for other cultural groups within our society to determine these matters in a way which they consider appropriate.

Material Cultural Heritage, Protection and Management

In this chapter the terms 'material cultural heritage', 'cultural property', and 'taonga tukuiho' are used as equivalents. Each refers to the physical evidence of human creativity and activity, including moveable and immoveable artefacts, buildings, and historic places, be they archaeological sites or wāhi tapu (sacred places). It is also recognized that cultural property is only one component of cultural heritage. Cultural heritage consists of both tangible and intangible elements which are closely interrelated. The traditions or history (oral or written) of artefacts, buildings or historic places must be preserved (recorded or remembered) if they are to retain their significance. Any strategy for the preservation of material cultural heritage should also recognize the importance of maintaining the relationship between the tangible and intangible elements of cultural heritage.

In this chapter 'protection of cultural property' refers to the mechanisms available in law making it illegal for people to export or destroy significant artefacts, buildings or sites (O'Keefe and Prott 1984, 1989). Management includes the collecting, documentation, conservation and interpretation of cultural property. It is important to observe that successful public programmes using cultural property resources must be based on sound documentation, research and conservation policy and practice. Heritage preservation is a term that will be used in this chapter to include both protection and management.

Formal and Informal Cultural Property Preservation

Formal management is that which occurs as a requirement or consequence of legislation or institutional practice. Informal heritage management is that which occurs as a result of the private initiative of one or more individuals. The line between formal and informal heritage management is fluid. An individual initiative can evolve into a group activity (still private) and then eventually into a public institution. Some landowners begin by privately preserving an archaeological site on their land but eventually recognize the value of using the legislative provision to place a Heritage Covenant on the site. Therefore, the formal and informal or public and private modes of cultural property management should not be seen as separate and closed systems.

An excellent example of the two systems working together is the New Zealand Historic Places Trust Māori buildings conservation programme (Geelan de Kabath 1986). Professional Māori conservators work with Māori communities to conserve whare tupuna (meeting houses) and other marae buildings. The objectives of the conservation programmes are controlled by the community and the buildings remain completely within the control of the community. The whare tupuna remains a living part of the community, not an artefact to be institutionalized.

The Role of Government

Central Government is involved in the protection and management of cultural property at many levels in Aotearoa/New Zealand. These include legislation, administrative functions, the establishment and resourcing of national collecting and interpretation institutions and the provision of project funding to non-governmental heritage agencies (i.e. museums, archives, and iwi authorities).

One means of evaluating the level of consensus within a society about heritage matters is to examine the legislative provisions for heritage preservation. This legislation provides both an expression of what is considered to be worthy of preservation and a range of resources and powers thought to be appropriate to ensure that this preservation occurs. As the attitudes of society change so there is a need to review and amend existing legislation.

Governments in Aotearoa/New Zealand have adopted a range of heritage strategies throughout this century and these have been periodically reviewed and amended (Cater 1989). These strategies range from restrictions on the export of important cultural property (Antiquities Act 1975), and the provision of funds to train cultural conservators (Cultural Conservation Advisory Council), to the provisions for the registration and protection of buildings and archaeological sites (Historic Places Act 1980, Resource Management Act 1991). These and other measures also provide a means for members of the public either individually or collectively to participate in the cultural heritage preservation process (e.g. District Committees of the New Zealand Historic Places Trust).

Governments in the Western world appear to be facing a fundamental dilemma in relation to heritage preservation. On the one hand governments generally recognize the importance of cultural identity in creating a sense of community and the importance of preserving heritage as a part of that cultural identity. On the other hand the dominant political philosophy at the present time advocates a more confined role for central and local government, privatization of government enterprises, and reliance on competition in the market place to determine value. Added to this is the traditional concept of the rights of the owner of property, particularly rights of landowners, to determine what happens to their property. This is an issue in all common law countries (Cleere 1989).

Since the early 1980s in Aotearoa/New Zealand the 'New Right' ideology has dominated politics and considerable economic (and consequently social) restructuring has occurred. During this period there has also been extensive review of the effectiveness of existing heritage preservation legislation. Though largely driven by a growing recognition of the rights of iwi Māori to determine appropriate processes for the preservation of their own cultural property, there has also been a considerable growth in public advocacy for more effective measures to improve heritage preservation generally. While there is an apparent political willingness to provide more effective legislative mechanisms for the protection of cultural heritage, there is no guarantee that an appropriate level of resourcing will be available to enable them to be used effectively.

Existing heritage legislation provides a broad framework for the protection and management of heritage by government agencies and public institutions. Within this framework it is necessary to determine what should be preserved and the most appropriate strategy for achieving that preservation. There are some areas of heritage management which are not specifically covered in legislation. Perhaps the most important is the establishment and management of museums and archives. Any individual or organization can establish a museum or archive to collect cultural property without demonstrating they have the skills or resources to do so adequately. While many of the individuals working in museums and archives think of themselves as professionals, they are not recognized by society as being part of a profession that requires legislative control. Society recognizes the need to preserve cultural heritage, but not the need to legislate to ensure appropriate standards of care and interpretation of these resources. This would be a very complex task and at present it is thought best to leave it to the professional organizations themselves to monitor. The establishment of the Ministry of Cultural Affairs in 1991 may lead to a more proactive government role in the development of a coherent cultural heritage preservation policy. Since establishment, the Ministry has undertaken a review of the Museum of New Zealand Te Papa Tongarewa project and the Queen Elizabeth II Arts Council. The Ministry should also have a role in co-ordinating dialogue between the full range of heritage agencies in the development of government policy. There have been a number of cultural heritage policy development initiatives at the Federal and State levels in Australia which would provide useful models for a policy development process in Aotearoa/New Zealand (Department of the Arts,

Sport, the Environment, Tourism and Territories 1990, 1991; Department of Arts, Government of Western Australia 1992).

Antiquities Act 1975

The Maori Antiquities Act 1901 was the first legislation designed to prevent the export of Māori cultural property of historical or scientific importance from Aotearoa/New Zealand. Minor amendments were made to the 1901 Act in 1904 and 1908. The 1908 Maori Antiquities Act was repealed by the Historic Articles Act 1962. This Act restricted the export of historic articles from Aotearoa/New Zealand. Historic articles were defined by the Act as Māori artefacts made before 1902, books and documents of historic, scientific or national value or importance and more than ninety years old, and type specimens. A process of application and appeal to seek permission to export a restricted item was established in the legislation. The Act made it an offence, liable on summary conviction to a fine, to export an historic article, as defined by the Act, without first obtaining a permit from the Minister of Internal Affairs. The Historic Articles Act was repealed by the Antiquities Act 1975. The major provisions of this Act are to restrict the export of antiquities, to establish and record ownership of Māori artefacts and to control the sale of Māori artefacts within Aotearoa/New Zealand.

Export Restrictions
The Antiquities Act 1975 restricts the export of the following antiquities:

> (1) any Māori artefact made prior to 1902:
> (2) any chattel of national, historical, scientific or artistic importance relating to the European discovery, settlement or development of Aotearoa/New Zealand and at least sixty years old. Some specific categories of cultural property are outlined in detail including books, documents, photographs, artworks, natural history specimens, ships and aircraft (section 2).

This is the most comprehensive attempt to date to define in legislation those elements of our moveable cultural property that should be preserved. In practice both the general public and the Department of Internal Affairs have found the definition too general. It is not always an easy matter to determine whether a particular antiquity requires a Certificate of Permission to be exported. This was demonstrated in the case of the *Department of Internal Affairs* v *The Poverty Bay Club Incorporated*. In this case the Department of Internal Affairs charged that 'without reasonable excuse and without the written Certificate of Permission of the Secretary of Internal Affairs, the club removed an antiquity from New Zealand, namely a letter from Captain James

Cook to Captain Charles Clerke dated the 10th day of July 1778 (referred to as the "Cook Instruction")'. Although the 'Cook Instruction' does not mention Aotearoa/New Zealand it relates to Captain Cook's third voyage of Pacific exploration during which he did spend a period of twelve days at Cook's Cove, Queen Charlotte Sound, in the northern South Island.

Evidence given in court confirmed that staff at the Alexander Turnbull Library, a section of the National Library of New Zealand, had advised the Club to sell the letter at Sothebys. When the Department of Internal Affairs was informed that the letter had been sent to London an investigation was undertaken to determine whether it was an antiquity as defined in the Antiquities Act 1975. The Department concluded, on the basis of expert opinion, that the letter was an antiquity within that definition and thus proceeded with the prosecution outlined above. Judge Thomas convicted the Club of the charge noting at the same time that the offence was an unwitting one. He also noted 'the legislation is in the nature of public welfare regulation and illustrates the determination of the Legislator to retain national treasures (if I may use that more neutral term) in the country'.

This case demonstrated a limited knowledge of the Antiquities Act amongst the museum and library professionals consulted by the Club as well as the members of the Club themselves. Because of the limited public education programme of the Department of Internal Affairs to educate the general public about the Antiquities Act this lack of knowledge is not surprising. The success of any heritage preservation legislation will be determined by the extent to which it is understood and supported by both the heritage professionals and the general public.

The Judge's finding demonstrated that the Act is open to very broad interpretation. Although the 'Cook Instruction' does not mention Aotearoa/New Zealand it is deemed to be within the definition of an antiquity (section 2(c)) in that it 'relates to New Zealand'. Although the Poverty Bay Club was convicted of the charge the letter remained in London for sale. Fortunately the New Zealand 1990 Committee in London was able to purchase the letter and return it to New Zealand.

The most comprehensively documented case of illegal export is that of the Motunui pataka panels. Legal initiatives by the New Zealand Government to have these carvings returned have become a classic case in the international repatriation literature (Greenfield 1989) and the failure to do so focused the Department of Internal Affairs on the need to review the Antiquities Act 1975 (Cater 1989).

Five pataka (raised storehouse) panels, carved by members of the Āti awa tribe of Taranaki on the west coast of the North Island before 1820, were illegally removed from Aotearoa/New Zealand in 1973 and sold to George

Ortiz in New York in April of that year. In 1978 Ortiz attempted to auction the carvings at Sotheby Parke Bernet in London. When the New Zealand Government issued instructions for counsel in London to seek an interim injunction to stop the sale of the panels, Sothebys agreed to remove the carvings from the sale. The New Zealand Government attempted and failed to establish legal ownership of the carvings in the English courts and the carvings still remain in the ownership of Mr Ortiz. It should be noted that another Māori carving offered for sale at the same auction by Mr Ortiz was purchased for the Canterbury Museum collection with assistance from the Government. Government funds have been made available to the National Museum on a regular basis to assist with the return of important items of Aotearoa/New Zealand's material cultural heritage.

The illegal export of the pataka panels was only discovered when they were offered for sale in London. There is no reliable information available to indicate the volume of material that has been illegally exported from New Zealand in recent years. This case persuaded the New Zealand Government of the need to participate in international initiatives to deter the illegal trade in material cultural heritage which continues to be a problem in many countries.

Establishing Ownership and Custody of Artefacts

Artefacts are defined in the Act as:

> any chattel carving object or thing which relates to the history, art, culture, traditions, or economy of the Māori or other pre-European inhabitants of New Zealand and which was or appears to have been manufactured or modified in New Zealand by any such inhabitant, or brought to New Zealand by an ancestor of any such inhabitant or used by any such inhabitant, prior to 1902 (section 2).

The Act states that any artefact found in Aotearoa/New Zealand after 1 April 1976 is prima facie property of the Crown and establishes a procedure for notifying the Secretary of Internal Affairs of the find. This includes all artefacts recovered from archaeological sites. Once notified the Secretary will determine whether custody will be given to the finder or a public institution. Any person who is given custody of an artefact under the powers of this Act must be a registered collector. The Act also provides a procedure for the registration of collectors.

Where an artefact has been recovered from the grave of a known person the Maori Land Court is empowered to determine ownership and custody. The Maori Land Court is also given very wide powers to determine the ownership or custody of any artefact where such a matter is referred to it by the Minister of Internal Affairs or any other person.

Artefacts may only be sold, or otherwise disposed of, to a registered collector, a public museum or through the offices of a licensed auctioneer or a licensed secondhand dealer. Before an artefact can be sold by a licensed auctioneer or a licensed secondhand dealer an authorized museum must issue a certificate of examination. A complete list of artefacts found each year and permissions for the removal of antiquities from Aotearoa/New Zealand must be published by the Secretary of Internal Affairs in the departmental report to Parliament.

This Act has been in operation for sixteen years. Although it has been most effective in controlling the public sale of artefacts, without more detailed research it is impossible to evaluate how successful the legislation has been in stopping illegal export of antiquities or ensuring that the appropriate action is taken when artefacts are found. There has been no independent review of the operation of this legislation during that period.

Review of Antiquities Act 1975
The Act has been under internal review by the Department of Internal Affairs since 1987. There have been three major foci in the review:
(1) The implications of the Treaty of Waitangi for the key issues of cultural heritage export control and the determination of ownership and custody of newly found Māori taonga tukuiho;
(2) Drafting a Heritage Control List which will specify categories of objects for which an export certificate is required; and
(3) Ensuring that the Act has all the components required to enable the New Zealand government to accede to the 1970 UNESCO Convention on the Means of Prohibiting the Illicit Import, Export and Transfer of Ownership of Cultural Property.

The Department of Internal Affairs (1990) circulated an issues paper which outlined a number of recommendations for discussion. Instead of newly found artefacts being prima facie property of the Crown, it is recommended that an appropriate process is needed to assist the Secretary of Internal Affairs to determine Māori ownership and custody. It is proposed that the artefacts now be termed Taonga Tukuiho and these be defined as 'any moveable object created by or modified by the Māori or their descendants or any other person:
(a) which is of cultural, spiritual, and historical, aesthetic or heritage significance and value to the Māori; and
(b) which:
   (i) has been handed down a descent line of not less than two

generations; or
(ii) is not less than 50 years old (Department of Internal Affairs 1990: 3).

Changes in legislation provide an insight into the changes that occur in public attitudes towards particular issues. This proposed new definition is expressed in quite different terms to those used to define an artefact in the 1975 Act. The underlying principles in the new proposals also recognize to a much greater extent the right of Māori to determine the ownership and custody of their cultural property. This reflects the extent to which the principles of the Treaty of Waitangi have gained recognition in heritage management. The challenge for the legislators is to find an appropriate mechanism for shifting the process of determining ownership and custody away from central control towards hapū and iwi (tribal) control. The Maori Land Court will also continue to have an important role in this area.

The inclusion of a Heritage Control List in the legislation would meet the requirement of the 1970 UNESCO Convention for a detailed outline of the cultural property covered by the Act. Such a list would also provide a much more comprehensive guide for the public. It is also recommended that a provision be included in the Act to prevent the import into Aotearoa/New Zealand of cultural property which has been illegally removed from another country. This is also a requirement of the 1970 UNESCO Convention. At the time of writing this chapter (September 1992) a draft of the new proposals in the form of a bill has not been made public and it is not evident when such a Bill will be introduced to Parliament. Given that 1993 is an election year the Bill will probably not be introduced until 1994.

The Antiquities Act was administered by the Arts and Cultural Heritage Division of the Department of Internal Affairs until 1991 when this Division ceased to exist because its functions were transferred to the newly created Ministry of Cultural Affairs. The Antiquities Act is currently administered by the Constitutional Branch of the Department of Internal Affairs.

Historic Places Act 1980

The Historic Places Act 1980 repealed the Historic Places Act 1954 and its subsequent amendments. The major provisions of this Act are to establish the New Zealand Historic Places Board of Trustees, to clarify and protect historic buildings, archaeological sites, historic areas, and traditional sites. The Act provides for the classification of buildings into four categories according to their historical significance or architectural quality:
(a) Those buildings for which permanent preservation is regarded as essential;
(b) Those buildings which merit permanent preservation;

(c) Those buildings which merit preservation; and
(d) Those buildings which merit recording.

The Protection Notice provisions of the Act have been replaced by the Heritage Order provisions in the Resource Management Act 1991 (see below).

The Historic Places Act requires the Historic Places Trust to establish and maintain a register of archaeological sites. Anyone intending to modify an archaeological site more than 100 years old, whether for research or any other purpose, is required to obtain an authority from the Historic Places Trust. The Trust may (a) decline such an authority if the modification will destroy the archaeological site, or (b) require an archaeological investigation to be completed before such modification can proceed.

The applicant for authority may be required to pay for such an investigation except where the proposed modification is for farming or agricultural purposes. If an authority is declined the applicant can appeal to the Minister. A significant number of appeals are upheld.

The Trust may require any territorial authority to record a registered archaeological site in a district planning scheme. This provides a mechanism for notifying prospective land purchasers of the presence of a site and assists planners to assess the impact of land use on the archaeological landscape.

Anyone proposing the scientific investigation of an archaeological site requires a permit from the Trust. No such authority may be granted by the Trust without the concurrence of the appropriate Maori Authority. The Trust may impose conditions on the permit. Artefacts recovered from such excavations are subject to the requirements of the Antiquities Act 1975.

The Historic Places Act also provides for the classification of Historic Areas and the notification of such classification to the territorial authority in whose district the historic area is situated. The territorial authority is only required to take into account the desirability of preserving or enhancing such an area. Such a classification has been placed on part of Napier because of the Art Deco architecture (See Chapter 18).

New Zealand Historic Places Trust

The Trust is responsible for administering the provisions of the Historic Places Act 1980 (section 5). Since its founding in 1955 the Trust has developed to an establishment of about forty staff (plus wage workers), administers a number of historic buildings throughout Aotearoa/New Zealand and serves a public membership of over 24,000 through a network of twenty-one district committees. To date, the Trust has classified nearly 5000 buildings.

The Trust's history reflects the evolution of government cultural and natural heritage preservation policy. Until 1987 the Trust operated as an semi-autonomous body funded by vote allocation through the Department of Internal Affairs. In 1987 the Conservation Act established the Department of Conservation with responsibility for the management, for conservation purposes, of all land and all other natural and historic resources included in the Crown estate. From 1987 the New Zealand Historic Places Trust was funded through the Department of Conservation. It was expected that the Department of Conservation would absorb all other government-funded natural and cultural heritage agencies thus forming a unitary heritage management agency. As part of this process the archaeological staff of the Trust moved into the Science and Research Division of the Department of Conservation.

However, the Trust has retained its identity and no other sections of Trust staff have been integrated into the Department of Conservation. At the present time the Trust administers the archaeological provisions of the Historic Places Act and the archaeologists in the Science and Research Division of the Department of Conservation provide professional archaeological advice and investigation services to the Trust as required. In relation to the classification and protection of buildings the Trust has retained a larger staff to meet the administrative and professional requirements, although use is made of consultant architectural conservators. The Historic Places Bill (see below) gives the New Zealand Historic Places Trust autonomy from the Department of Conservation, thus reversing the initiative to bring heritage functions together under the Conservation Act.

The Trust has given increasing recognition and resources to its role of interpreting historic places for the public visitor. Unfortunately, apart from one visitor survey (Shum 1986) which provides basic proportions of adult and child visitors at a range of Trust properties, there has been no comprehensive user and non-user survey. Thus it is not possible to evaluate the Trust's public programmes. Nor is there any evidence in the literature of the development of innovative site interpretation or public programmes, despite considerable resources having gone into conservation projects on several Trust properties. The Trust has been an active partner with ICOMOS New Zealand and the New Zealand Professional Conservators Group in developing the draft ICOMOS New Zealand Charter.

Conservation Act 1987

The Conservation Act established the Department of Conservation with responsibility for the management, for conservation purposes, of all land and all other natural and historic resources included in the Crown Estate (the Conservation Estate). The Conservation Estate includes significant building and archaeological resources including the Mansion House on Kawau Island and the archaeological sites on Motutapu Island (see the Annual Report to Parliament).

The historic resources role of the Department of Conservation can be classified into four primary functions:

(a) *Policy*: the priority in this area has been the review of the Historic Places Act. In the future this function will focus on the policy for the DOC Estate;

(b) *Implementation of Legal Protection*: including the provision of Heritage Orders and the development of the Historic Resource Inventory;

(c) *Management Service—Conservation Estate*: including the management of historic resources at conservancy level; and

(d) *Servicing of Crown Agencies*: servicing the Historic Places Trust (Department of Conservation 1990: 5–6).

Staffing for these functions is currently inadequate. There are 14 full-time archaeologists (4 at head office and 10 employed at conservancy level) and 10. 5 Historic Resources staff (2 at head office and 8.5 at conservancy level). There are currently 14 conservancy regions. There will need to be significant increases in staff if the Department of Conservation is to meet its mandate to protect and preserve the historic resources on the Conservation Estate (see Chapter 5).

Resource Management Act 1991

The Resource Management Act is based on the principle of 'sustainable management of natural and physical resources' (section 5(1)). Sustainable management is the use and development of resources in a way which enables people and communities 'to provide for their social, economic, and cultural well-being'. Territorial authorities are required to recognize and provide for 'the relationship of Maori and their culture and traditions with their ancestral lands, water, sites, wāhi tapu and other taonga' as a matter of national importance (section 6(e)). General protection for the heritage value of the sites, buildings, places and areas of all peoples is specifically provided for in the Act (section 7).

This Act will be increasingly influential in the protection and management of cultural heritage resources. Broadly speaking it will encourage the Trust to focus on the identification and registration of sites and buildings while protection and ongoing management become increasingly the responsibility of territorial authorities.

The Resource Management Act 1991 enables any Heritage Protection Authority to give notice to a territorial authority of its requirement for a Heritage Order for the purpose of protecting any place or area of special interest (cultural, architectural, historical, scientific, ecological), character, intrinsic or amenity value or visual appeal, or of special significance to the tangata whenua (local Māori tribe) for spiritual, historical or cultural reasons. At the present time it is probable that very few Heritage Orders will be sought because of the cost of the process and the chance that if an appeal against an Order is successful the Heritage Protection Authority will be required to purchase the building or site or remove the Heritage Order (Guthrie 1991). To date Heritage Orders have been placed on the Hoffman Kiln at Benhar and the Sacred Heart Chapel in Invercargill.

Guthrie (1991: 127) has noted that iwi Māori will now be able to protect a much wider range of wāhi tapu than was previously possible. However, the broader implications for cultural heritage protection and management are inherent in the requirement of regional and district government to take account of the effect of any planning application on historical or cultural sites, landscapes and wāhi tapu. There is a requirement on the local authority to develop policy and processes for dealing with issues relating to such resources (Lawlor 1991; Hawkes Bay Regional Council 1992). Some Māori authorities have also been active in preparing studies which will provide a basis for establishing recognition of their historic resources under the terms of the Act (Tau, Te Maire et al. 1990; Te Runanga o Ngatihine 1990). This Act will necessitate a much greater level of communication between local authorities and community groups to arrive at a consensus about which historic resources are to be protected and preserved and how this is to be achieved.

Historic Places Bill 1992

The objectives of the bill include:
(1) to increase Māori representation on the Trust Board;
(2) to provide more appropriate mechanisms for the protection of Māori cultural heritage;
(3) to integrate the Historic Places Act with the Resource Management Act 1991;
(4) to unify the registration of historic places, archaeological sites, and wāhi tapu; and
(5) to increase penalties for convictions under the Act.

The background section of the explanatory notes published with the bill state:

> The Bill deals principally with the registration system of historic places and the administration of that system. The enforcement of heritage protection will be achieved largely through the mechanisms in the Resource Management Act 1991.

Māori representation on the Trust Board will be increased from one to three and total Board membership is reduced from fifteen to ten. A Maori Heritage Council will be established with responsibility for the identifying, conserving, and registration of wāhi tapu, and advising the Trust on matters referred to it by the Trust, such as applications to modify or investigate archaeological sites. This bill provides the enabling legislation for the Historic Places Trust within the broader context of the Resource Management Act. For example, a local territorial authority will be required to advise the Trust of any application for a resource consent or permit or approval affecting any registered historic place (clause 29). Of particular note in the bill is the list of criteria for registration of historic places and areas (clause 21). This is the most comprehensive statement to date in legislation of such criteria, and takes in a much wider range of considerations than previously. In relation to the broader concerns of heritage management the inclusion of the potential of the place for public education is of particular importance. The penalties for conviction in the bill are significantly greater than those in the 1980 Act. This bill is currently (September 1992) before a Select Committee and has drawn considerable criticism particularly from the archaeological community (NZAA 1992).

National Collecting and Interpretation Institutions

Government has established three major collecting and interpretation institutions to care for cultural property of national importance. The National Library Act 1965 requires the National Library/Te Puna Matauranga o Aotearoa (including the Alexander Turnbull Library) to develop and maintain a national collection of library materials including a comprehensive collection of library materials relating to Aotearoa/New Zealand. This latter is a collection of 'last resort' because the library is responsible for ensuring the survival of at least one copy of every book published in Aotearoa/New Zealand. The Archives Act 1975 established National Archives/Te Whare Tohu Tuhituhinga o Aotearoa and provides for the preservation of public archives. This Act has been under review for some years and a draft Bill has been completed, though it is not yet a public document.

The Museum of New Zealand Te Papa Tongarewa Act 1992 has united the National Art Gallery and National Museum within one organizational structure. This museum will 'provide a forum in which the nation may present, explore and preserve both the heritage of its cultures and knowledge of the natural environment'. The functions of the museum as outlined in the legislation are to collect, preserve, exhibit, research and educate. The museum is organized into four departments: Art, History, Māori, Natural History.

Each of these departments must contribute to the development of an accessible national repository of cultural and natural heritage collections. This accessibility implies an enjoyable and enriching experience (see Chapter 15).

As a national institution the Museum of New Zealand places primary emphasis on collecting objects of national importance which will meet the needs of its public programmes, including its research programmes. This objective signals a significant change from developing research collections to developing collections which are primarily to meet the needs of exhibition and education programmes. The collections will also reflect the bicultural commitment of the museum. In recognition of the importance of providing quality public programmes the museum has developed a Public Programmes Department. This department co-ordinates exhibition planning, education programmes and marketing. During the last two years this Department (which existed before the transition to the Museum of New Zealand) has commissioned a number of visitor surveys to develop visitor profiles and to evaluate particular exhibitions.

The Museum of New Zealand Te Papa Tongarewa Act requires the museum to provide 'national services' to other museums. Exactly what this means is uncertain at the present time. However, there is an expectation on the part of some museums that this will mean access to government funding to assist in the preservation of collections of national importance in their institutions. The challenge of the Museum of New Zealand Te Papa Tongarewa and the Ministry of Cultural Affairs will be to find a process which allows all museums to participate in the debate about what form 'national services' should take. One can assume that government included the provision for 'national services' in the Act to ensure the distribution of both services and resources to the whole museum sector.

Cultural Conservation Advisory Council (CCAC)

This ministerial advisory committee was established in 1987 to identify, set and promote national priorities for the conservation of our material cultural property; to decide allocations of funding made available for conservation purposes; and to identify and arrange employment and training opportunities for people to carry out conservation work (CCAC 1988). CCAC is funded partly from the Vote for Internal Affairs and partly from the New Zealand Lotteries Board.

To achieve its objectives CCAC decided it would need to establish the current extent of the nation's taonga tukuiho/material cultural property and to assess the available and required resources for its conservation. To this end the Council agreed to fund conservation surveys of public collections.

Unfortunately, it has not yet found a mechanism for evaluating the needs of collections outside public institutions.

The Council established a subsidy scheme for conservation projects proposed by public institutions and some community groups. Funding to train cultural conservators overseas is also granted in the form of three-year scholarships. A limited number of research proposals have also been funded including a project at Otago University to try and discover a way of stabilizing taonga made of harakeke (flax) which are deteriorating.

CCAC has enabled many museums, archives and libraries to improve the storage of their collections and to undertake projects to conserve important items or collections. A number of conservators have obtained degrees in Conservation Science at the Canberra College of Advanced Education and returned to work in Aotearoa/New Zealand. For example, two Māori conservators currently employed by the New Zealand Historic Places Trust to conserve Māori buildings had their training funded by CCAC.

Through CCAC government has been able to provide a delivery structure for some of the funding needed to facilitate the heritage preservation policy embodied in legislation such as the Antiquities Act 1975 and the Historic Places Act 1980. However, CCAC is currently under review and it is not known what changes may occur to the terms of reference or funding of the Council.

Conclusion

This chapter has outlined the extent to which government has legislated to ensure the protection and management of cultural heritage of the nation's peoples. The willingness of government to acknowledge the limitations of existing legislation and the significant increase in public interest in cultural heritage is perhaps reflected in the substantial changes which have occurred in the institutional environment for heritage management. During the last five years three major pieces of legislation affecting cultural heritage preservation have been enacted: the Conservation Act 1987; the Resource Management Act 1991 and the Museum of New Zealand Te Papa Tongarewa Act 1992. The Historic Places Bill is currently before a Parliamentary Select Committee and the Antiquities Act 1975 and the Archives Act 1975 are currently under review.

A common theme throughout the review of all these Acts has been the need to provide appropriate recognition of the rights of iwi Māori to control their own cultural heritage. This is part of a more general recognition of Māori rights in relation to the care and interpretation of taonga tukuiho (Butts 1990). While significant progress might be anticipated in legislative change that will facilitate increased Māori control of their cultural property there is as yet no evidence that the New Zealand Government is considering introducing legislation equivalent to the Native American Grave Protection and Repatriation Act 1990. This law requires federal agencies and federally funded museums to inventory their collections of Native American human remains and associated funerary objects in five years and repatriate them if requested, to culturally affiliated tribes or native groups (Monroe and Echo-Hawk 1991). The same agencies and museums are also required to summarize Native American cultural items and notify appropriate tribes within three years. The next decade will most likely see the development of iwi Māori museums, and even a Māori cultural heritage foundation. In addition, a concept worthy of consideration in the New Zealand context is the Living National Treasures component of the Japanese Cultural Properties Protection Law (Adachi 1973: 5). This law recognizes both individuals and groups as holders of intangible cultural properties. This would be an appropriate way of recognizing, for example, the skills and knowledge of certain Māori weavers and carvers.

Another far-reaching change is the increased responsibility for cultural heritage protection and management placed on regional and district authorities by the Resource Management Act. Local Governments are now required to establish processes for evaluating the impact of planning proposals on historic resources. These same bodies will be accountable for the decisions they make.

There is a need for the new Ministry of Cultural Affairs to begin to co-ordinate the development of a coherent cultural heritage preservation policy which provides a framework within which the various cultural heritage agencies can operate. Legislation alone is not enough. Government has a role to set objectives and provide some incentives for cultural heritage agencies to achieve the highest possible standards in the care and interpretation of the taonga tukuiho of the nation's peoples.

References

Adachi, B. 1973, *The Living Treasures of Japan*, Wildwood House, London.
Butts, D. J. 1990, 'Nga Tukemata: Nga Taonga o Ngati Kahungunu (The Awakening: the treasures of Ngati Kahungunu)', in *The Politics of the Past*, eds. P. Gathercole and D. Lowenthal, Unwin Hyman, London.
Cater, R. 1989, 'Threats to New Zealand's moveable cultural heritage', in *Protection or Plunder? Safeguarding the Future of Our Cultural Heritage*, Australian National Commission for UNESCO, Canberra.
Cleere, H. F. (ed.) 1989, *Archeological Heritage Management in the Modern World*, Unwin Hyman, London.

Cultural Conservation Advisory Council 1988, *Policy Statement*, Department of Internal Affairs, Wellington.
Dalziel, R. 1981, 'The politics of settlement', in *The Oxford History of New Zealand*, ed. W. H. Oliver with B. R. Williams, The Clarendon Press, Oxford.
Davidson, J. 1984, *The Prehistory of New Zealand*, Longman Paul, Auckland.
Department of the Arts, Sport, the Environment, Tourism and Territories 1990, *What Value Heritage?*, Department for the Arts, Sport, the Environment, Tourism and Territories, Canberra.
Department of the Arts, Sport, the Environment, Tourism and Territories 1991, *A Plan for Cultural Heritage Institutions to Reflect Australia's Cultural Diversity*, Consultative Committee on Cultural Heritage in a Multicultural Australia, Department for the Arts, Sport, the Environment, Tourism and Territories, Canberra.
Department of Arts, Government of Western Australia 1992, *Into the Twenty-First Century, The Report of the State Taskforce for Museums Policy in Western Australia*, Department of Arts, Government of Western Australia, Perth.
Department of Conservation 1990, *Head Office Historic Resources/NZHPT*, Department of Conservation, Wellington.
Department of Internal Affairs, 1990, *Protection of Moveable Cultural Property Bill—Issues Paper*, Department of Internal Affairs, Wellington.
Geelan de Kabath, A. 1986, 'Restoration of Maori buildings in New Zealand', in *Symposium 86: The Care and Preservation of Ethnological Materials—Proceedings*, eds. R. Barclay, M. Gilberg, J. C. McCawley and T. Stone, Canadian Conservation Institute, Ottawa.
Greenfield, J. 1989, *The Return of Cultural Treasures*, Cambridge University Press, Cambridge.
Guthrie, J. 1991, 'Heritage orders', in *Implementing the Resource Management Act: Conference Proceedings, 15–16 August 1991*, eds. R. Morgan, P. Mernon, and M. Miller, Environmental Policy and Management Research Centre, University of Otago, Dunedin.
Hawkes Bay Regional Council 1992, *Historic Resources, Hawkes Bay Region, Resource Management Act 1991*, Regional Policy Statement, Working Paper No. 1, Hawkes Bay Regional Council, Napier.
Lawlor, I. 1991, *Cultural Heritage Inventory: A Scoping Exercise for the Auckland Region*, Auckland Regional Council, Auckland.
Monroe, D. and Echo-Hawk, W. 1991. 'Deft Deliberations', *Museum News*, July/August.
New Zealand Archaeological Association 1992, 'Historic Places Bill No. 149–1: Written submission', *Archaeology in New Zealand*, vol. 35, no. 2, pp. 88–91.
O'Keefe, P. and Prott, L. 1984, *Law and the Cultural Heritage: Discovery and Excavation*, Professional Books Ltd, Worcester.
O'Keefe, P. and Prott, L. 1989, *Law and the Cultural Heritage: Movement*, Butterworths, London.
O'Regan, S. 1990, 'Maori Control of Maori Heritage', in *The Politics of the Past*, eds. P. Gathercole and D. Lowenthal, Unwin Hyman, London.
Shum, D. 1986, 'Admissions to Historic Places Trust properties 1979–83', in *Historic Places Trust: Admissions 1979–83, Membership Trends 1976–1984*, Research Unit, Department of Internal Affairs, Wellington.

Tau, Te Maire, et al. 1990, *Te Whakatau Kaupapa: Ngai Tahu Resource Management Strategy for the Canterbury Region*, Aoraki Press, Wellington.

Te Runanga o Ngatihine 1990, *An Introductory Perspective to Resource Management Planning*, Te Runanga o Ngati Hine.

Thomson, K. W. and Trlin, K. W. 1970, *Immigrants in New Zealand*, Massey University, Palmerston North.

16

Cultural Tourism, History, and Historic Precincts[*]

Martin Davies

Cultural tourism is about resources, the most important being the resource of the 'fabric'—the physical bricks and mortar of which a place is made. This fabric is not confined to buildings, as is often the case, but includes vegetation, pathways, roads, fences, walls, earthworks, machinery, street furniture—what could be encompassed in the term 'landscape', both urban and rural. Without this physical fabric there is no resource for cultural tourism to use, let alone build upon.

This chapter addresses the physical fabric of several Tasmanian heritage sites, and outlines preservation efforts by management for current and future generations. It also looks at the wider issue of historic precincts and the nature of the heritage being presented.

Conserving and Managing for the Present and Future

The Department of Parks, Wildlife and Heritage (DPWH) manages and administers over 160 State Reserves throughout Tasmania. Some are designated Aboriginal and Historic Sites and range from such complex precincts as Port Arthur to the landing site of Abel Tasman and the monument to the wreck of the *George III*. The majority of administered lands are State Reserves such as national parks, within which lie an enormous number of Aboriginal and historical sites.

The DPWH's primary role is the conservation, management, and interpretation of these sites to ensure the retention of their cultural significance and the presentation of this significance to the public. The Department also provides advice and guidance to other government

---

[*] Paper delivered to the Royal Australian Institute of Parks and Recreation 1992 Conference on 'Heritage Management'.

institutions and private institutions as well as undertaking long-term research programmes to identify aspects of the State's heritage.

Whilst a great number of sites are in isolated locations or comprise minimal physical remains, the DPWH is aware of the importance of a number of its larger sites—those which probably qualify for the term 'precinct' to the various local communities and the tourist industry. The most obvious is Port Arthur, presently operated by the Port Arthur Management Authority. Others include Highfield at Stanley (an 1820s agricultural settlement), the Coal Mines on the Tasman Peninsula (a convict operated mine from 1833 to 1848 and at one time the punishment station for Port Arthur), Sarah Island in Macquarie Harbour (an 1820s convict settlement closed when Port Arthur was opened), Entally (an 1830s rural property now leased and operated by the National Trust), and Darlington on Maria Island off Tasmania's East Coast (a site which underwent seven different phases of occupation included two convict settlements and two industrial operations).

Up until the 1980s many of these historic sites suffered from lack of professional heritage input, inadequate assessment as a basis for conservation, *ad hoc* decision making, lack of funds, and neither management strategies nor procedures for their protection. With a few exceptions, the result was the continued deterioration and destruction of the heritage value of these sites through a combination of natural and human actions. In many instances the available monies were either spent on detailed recording works or on infrastructure. Neither is unnecessary or wasted, but the fabric's continued deterioration attested to the fact that these monies were misdirected away from the conservation of the resource. An example is Entally House, which suffers from 'caretaker flat' syndrome—five at the present time and none occupied by caretakers. Meanwhile the historic fabric of the main house, its contents and the unique garden conservatory continued to fall into disrepair.

As a conservation body, the DPWH's primary role must be to preserve what is important about the sites under its control and to strike a balance between this and the often competing requirement to provide infrastructure for visitors, including interpretation facilities.

However, these are not the only tensions associated with cultural tourism. The roles of volunteers and sponsors can create their own problems. In addition, the physical capacity of a site may well be a factor in limiting visitor numbers or requiring intrusive protective measures (walkways, barriers, and screens) which change and restrict the visitor experience (Plate 16.1). For example, there is the effect of large numbers of visitors to a town or village with increased congestion, parking problems, invasion of privacy, the change of one's town into a tourist destination, and resentment towards newly arrived tourist entrepreneurs.

Plate 16.1: The construction of protective measures which impact the visitor experience, Port Arthur, Tasmania

Conservation Practice

In the late 1970s and 1980s a great change occurred in heritage conservation, with the formulation of the Australia ICOMOS Charter for the Conservation of Places of Cultural Significance (Burra Charter). The DPWH is now committed to professionally managing its historic sites and to undertaking research to identify significant sites which may become future reserves.

The heritage procedures which the DPWH has in place on its State Reserves, and which are suggested as sound conservation practice for all sites and precincts are:

- *Understanding the place*: this encapsulates the question of 'what is it that we're dealing with?' It comprises identification, analysis, and assessment. So often poor decisions have been made because this initial stage was not addressed (in some cases leading to very costly mistakes). This stage is usually undertaken by a heritage practitioner, but is more successful when done by a multi-disciplinary team comprising historian, historical archaeologist, and architectural historian.
- *Structural fabric or material conservation assessment*: this basically asks what is the physical condition and what are the treatments or options necessary to ensure survival of the existing fabric. This can be undertaken concurrently with the first stage, though it requires different skills (e.g. a structural engineer or architect with a sensitivity and awareness of conservation issues and principles).
- *Preparation of a Conservation Plan*: this incorporates the first two stages but goes further to establish the policies with which to conserve the site. The policies are formulated from the range of constraints, opportunities, feasible end-uses and requirements which arise from the significance of the site, those of the client or managing body, the desires or wishes of other interested parties, the physical condition of the place and external factors such as legislation or planning requirements. The Plan also provides the implementation strategy by identifying the conservation and management priorities, i. e. it attempts to strike the balance between the physical conservation works to the site and the necessary management requirements of visitor facilities, interpretation (displays, events, publications) and departmental infrastructure (office, plant, storage, and staffing). The model for the plan is that provided by Dr J. S. Kerr in his *The Conservation Plan* (1991). It is a common sense, plain English guide to the process and is highly recommended to all those involved in making decisions on historic sites, or sites thought to be of significance.
- *Careful management*: this involves thoughtful implementation and a constant process for assessing new proposals (once immediate works are

completed), an established maintenance programme and a monitoring programme to assess deterioration through natural causes and/or visitor impact.

It is important to stress that such a process does not necessarily mean that a site must be preserved in its present state or that it should be 'restored' to some earlier form. In fact a number of recently commissioned plans for the DPWH have identified tourist accommodation as being a compatible and desirable use in a number of historic structures, and commercial opportunities at a number of other sites. Paramount throughout the process is the idea that such developments can be achieved in tandem with ensuring that what is significant about the site or precinct is retained and preserved.

The changes in conservation practice on historic sites have also been matched by a period of economic recession and a new economic pragmatism. Increasingly, these sites are seen as significant in economic terms as generators of income and opportunities for employment. Some of the sites may be able to generate enough money to cover ongoing expenses, most not, but it is unlikely there will be enough profit to fund further conservation or development works. However, this is not to say that these sites do not benefit the wider community economically:

> Tourism by itself will not provide all the funds necessary . . . Indeed the costs of tourism, in the form of the payment of staff for guiding, security, extra facilities and wear-and-tear, will sometimes exceed the revenue from visitors . . . [yet] the main economic benefit will be derived by transport, accommodation, catering and retailing businesses. In this context the historic building is a classical example of the 'loss leader' (SAVE Britain's Heritage 1983).

SAVE's comments are as relevant to precincts such as Highfield on the outskirts of Stanley in northwest Tasmania or Port Arthur on the Tasman Peninsula as they are to the historic buildings in Britain which originally inspired them. There is a change in perception from historic sites being significant in their own right to their existence being justified on the grounds of being an economic resource and serving the interests of economic regeneration. This can also be applied to cultural institutions and the arts generally. Robert Hewison put it succinctly:

> In the nineteenth century museums were seen as sources of education and improvement, and were therefore free. Now they are treated as financial institutions that must pay their way, and therefore charge entrance fees. The arts are no longer appreciated as a source of inspiration, of ideas, images or values, they are part of 'the leisure business'. We are no longer lovers of art, but consumers for a product. And as the marketing managers of the heritage industry get into full swing, the goods that we are being offered become more and more spurious, and the quality of life more and more debased (1987: 129).

Cultural Tourism, History, and Historic Precincts

Cultural Tourism and History

The notion of cultural tourism and historic precincts is bound up with history. It is history which is being used. The question is 'what history is being presented?' Are the 'goods that we are being offered becoming more and more spurious' as Hewison claims? Is the image we have of the past or are promoting of the past based on reality?

The Director of the Ironbridge Gorge Museum, one of the leading industrial historic precincts in England, was aware of the problem: 'If you are not careful you will wallow in nostalgia, in this sort of myth that the past was wonderful. I personally believe the past was awful' (Hewison 1987: 143). Yet what is being promoted in the heritage industry verges on the wonderful. 'The past is made more vivid than the present. It never rains in a heritage magazine. . . The past is domesticated and, by regulation, made safe; it is rescued, removed, rebuilt, restored and rearranged' (Hewison 1987: 137).

Life in the nineteenth century, certainly the early half of that century, was not pleasant especially if you were a convict or belonged to the lower socio-economic group. The pleasant rural English surroundings of Port Arthur belie the conditions of the convicts and assigned servants. The same can be said for the Coal Mines, another penal station not far from Port Arthur. The soft textured mellowness of the stone ruins set amongst open grasslands with stunning views across Norfolk Bay distract from the horrors of working 30–50 metres underground in the stifling, cramped and filthy mine workings. At this station so-called underground cells lived up to their description. There were four punishment cells situated 70 m from the mine entrance, some 25 m below the surface. Yet how do visitors experience this site? Can visitors get the feeling what it was like to be a convict at this site or at Port Arthur?

In a similar vein the profusion of colonial accommodation outlets throughout Tasmania, whilst offering a welcome change from the standard motel, hotel or pub accommodation, distort the historic experience. Food served hot, hygienic bathing facilities, electric blankets, flushing toilets are all expected as part of modern conveniences, but they have nothing to do with a colonial experience.

The use of the term 'colonial', particularly in Tasmania, also serves to break the continuity of history, denying the contribution of much that went on after that period. This was also true of conservation organizations such as the National Trust (for whom this author worked for two and a half years) who restored their properties to their earliest form thus obliterating their later history. Where the original bits were missing they were made up, their form being borrowed from other unrelated structures. The sites were then presented as what it was like to live (as the owner) in this or that (usually stately) home. Slowly this attitude is changing and interpretation is being directed towards presenting the whole history of a site, not just its earliest or grandest manifestation. Similarly, the creation of 'historic precincts' serves to sever continuity of development. What is old is kept within a defined boundary to allow 'normal' development to proceed outside it, thus furthering the artificial divide between conservation and development. Does a town or area have to have a historic precinct in order to retain the physical fabric of its history or to attract the cultural tourist? And what of those historic places outside which do not form part of the precinct, not to mention completely unsympathetic development which can occur adjacent to the precinct?

One of the rare things about Tasmania and about Hobart in particular is that very continuity of history: scratch a seemingly 1920s facade and you may find an 1820s structure beneath it. (It doesn't mean you have to rip down the facade, you just have to be aware and sensitive to the fact that such places are components of the history of the city or town or district—in fact the history of the country—and are worthy of interpreting and presenting to the tourist and local alike.) The concentration on historic precincts can be to the detriment of the larger landscape. For instance, the Midlands of Tasmania are dotted with hedgerows, windbreaks, clumps of trees marking farming establishments, mostly relating to the nineteenth-century occupation of the region. Yet these landscape features do not easily fall into historic precincts. The farm buildings may be on a heritage register or schedule, but not their context. The presence of these items greatly enhances the experience of visitors—some of the most delightful drives in Tasmania are on the hedgerow backroads through the Midlands—yet I doubt whether any of the landscapes are either promoted or specifically protected in any legislation or planning schedules.

As part of a SWOT analysis (enumerating strengths, weaknesses, opportunities, threats) during a local planning workshop for the Highfield Historic Site, one of the overriding strengths identified by the local Stanley community was that their town was 'real', 'authentic', 'not artificial', 'not like Richmond'. The overwhelming attitude, and this came from tourist operators in the district, was that somehow Richmond had become fake through over-exploitation, while Stanley had retained its character as an old town, not a 'heritage' site. Stanley was established in the 1820s and served as the company town for which Highfield was the headquarters. The majority of the structures in the 'old' part of the town date from the 1830s–1860s and the area is a recognized historic precinct in the local planning scheme. However, it is not just this core area which is important. The surrounding landscape and township also contribute to the experience of the place, an experience under some threat as new residential development creeps further along the approach road.

Highfield sits on a prominent hill two kilometres from the town—the visual link between the two is important historically. The isolation of Highfield amongst grassed paddocks with their box-thorn hedging and macrocarpa windbreaks is also important. Yet while Highfield and the Stanley historic precinct are subject to various planning controls, the surrounding landscape is not, one of the more recent intrusions being the location of the sewage ponds between Highfield and the town.

The concentration on precincts also distorts history: as though the town or settlement was self-sufficient and operated autonomously. Interpretation on our historic sites has reinforced this with site-specific material. One of the interpretation opportunities identified at Highfield has been to develop tourist packages which will link this site with its agricultural outstations. One of these sites—Woolnorth (still owned by the Van Diemens Land Company which set up Highfield and Stanley)—has already a successful tourist programme operated by the property manager. The others are located throughout northwest Tasmania and, although little tangible remains still exist, the development and exploitation of this area of the State can be explained. The remains of a number of the earlier Company tracks also survive and the possibility exists of opening these for day or overnight walks. I doubt if one would experience what it was like to have lived at one of these isolated lonely outposts, but one may build up a picture of the processes of history and more clearly understand the present by reference to the past.

Tourists are looking for different experiences to those which they normally encounter. I would like to think that this does not mean driving between isolated 'heritage' sites to find them filled with souvenir shops, museums, colonial accommodation, devonshire teas, and the local population attired in period (i. e. colonial) costume. I would like to think the experience would be the sense of discovery of history throughout the various towns they visit and the landscapes through which they travel.

I suggest that what is needed is not development of isolated historic precincts complete with the ubiquitous heritage colour schemes. What is needed is initial proper identification of what is out there, protection of individual buildings or site complexes through tax incentive schemes, conservation works based on sound professional advice and principles, and sympathetic contextual development. A rigorous approach to public interpretation and education is required to provide visitors with an informed understanding of history, not just experiences in heritage areas, and the formulation of effective marketing and management strategies is needed to preserve the resource and maximize the returns, both economic and cultural. Then we could create places and environments which are desirable both to live in and to visit.

References

Hewison, R. 1987, *The Heritage Industry*, Methuen, London.

Kerr, J. S. 1991, *The Conservation Plan: A Guide to the Preparation of Conservation Plans for Places of European Cultural Significance*, National Trust, Sydney.

SAVE Britain's Heritage 1983, *Preserve and Prosper: The Wider Economic Benefits of Conserving Historic Buildings*, SAVE Britain's Heritage, London.

17

A Regional Approach to Heritage Management
A Case Study of Otago

G. W. Kearsley

The Otago region lies in the south of the South Island of New Zealand. The area encompasses a great diversity of geographical forms. These range from the high Alps, through the arid block mountains of Central Otago to a richly varied coastal region. It shares in the unique biota of New Zealand with distinctive wildlife and vegetation. It is a district that also bears a substantial cultural heritage, significant within which are instances of Māori rock art, fine assemblages of Victorian architecture, and an extensive range of sites from the goldfields era that began in the 1860s (Kearsley and Fitzharris 1991) (Plates 17.1 and 17.2).

Always well regarded, the region's physical and cultural heritage has come to be even more valued in recent years, both intrinsically and as a major resource for recreation and tourism. Otago has suffered considerably from changing economic fortunes and the consequences of the restructuring that has taken place since the mid-1980s. As a consequence, the region has come to rely on tourism much more than was previously the case. However, as tourism has grown it has brought new pressures, for it is the physical and cultural heritage of the region that has proved to be so attractive to visitors, but resources are scarcely adequate for protection and management (Department of Conservation 1992).

Tourism, though, does not simply offer problems and threats. Rising visitor numbers have created an awareness of, and demand for, heritage values and environments. Thus, both royal albatrosses and yellow-eyed penguins have been accorded a high measure of attention as visitor attractions; both Dunedin and Oamaru have been able to restore and protect significant precincts and buildings, so that the region now offers perhaps the finest examples of Victorian architecture in the Southern hemisphere. Goldfields

Plate 17.1: The University of Otago

Plate 17.2: Lake Wanaka from Treble Cone

sites have been acquired, protected, and restored as part of a developing Otago Goldfields Park, and wild rivers, such as the Kawarau, have been protected, not least because of their value as venues for adventure tourism in the form of white-water rafting.

Taken together, the natural and cultural phenomena of Otago form a heritage that is both locally unique and regionally complementary, setting historical culture alongside magnificent wilderness. Statutory requirements, through the Conservation Act, the Resource Management Act and others, mean that a base of protection and management would be maintained, but, particularly in respect of cultural heritage, recognition of tourism values means that local authorities, private companies and voluntary agencies have combined to offer a higher level of management and development than could possibly have been the case otherwise.

It is the region's natural heritage that primarily acts to attract visitors; the cultural realm adds interest, diversity, and character. Because the geography of the region is so varied, it has been possible to recognize a number of distinctive natural areas in the province, and these form the basis of conservation management regions. Because of their particular nature, the cultural manifestations of heritage tend to vary along a similar pattern.

The Coastal Belt

Otago possesses some 450 kilometres of coastline. With a variety of habitats, it is perhaps not surprising that many types of seabirds should be present, including royal albatross, yellow-eyed penguins, shags, little blue penguins, and spoonbills.

The royal albatross is not a highly endangered species, but Taiaroa Head, at the head of the Otago Peninsula, is the only site in the world where such birds breed on a mainland. The colony is relatively recent—the first egg was laid around 1920. This was taken, either by a predator or collector, and such was the fate of all eggs laid until 1935, in which year a chick was hatched, only to be killed. Fortunately, in 1937, a local ornithologist, Dr L. E. Richdale, took up the virtually full-time task of protecting the birds, with the result that the successful rearing of a chick was accomplished almost the following year. Eventually, the birds came under the protection of the then Wildlife Service through the fencing off of a formal reserve.

Development of the albatross colony as a tourist resource began in 1967 with the formation of the Otago Peninsula Trust, a non-profit organization dedicated to the conservation and management of the scenic and historical heritage of the Peninsula. A first visitor centre and observatory was opened in 1972, and visitor numbers grew rapidly. As a result a much larger centre was opened in 1989, with commercial sponsorship, and visitor numbers have reached over 60,000 in 1990, not least because of extensive promotion, both by the Trust and by Tourism Dunedin, who regard the colony as one of the city's central attractions. Until recently, it was thought that the observatory had no adverse impact upon the birds, but new research is beginning to suggest that they are nesting ever further away from the observatory, and thus moving into less visible and less hospitable environments. If this proves to be correct, then the Department of Conservation, who have complete control of the birds and their environment, will have the difficult task of deciding whether or not to restrict visitor numbers and access. Fortunately, it is possible to view the birds from the sea, and a private boat operator already provides this service as part of a broader wildlife cruise.

The Otago Peninsula is also the principal habitat of yellow-eyed penguins, which nest on remote and inaccessible beaches. They, too, have been recognized as a visitor attraction, and, since 1967, a local farmer has charged for access to a cliff-top viewing site. Further protection has been afforded by the formation of a Yellow Eyed Penguin Trust which, in consort with the Department of Conservation and others, has acquired land, created hides, and set out to re-vegetate nesting areas and eliminate predators. The Trust has used inventive commercial sponsorship to raise substantial sums, one result of which has been the opening of a new reserve in 1992, representing a shared commitment by the Trust, the Department of Conservation, the Dunedin City Council, and local Māori. This effort is greatly assisted by a privately self-funded conservation tourism programme, Wild South Limited, which also recreates habitat and viewing opportunities, using revenue from its tour operation to fund this.

In Oamaru, the rising public awareness of penguins has prompted the acquisition of land to protect the little blue penguin, and the elimination of pollutants that may be affecting the birds, while the presence of spoonbills and other birds at Moeraki has generated the development of a Māori-sponsored sea trip and created a vested commercial interest in their protection.

Geologically, the coast has a number of significant heritage sites, based largely upon volcanic landforms, although the most famous, the Moeraki Boulders, are actually large spherical concretions exposed by sea action. Visitor interest has made possible a profitable restaurant, presently owned by the Ngāi Tahu as part of their strategy of investing in environmental tourism ventures, and the Department of Conservation have begun a programme of forest regeneration and gorse eradication in the surrounding area. Other wetlands and beaches are also of major significance, especially in the extreme south-east of the province, in the Catlins district.

A Regional Approach to Heritage Management

The Catlins is presently the site of a major, if fragmented, Forest Park, the only one of significance in the southern South Island, and the only remaining area of extensive natural lowland forest. Although much is protected as conservation land, considerable areas of forest are still in private hands, and very much at risk from commercial logging for woodchips, or from agricultural clearance. The Royal Forest and Bird Protection Society have been instrumental in protecting some key areas through outright purchase. A very small tourist industry in the area caters to a rising number of foreign and domestic travellers, but this has not been helped by the removal of State Highway status from the principal route through the region, which may well now deteriorate from lack of maintenance. Containing several wholly forested catchments, and a number of coastal features such as caves, blowholes, and untouched beaches, the Catlins has a romantic early history based upon Māori settlement and forestry. Very little has yet been done to interpret any of this, and conservation management is presently concerned with controlling possums, feral pigs, and goats and wandering farm stock. Here, as elsewhere in Otago, the Conservation Estate is highly fragmented, and suffers considerably from such 'edge effects' as inadequate fencing and stock invasion.

A principal need is to aggregate sufficient land to provide for a representative sequence from bush-edged beaches to tussock grassland tops. At present, tourism is seemingly insufficient to justify further facilities and investment, as, for example, in accommodation, or in the restoration of the former Tahakopa railway line as a walking/cycling track, but without these, tourist numbers will not increase quickly, and the benefits to conservation and heritage management that are seen elsewhere in the province may not be realized.

Overall coastal management awaits the publication of the Otago Regional Council's Coastal Plan, which is a requirement of the Resource Management Act, as well as the New Zealand Coastal Policy Statement, both of which are expected in 1992. In a major co-operative enterprise, Dunedin City Council and the Otago Regional Council have joined forces to produce an Otago Harbour Planning Study, due for completion in 1992/3, and it is expected that heritage conservation values will loom large in this.

Finally, the coastal belt is the longest and most densely settled part of Otago. As has been stated, significant Victorian architecture is to be found in both Dunedin and Oamaru but, outside the larger settlements, numerous smaller sites offer historic associations with the early development of agriculture, such as mills, early agricultural estates, engineering works, stone walls and cottages, as well as Māori settlement sites and rock drawings (see Chapter 10). The Historic Places Trust has been of great importance in identifying, classifying and, in some cases, restoring and operating these. The role of district authorities in the restoration and promotion of historic sites and values is described in more detail below.

The Dry Uplands

Inland from the coastal belt, a dry rain-shadow region with a continental climate is based upon a sequence of block mountains and faulted basins. In the uplands, a schist basement has eroded into tors and fretted landscapes that, with numerous periglacial landforms, provide a distinctive natural heritage. It is here, too, that many of the now abandoned sites of Victorian gold-mining are to be found, ranging from small sluicings and rock shelters to the huge tailings left by massive river dredges.

The natural vegetation is tussock grassland, and while much has been modified through burning and overseeding, much remains in a natural state. In general terms, native grasslands are not well represented in the Conservation Estate, and the schist uplands are largely unprotected at the present time. This is seen as a major shortfall in the regional portfolio of protected lands.

Perhaps because it is largely unprotected, the tussock area is diminishing. Pastoral farming, carried out on perpetually renewable Crown leases, allows grazing over extensive areas, although the most vulnerable and erosion-prone districts have been retired, either through agreement or by compulsion. A controversial issue concerns the practice of burning off to encourage new growth, and farmers and conservationists are at loggerheads about this practice, especially when carried out above the snow line. It is in this region, too, that rabbit infestation reached plague proportions in the late 1980s, and, although a Rabbit and Land Management Programme has achieved some success in reducing rabbit numbers to a small percentage of their peak, a consequence has been the adoption of more intensive agriculture or commercial forestry. An explosion of hawkweed (*hieracium*) in some areas, and the advance of wilding conifers in more favourable districts, have further impacted upon tussock environments. Elsewhere, high-altitude cushion fields and wetlands offer distinctive ecosystems and, while less vulnerable to the pressures described above, they are subject to careless recreationist damage through the increasing use of mountain bikes and off-road recreational vehicles.

Pressures for further land protection have come from ecological concerns and local recreationists (Mason 1988) rather than from explicitly tourist interests, although limited cross-country skiing and four-wheel drive safaris are beginning to appear. Consequently, the chosen instrument for preservation comes from the Protected Natural Areas (PNA) programme. Very many potential reserves have been identified, but few have been set up, at least in part because of the lack of resources to carry out PNA surveys and preparation of reports. However, Mark (1991) proposed a conservation park covering some 29,000 hectares between the Mataura and Clutha Rivers. Part of this area has also been recommended as a winter wilderness (Molloy 1983; Hall 1988). When Federated Mountain Clubs set out to identify ten wildernesses throughout New Zealand, they nominated the Garvie Mountains for this status, the only such in the country. In practice, a similar part of the area, the Remarkables, has been proposed by the Department of Conservation as a conservation park, and ministerial approval was sought in 1992. Land for this and other PNA reserves is not always purchased outright. Much is voluntarily surrendered by farmers, and much more is subject to agreed covenant. In at least one case land was surrendered for conservation in return for the right to operate a Nordic skiing operation on Crown Land; this was not without acrimony, but, again, it sets a precedent for commercial recreation and tourism to act as the catalysts for heritage conservation.

The cultural heritage of the area is very much bound up with the goldfield days; much of the best of this heritage is protected by the Department of Conservation in the form of the Otago Goldfields Park. This is a growing collection of over twenty sites, most of them small, and reflecting most forms of mining, abandoned townships, water races and machinery, as well as evidence of the Chinese contribution to goldfields history. The principal aim of the Park is protection and restoration, much of it carried out by volunteers, but interpretation and promotion are growing tasks. To complement this, a non-profit trust has organized a Heritage Trail and an annual event in which a Cobb and Co stagecoach travels from site to site and to the settlements with a goldfields association, to the accompaniment of suitable festivities (Getz 1991).

The Lakes District and The Western Park Areas

Further inland, the Lakes District forms the heart of the South Island's principal tourist axis, focused upon Queenstown (Kearsley 1990). More folded and higher mountains and more plentiful moisture provide a grander environment. There is extensive tourism use of the heritage estate. Three of the major ski-fields are on conservation land, with attendant problems of ski-run remodelling and waste disposal; the wild rivers such as the Kawarau and Shotover are the venue for extensive white-water rafting and jet-boating operations (KRTA and Kearsley 1982; Kearsley 1983, 1993) and extensive guiding operations take place throughout much of the back country.

Closely associated with the Queenstown–Wanaka axis of the Lakes

District is the westernmost part of Otago, comprising Mount Aspiring National Park (355,543 ha) and associated Conservation Forests, which were inherited by the Department of Conservation in 1987, when the former Forest Service was disbanded. Part of the South West New Zealand World Heritage Area, Mount Aspiring National Park continues to grow as further land is added. A region of extensive beech forest, alpine scrub and permanent snow, the Park contains many popular walking tracks, the best known of which is the Routeburn track, although the bulk of Otago's 450 km of track is within this area.

Overcrowding is a critical management problem on the Routeburn track (Harris 1983; Keogh 1991). While the track has an unspecified capacity for walkers on the track itself, numbers are clearly controlled by the number of beds available in the huts, given that there are few camping opportunities. At peak times, huts are grossly overcrowded, up to double their nominal capacity not being unusual. This leads to a competition, a race as it were, to reach the next hut, and the whole experience is degraded. Clearly a far more effective allocative mechanism is required than the present 'first come first served' situation. The huts themselves are a critical instrument of management, not least because they return virtually the entire commercial revenue of the Otago conservancy. In return, the high-use tracks swallow almost all of the maintenance resource. Thus, some form of rationing based upon price seems to be indicated, especially as concessionnaires are able to charge substantial sums for a largely similar experience.

Provision of wilderness experiences is a key component of heritage management in the region, although plans by the Otago Conservation Board (Department of Conservation 1990) to extend wilderness areas in Mount Aspiring appear to have been dropped. Wilderness, however, has both an ecological and a perceptual component, and it is clear that many people find wilderness in areas that display at least some modification (Kearsley 1983, 1990, 1992; Shultis and Kearsley 1988; Kliskey and Kearsley 1991). This may well prove to be the key that protects pristine wilderness from invasion and damage, if it is possible to divert visitors to less vulnerable areas without loss of satisfaction for them.

It is estimated that more than 15,000 people use the region's tracks, and more than 200,000 take day walks or shorter trips. Overall, some 1. 5 million visits of all types were made to Department of Conservation sites in 1991, with growth rates as high as 25 per cent being recorded. Partly in response to this, a Recreational Opportunity Spectrum (ROS) analysis has been carried out for Otago, and a major recreation strategy is to be undertaken in 1993.

Despite resource shortages, an active interpretation programme continues, although it is less than has been the case in the past. Summer holiday programmes are run from Dunedin, Alexandra, Wanaka, and Queenstown, but that in the Catlins has been dropped. Visitor centres are maintained, with the Wanaka centre being shared with the newly formed Wanaka Promotions group, to the considerable advantage of both. While leaflets and on-site interpretation are provided at the Goldfields Park sites, little in the way of interactive interpretation is offered, and the educational possibilities of the Park remain under-exploited.

As visitor numbers grow, and in the light of projected large increases in incoming international tourists, it seems self-evident that the principal conservation agencies are in no position to cope with expected impacts under present resource levels (see Chapter 5). Thus, in the future, it is apparent that management of the natural heritage of Otago requires a greater partnership between private enterprise and the Department of Conservation, and a more entrepreneurial approach from that body, so as to make heritage resources available for the long-term benefit of all stakeholders. Similarly, while the Otago Regional Council has no tourism policy as such, and really has no role to play in promotion (Kearsley and Coughlan 1991), it has a critical task in the statutory regulation of impact and impact mitigation in the broadest sense.

Dunedin and Other Settlements

Dunedin was once the premier city of New Zealand as the wealth generated by the 1861 gold rush poured through the new settlement. The result is a legacy of fine Victorian civic buildings, business premises, and private homes. After the gold rush died and influence moved to Auckland, Wellington and Christchurch, Dunedin grew only very slowly. As a consequence, no great development pressures eradicated the early structures, although, of course, some were inevitably lost, most notably the very fine Stock Exchange, in the 1960s.

After the decades of slow growth, Dunedin began to face real adversity in the 1970s and early 1980s, as national and global recession and restructuring began to take effect. In the city, the population began to fall, the University roll declined, and many long-established manufacturing and processing companies failed, while the head offices of financial companies that had been founded in the gold rush era moved north. In the region, farming faltered and the hoped-for benefits of energy programmes disappeared as a succession of hydro schemes were postponed and lignite processing ventures and alumina smelter plans put on hold (Kearsley and Hearn 1985). However, in 1984 and 1985 the city launched an ambitious civic participation programme, called *Dunedin in the year 2000*. A research-based public discussion programme, *Dunedin 2000* recognized that future social well-being depended very much on new economic directions being taken, and that the Dunedin

City Council was the only agency capable of mounting such an effort (Kearsley and Parry 1986).

The challenge was taken up, and a vigorous Economic Development Unit (EDU) was formed. Armed with a million-dollar electricity profit, the EDU set out to promote the city and to encourage restructuring of the economy. A key element in this was to be tourism, and the vital components of the tourism programme were to revolve around both natural and cultural heritage. For example, the City's 'Its all right here' campaign, based upon careful market research, plays heavily on heritage values.

Three themes were promoted: 'Natural Wonders', 'Architectural Wealth', and 'Tradition Alive'. The natural world of penguins, albatrosses, and geological features has been described, and the city certainly had an abundance of architectural wealth. Some of this was well maintained, with buildings such as the law courts, university clocktower, ANZ bank main office, 'Olveston', 'Larnach's Castle', churches and cathedrals, and the main block of the Otago Boys High School undergoing major restoration. However, other buildings were not so safe, but a strong leadership role has been adopted by the city. In the first instance it has spent several millions of dollars in restoring the municipal chambers and town hall, and in paving the main street and central Octagon to encourage maintenance of main street buildings. Similarly, the city has required sympathetic period reconstruction where significant façades have been lost to fire or decay. More recently, the city has acquired the railway station for a very small sum, but with a large maintenance cost, and with no immediate use, although both a casino and a gallery or museum have been suggested.

Dunedin's renaissance strategy involves more than active tourism based upon heritage. It has successfully brought in major new industries and facilitated the expansion of existing concerns, and it has made significant efforts in educational development, so that heritage tourism is but one part of a wider development strategy.

Similar striking achievements have taken place in Oamaru. Here, an early wealth led to a magnificent commercial area being constructed out of white limestone in the Victorian era. This too had quietly declined but without any pressure for removal. As recession began to bite in this smaller town, it was recognized that tourism through heritage values might provide a new economic dimension here as well. After a 1987 feasibility study, funded by the then Minister of Tourism and various Trusts and sponsors, Oamaru Borough Council moved to set up the Whitestone Civic Trust in 1988, with the backing of the Historic Places Trust. So far the Trust has purchased ten buildings and is progressively restoring them; plans are afoot to create a cobblestoned precinct in the central street of the area. Work is carried out by a paid foreman, work scheme trainees, and volunteers; even so, over a third of a million dollars has been spent on restoration work. Once restored, buildings are leased out to, for example, a furniture manufacturer, and leases return a high proportion of ongoing costs. Tours are an important part of the project, which aims to be wholly commercially viable, and a visitor centre has been opened in the Criterion Hotel. It is expected that the project will last some twenty years, and that a viable and sustainable heritage tourism industry will result.

Conclusions

Otago's rich heritage has become a major source of tourist interest and, hence, revenue. In the main, the natural world has begun to come under great visitor pressure, although this pales into insignificance, except here and there, when agricultural, biological and extractive influences are considered. Nevertheless, considerable progress is being made in the development and maintenance of a comprehensive conservation estate, and there is no doubt but that tourism values have assisted in this. The task, though, is enormous, and even the substantial resources available are nowhere near ideal.

In some cases, easily observable wildlife has become much more protected through the activities of specialized Trusts and other bodies; conservation tourism is also growing, and these efforts complement the work of the Department of Conservation. The early work of the Historic Places Trust has been given an enormous boost by the activities of local bodies, who have come to recognize that cultural and historic heritage has a major tourist value. The restructuring of the region's urban economies towards a greater tourism emphasis has served to galvanize attitudes towards architectural conservation, and it is this field more than anywhere else that the oft-quoted phrase that 'tourism justifies conservation' has been shown to be true.

References

Department of Conservation 1990, *Mount Aspiring National Park Draft Management Plan*, Otago Conservancy, Dunedin.
Department of Conservation 1992, *Otago Conservancy Business Plan 92–93*, Otago Conservancy, Dunedin.
Getz, D. 1991, *Festivals, Special Events, and Tourism*, Van Nostrand Reinhold, New York.
Hall, C. M. 1988, 'Wilderness in New Zealand', *Alternatives: Perspectives on Science, Technology and the Environment*, vol. 15, no. 3, pp. 40–6.
Harris, C. 1983, 'Recreation on the Routeburn Track', Unpublished Honours Dissertation, Department of Geography, University of Otago, Dunedin.

Kearsley, G. W. 1983, 'Accessible Wilderness: Images of Wilderness and Their Implications for National Park Planning', Paper presented at the First International Imagery Conference, Queenstown, New Zealand.

Kearsley, G. W. 1990, 'Tourism development and users' perceptions of wilderness in southern New Zealand', *The Australian Geographer*, vol. 21, no. 2, pp. 127–40.

Kearsley, G. W. 1992, 'Using geographic information systems to order multiple perceptions of the environment as management tools', in *Proceedings of the Fourth Colloqium of the Spatial Information Research Centre*, University of Otago, Dunedin, pp. 155–69.

Kearsley, G. W. (forthcoming), 'Tourism and resource development conflicts on the Kawarau and Shotover Rivers', *GeoJournal*.

Kearsley, G. W. and Coughlan, G. 1991, 'Selling southern landscapes: the role of local bodies in tourism promotion and development', in *Southern Landscapes: Essays in Honour of Bill Brockie and Ray Hargreaves*, eds. Kearsley G. W. and Fitzharris B. B., University of Otago, Dunedin, pp. 275–84.

Kearsley, G. W. and Fitzharris, B. B. 1991, *Southern Landscapes: Essays in Honour of Bill Brockie and Ray Hargreaves*, University of Otago, Dunedin.

Kearsley, G. W. and Hearn, T. J. 1985, *Dunedin in the Year 2000*, Allied Press, Dunedin.

Kearsley, G. W. and Parry, G. 1986, *Dunedin 2000 Final Report*, Council of Social Services, Dunedin.

Keogh, C. 1991, 'Routeburn Track Market Study', unpublished MBA dissertation, Otago University, Dunedin, New Zealand.

Kliskey, A. and Kearsley, G. W. 1991, 'Mapping multiple perceptions of wilderness so as to minimise the impacts of tourism on natural environments: the case of the northwestern South Island of New Zealand', Paper presented at the World Leisure and Recreation Association Congress, Sydney, Australia.

KRTA Planning and Kearsley, G. W. 1982, *Upper Clutha Development Kawarau River Recreation Study*, Ministry of Works and Development, Wellington.

Mark, A. F. 1991, 'Ecological and nature conservation values: the case for a conservation park', in *Southern Landscape: Essays in Honour of Bill Brockie and Ray Hargreaves*, eds. Kearsley G. W. and Fitzharris B. B., University of Otago, Dunedin, pp. 233–74.

Mason, B. 1988, *Outdoor Recreation in Otago: a Conservation Plan*, Federated Mountain Clubs of New Zealand (Inc.), Wellington.

Molloy, L. F. (ed.) 1983, *Wilderness Recreation in New Zealand*, Federated Mountain Clubs of New Zealand (Inc.), Wellington.

Shultis, J. and Kearsley, G. W. 1988, 'Environmental protection in protected areas', in *Proceedings of the Symposium on Environmental Monitoring in New Zealand*, Department of Conservation, Wellington, pp. 166–77.

18

Napier, The Art Deco City

Robert McGregor

Historical Background

Napier is the oldest European settlement in the province of Hawke's Bay, on the East Coast of New Zealand's North Island. Blessed by a beautiful natural setting for their town, Napier's citizens early displayed a considerable degree of civic pride and by 1930 had built a solid commercial centre with some imposing buildings, including a fine brick cathedral designed by Benjamin Mountfort.

On 3 February 1931, a massive earthquake of magnitude 7.9 on the Richter scale and 2.5 minutes duration levelled most of the buildings in the town centre, the exceptions being those constructed of reinforced concrete in the preceding twenty years, although many of these lost facades or parapets. Fires quickly broke out and added to the destruction. Casualties in Napier numbered 162, with 258 in the whole Hawke's Bay area.

The Borough Council was replaced by a benign dictatorship of two commissioners who masterminded the reconstruction of the town, from which all but able-bodied men were evacuated. A moratorium on building in the commercial area was imposed while decisions were made on street widening, the splaying of corners, the undergrounding of services including power and telephone lines, the provision of service lanes and the design of suspended verandahs.

Because ornate embellishments, insecurely attached to the buildings, had caused many deaths and injuries and because there was so little of the past left to revere, the new and reconstructed buildings were almost without exception designed in modern styles—Stripped Classical, Spanish Mission Revival and in particular what is now known as Art Deco but was then called simply 'Modern' or 'Modernistic'.

Between 1934, when the rebuilding was largely complete, and the outbreak of World War II, beautification was carried out along the foreshore, now doubled in width by the earthquake's uplifting of the entire Napier area

Plate 18.1: The new Masonic Hotel in 1934, beyond the Marine Parade Gardens, Napier, New Zealand

by two metres. Upon the earthquake rubble, formal geometric landscaping and architectural features—an illuminated fountain, a sound shell, a skating rink, arches and colonnades—created a front garden to the business area, providing an unusually happy relationship between city and sea. Palm trees and Norfolk Island pines, planted between 1890 and 1920, enhanced the new buildings with their spiky and geometric forms. Napier could then be truly described as the world's most modern city (Plate 18.1).

The uplifting of Napier created over 2000 hectares of dry land which had once been swamp and salt-water lagoon. Because this land became the property of local authorities, it was developed in association with the Borough, and later the City Council to create new planned residential suburbs in which house design tends to reflect the decade in which the area was laid out. Marewa, developed in the late 1930s and late 1940s, is therefore the Art Deco suburb for those tourists interested in building design.

For a small, remote and conservative town to embrace modernism so thoroughly is today one of the aspects of Napier which appeals to overseas visitors, who are often surprised that the Art Deco style reached New Zealand at all. Yet in New Zealand generally, modernism seems to have been more widespread in the 1930s than in most of the United States, the exceptions being Florida, California, the South West and the major cites. Paul Walker (1991) suggests that the Napier earthquake marked the beginning of modernism in New Zealand and its acceptance in the 1930s.

In the early 1980s, a few visitors to Napier pointed out what its residents were too familiar with to recognize—that here was a unique collection of buildings, cohesive in scale, materials, and design, built in the trough of the Depression when the building industry worldwide had all but shut down (Figure 18.1). Barry Marshall, District Architect for the Ministry of Works and Development, persuaded the Ministry to publish the book T*he Art Deco Architecture of Napier* which, in turn, inspired a photographic exhibition at the Hawke's Bay Museum. Peter Wells followed with a film for television. This growing awareness coincided with several demolitions during the 1980s building boom, including two bank buildings which if still in existence today would be among Napier's gems.

The Art Deco Trust

In 1985 a small group of people formed the Art Deco Trust with the object of preserving, enhancing and promoting Napier's Art Deco era buildings. Their aim was to save them for their importance not just as local or national heritage but because they considered them to be of global interest. But they also believed that they were a resource which could benefit the city and the district, and that most local people would only be persuaded to value them if they were seen to be of commercial benefit to the city.

From the start, the Art Deco Trust set out to attract tourists to Napier by emphasizing its Art Deco character. This did not mean just attracting architectural historians, but stressing all those aspects of the 1920s and 1930s which had, by the 1980s, become once again of interest, especially to people in the under 30 age group. With its high-life associations—jazz, cocktails, streamlining, cars, planes, and Hollywood—Art Deco could be the brand name which gave Napier a competitive edge in tourism.

Preservation through tourism is successfully practised in other places, and the Trust has since had contact with American organizations such as the Historic Savannah Foundation, the Historic Charleston Foundation, the San Antonio Conservation Society, and the Miami Design Preservation League. But at the beginning, the Trust did not know of this policy being practised elsewhere.

The Trust encouraged shops, restaurants, and businesses with authentic interiors to retain and improve them, and promoted them in its literature. The Art Deco Walk, which began in 1985 and is the staple activity which the Trust offers tourists, either as a freedom walk with the aid of a leaflet or as a twice-weekly guided walk, leads them past these businesses every day. The Trust also promoted the Art Deco city by sending information to the writers of travel guides, publishing a promotional flyer which it sent to information centres around the country and to New Zealand Travel Offices overseas, and

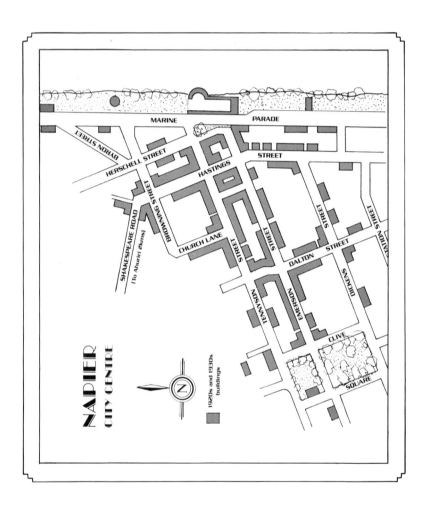

Figure 18.1: Napier City centre showing present extent of 1920s and 1930s buildings

by providing articles for magazines and newspapers or assisting journalists to write them. Contact was made and maintained with Art Deco societies, their number continually increasing, in Canada, Britain, the USA, and Australia.

By 1988, the number of tourists consulting their leaflets and photographing the buildings had become so great that nobody could fail to be aware of them. At this time, a marked change was evident in the attitude of building and business owners, City Councillors and the general public.

That year the Trust staged its first annual Art Deco Weekend which has since grown into a packed programme of house tours, jazz, film and stage events, wining and dining, harbour cruises, Tiger Moth rides, vintage cars, a Deco antique fair, and other entertainments at which 1920s and 1930s dress is encouraged. Although the Weekend can only attract a limited number of tourists to Napier, it creates publicity which reinforces the city's style as a year-round attraction.

The production of promotional merchandise has been important, not only to advertise Art Deco but to generate income. Tee shirts, badges, spoons, pens, postcards, notecards and of course the walk leaflet are produced by the Trust and other items manufactured independently. The book *Art Deco Napier*, first published in 1987, has been a resounding success and is now promoting Napier on bookshelves and coffee tables around the world. The Trust has also acted as a pressure group, mainly working to persuade the Napier City Council that preservation will bring more benefits to the city than redevelopment. Although progress was slow at first, a Council Working Party formed in 1988 recommended innovative policies which have since been adopted.

To maximize public awareness in Napier, the Trust has used every opportunity to provide the news media with publicity material resulting in a high public profile for the Trust and for Art Deco preservation. The fact that Napier's newspaper, the *Daily Telegraph*, owns the city's most exuberantly Art Deco building, which is more often than not being photographed by a tourist, has not been a disadvantage.

As a result of much hard work in all these areas by a small but dedicated committee, Napier is now very conscious of its Art Deco assets. Changes in 1991 in the City Council's tourism policy have brought two new appointments to key Council positions, both fully appreciative of the potential for growth in Art Deco tourism. But tourism is not the only benefit to have resulted from the Trust's work. Now aware of the importance of what were once thought of as very ordinary buildings and assisted by the Art Deco Improvement Grants, building owners have given central Napier a new look—bright, colourful, and immaculate. And Napier has gained confidence and pride as it has realized that it is unique, and a place that well-travelled foreigners describe as 'very special'.

Heritage Management

Napier City Council Initiatives

From the start, Council's attitude has been to encourage preservation rather than to require it, and this is only to be expected given that the 1980 Historic Places Act (superseded by a new Act in 1992) did not provide a legal framework for absolute protection. Even the Conservation Area designation placed on Napier's central business area in 1985 by the New Zealand Historic Places Trust conferred no protection on its buildings. The Resource Management Act 1991 now allows registered protection authorities to place heritage orders on buildings to protect them. However, in the event of a dispute, the Planning Tribunal could be expected to rule in favour of private ownership rights and to require any preservation authority to purchase the building or to compensate the owner. But the City Council has taken a positive approach with a number of initiatives. These are:

- *Art Deco Improvement Grants.* Council contributes $25 per linear metre per floor to building owners who are painting their façades in colour schemes approved by the Art Deco Trust. From 1993, these grants may be given for exterior and interior restoration work.
- *The redevelopment of the main shopping street* as a mixed vehicle/pedestrian precinct with an Art Deco/Mediterranean theme.
- *The publication of a design guide*, aimed at architects, developers and building owners who are modifying existing buildings or building new ones, to assist them in creating harmonious designs.
- *District Scheme changes.* The Historic Places Trust Conservation Area has been confirmed as a Heritage District, within which is an Art Deco Quarter where an absolute height limit of ten metres applies, the range of predominant uses has been broadened, performance standards relaxed and on-site parking requirements removed.

In 1987 the Trust presented a submission to Council proposing that the central business area be identified as a special area by means of signage, street design, and planting, and subsequently applied to the Ministry of Tourism for a Tourism Facilities Development Grant to subsidize the extra cost of special designs necessary to implement this concept when the Council carried out its already planned redevelopment of Emerson Street. A grant of $127,000 was received and this has contributed to the cost of specially designed lamp standards, gratings, street furniture, art-works, and paving, as well as floodlighting and seven information kiosks in the commercial area generally.

Between 1992 and 1994, the Trust would like to work with the City Council in the review of the District Scheme. It is hoped that consideration will be given to restrictions on the design of signage in the Heritage District, the enlarging of the Art Deco Quarter, and the setting up of a revolving fund to acquire, refurbish and then resell buildings which are at risk.

Hastings

Hastings City, only 20 km from Napier and with a similar population, was also damaged in the 1931 earthquake, although not as severely as Napier. Conscious of Napier's new Art Deco identity, the Hastings District Council adopted a consultant's recommendation in 1988 that the Spanish Mission style be used as the theme of the business area. This was an understandable move, although Spanish Mission does not generate the tourism opportunities that Art Deco can, with its international associations and wide network of interest and enthusiasm. It also meets with resistance from architects who are less happy to use Spanish Mission elements in the design of new buildings than they are with Art Deco motifs.

The Art Deco Trust has published a walk guide for Hastings, conducted several guided walks there and includes it in the bus tours it sometimes organizes. In 1992 it assisted a new 'Architectural Heritage Hawke's Bay' group to initiate guided walks in Hastings. This group has been set up by the Hastings District Council which is investigating ways of encouraging building refurbishment, as Napier has with its improvement grants. In addition, *Spanish Mission Hastings*, a companion volume to *Art Deco Napier* was published in 1991.

Factors Affecting Art Deco Preservation in Napier

The Art Deco Trust's success in the relatively short period of seven years has been assisted by a number of factors specific to Napier:
- *The uniqueness of a modern historic city*, constructed during the Depression, enhanced by its landscape and with suburbs which are also of interest to planners and architects. With the exception of Hastings, the only other known city in the Art Deco style is Miami Beach in Florida. There the buildings date from a building boom in the late 1930s and are mostly in the 'Streamline Moderne' variation of the Art Deco style.
- *The quality of the buildings*, which although usually simple and small, are well-crafted and are often decorated lavishly considering the harsh times in which they were built and the hardship experienced by their original owners who were often still paying off the building that they had lost.
- *The timing of this preservation effort*, coinciding with the revival of decoration in design and of the Art Deco style.

- *The isolation of Napier.* Many people are entranced by the discovery of an Art Deco city at the end of the world.
- *The role played by the Hawke's Bay Museum* in supporting the Trust and interpreting the earthquake, the townscape and the Art Deco style in a series of temporary and permanent exhibitions.
- *The fact that Napier's historic area is its commercial heart,* not a stagnating enclave of buildings that time has passed by. Because the buildings house operating businesses, they are not neglected or decayed. In addition, the Trust has a positive relationship with business, exploiting sponsorship opportunities, and is able to deliver tourists into the midst of shops, restaurants and bars.
- *The size of the community.* In a city of 50,000 people, it is possible to change the civic state of mind, something not so easily achieved in a large city.
- *The earthquake story is a tale of fire, death, rebirth and triumph over adversity.* This dramatic backdrop to the architecture makes its interpretation easy.
- *The economic recession of the late 1980s and early 1990s has created a breathing space* in which unsympathetic development has been infrequent, although twelve buildings have been destroyed or altered beyond recognition between 1983 and 1992.

Nevertheless, there have been other factors which have worked against the Trust:

- To many people, at least initially, these buildings were too young to be important, not yet 'heritage'.
- Many of the buildings are not architecturally important taken individually. In any other city they would be demolished without comment. It can be difficult to convince owners that in a concentrated historic area like this one, each building makes an important contribution. This problem is greatest with national operations which see a city like Napier as a place from which to draw profits, and have no interest in what makes it unique, even when that uniqueness is contributing to the economic health of the community.
- Because Napier's historic area is the commercial heart of the city, it is subject to commercial pressures which can be difficult to resist.

The Future

In 1992, the Trust is beginning a new era with the establishment of its own premises and the appointment of an executive officer. This has been made possible by the acceptance of a proposal to the Napier City Council that the Trust sell its tourism services to the city in return for a payment which is expected to diminish each year as the Trust builds up its income-generating activities. This proposal was based on a tourism business plan which defines a contract of services to the city, the emphasis on tourism ensuring that this arrangement is quite apart from any preservation and political activities which may lead to areas of conflict with the City Council. Therefore, in the future, the Trust will assume several roles:

- A tourist operator, with an emphasis on encouraging the provision of attractions and activities which will enhance the visitor experience for Art Deco tourists;
- A consultant, assisting building owners to enhance their premises and businesses to provide services of the type that Art Deco enthusiasts want. Because many of the tourists are knowledgeable about design and social history, it is important that the design and decoration of buildings be historically correct;
- A retailer and producer of Art Deco related merchandise;
- A promotional body for Napier; and
- An information base, offering informed personal contact for Art Deco and architectural enthusiasts.

Should the need arise, the Trust will also tackle developers who intend to further erode the stock of buildings. Indeed, a more aggressive approach in this is planned for the future. However, the Trust will also be working to ensure that visitors to Napier will discover not an exploitative, commercial environment but a Kiwi town where it is possible to savour an unself-conscious way of life in a unique setting.

Reference

Walker, P. 1991, 'Shaky Ground', Paper presented to PAPER Conference, Auckland.

Further Reading

Art Deco Trust 1992, *Tourism Business Plan*, Art Deco Trust, Napier.
Conly, G. 1980, *The Shock of '31*, Reed, Wellington.
Galloway, A. 1992, *Art Deco Napier—A Design Guide*, Napier City Council, Napier.
Ives, H. 1982, *The Art Deco Architecture of Napier*, Ministry of Works and Development, Napier.
McGregor, R. B. 1985, *Take a Walk Through Art Deco Napier*, Art Deco Trust, Napier.
McGregor R. B. 1989, *The Great Quake*, Regional Publications, Napier.
McGregor, R. B. 1991, *Take a Walk Through Historic Hastings*, Art Deco Trust, Napier .
Shaw, P. and Hallett, P. 1987, *Art Deco Napier—Styles of the Thirties*, 2nd ed., Cosmos Publications, Napier.
Shaw, P. and Hallett, P. 1991, *Spanish Mission Hastings—Styles of Five Decades*, Cosmos Publications, Napier.

19

Perspectives on Urban Heritage Tourism in New Zealand

Wellington in the 1990s

Stephen J. Page

Introduction

The tourism industry in New Zealand has seen different trends emerge over the last decade (Page 1989; Page and Piotrowski 1990; Pearce 1992), as new products and tourist experiences have been provided for domestic and international visitors in relation to 'special interest tourism' (Zeppel and Hall 1991; Weiler and Hall 1992), with heritage and cultural tourism featuring prominently in these developments (Young 1989; Mitchell, Hall, and Keelan 1991). This chapter examines heritage tourism in Wellington, where future tourism projects are emphasizing the city's heritage and cultural resources. It is argued that tourism-related projects associated with the waterfront, such as the new National Museum of New Zealand—Te Papa Tongarewa, are using heritage interpretation as a 'value added product' for the tourism industry (Uzzell 1989).

Various reasons have been advanced to explain how tourism has been used to revitalize urban areas, although it is research on urban political economy and leisure theory (Henry and Bramham 1990) which has identified the processes shaping these areas in capitalist society. Such research has emphasized shifts in regimes of capital accumulation from 'Fordism' to 'post-Fordism' (Esser and Hirsch 1989; Mullins 1991) and the consequences for the broad area of leisure and tourism policy. Although it is not possible within this case study to discuss the theoretical framework implied by these developments in leisure theory, it is useful to highlight their significance in relation to Wellington. Henry and Bramham (1990: 8) examined the change from Fordism to post-Fordism (Table 19.1) and argued that local government strategy based on the social democratic structures of Fordism has been replaced by a new ethos and political ideology. Local government policy, especially in leisure provision, has responded to the changing regime of capital accumulation with an emphasis on an economic rationale for tourism and leisure policy in the public sector compared to the former concern with the public good under a Fordist regime. Within this context, it is interesting to acknowledge the role of a development agency such as Lambton Harbour Management Limited (LHML), responsible for the redevelopment of Wellington's waterfront. LHML's role in urban redevelopment involves the attraction of international investment in new service industries and the provision of a cultural infrastructure to attract and retain the 'geographically and socially mobile core workers, such as financial service and information technology personnel' (Henry and Bramham 1990: 11). Such a process is evident from the development plans for Wellington's waterfront in relation to the role of cultural and heritage tourism. Although this case study cannot expand this debate, it does provide an appropriate theoretical framework for understanding the political and economic changes which are shaping the cultural landscape in Wellington in the 1990s.

The chapter commences with an examination of the demand, supply, organization, and management of tourism in Wellington to illustrate how heritage tourism has been identified and developed as a niche market. Reference is also made to the Lambton Harbour Development Project (LHDP) and its plans for heritage tourism on Wellington's waterfront. The National Museum project is then considered in relation to the presentation and development of the nation's material culture and the implications for heritage and cultural tourism are discussed.

Urban Tourism in Wellington: Patterns, Problems, and Prospects for Heritage Tourism in the 1990s

Research on tourism within capital cities is often neglected because of the problem of disaggregating it from other economic activities in large urban areas. Apart from a small number of exceptions, research on tourism in New Zealand has largely overlooked the role of tourism in Wellington (e.g. Wellington Regional Council 1986; New Zealand Tourist and Publicity Department 1989a; Pearce 1990; Wellington Regional Council 1991) in view of the importance attached to Auckland and Christchurch as international gateways (Page 1989) and as centres of demand for domestic tourism (Mayson and Williams 1989). Yet the scale of tourism demand in Wellington in 1990 indicates its significance for the urban economy as the Wellington region received 1.1 million domestic and 253,000 overseas visitors, generating a gross visitor expenditure of $NZ400.3 million in 1990 (Figure 19.1). The reasons for visiting Wellington and its hinterland show

Table 19.1: Illustrations of Fordist and Post-Fordist regimes of accumulation and methods of regulation

	Fordism	Post-Fordism
Local Government	Large-scale bureaucratic corporate policy and management approach to social provision and accountability	Flexible forms of management and policy control: introduction of area management, decentralization: Enterprise Zones, Urban Development Corporations (UDCs) and Compulsory Competitive Tendering bring with them new management approaches and structures.
Orientation of Local Government Professionals	Bureaucratic and (liberal welfare) professionalism	Entrepreneurial and 'industrial' professionalism (e.g. accountancy)
Central–Local Relations	Local determination/influence on local spending and taxation levels; local management and policy for major consumption services, central responsibility for economic planning	(a) *Service provision* Central control of minimalist policy—local concern for locally flexible and appropriate means of implementation (b) *Economic development* Centrally devised policy implemented by local organs of the central state e.g. UDCs and Enterprise Zones (c) *Taxation levels* Largely decided centrally
Leisure Policy Emphasis	Social democratic orientation —leisure opportunities are a right of citizenship —leisure investment may achieve externalities (reduce anti-social behaviour and improve health)	—Provide cultural infrastructure to attract investment from new industries —Generate tourism multiplier effect —Provide infrastructure for new cultural industries (in some authorities) —Provide safety net welfare services in inner city —Minimize costs of achieving externalities
Leisure Policy Rationale	Largely social with some economic benefits	Largely economic with some social benefits

Source: Adapted from Henry and Bramham (1990)

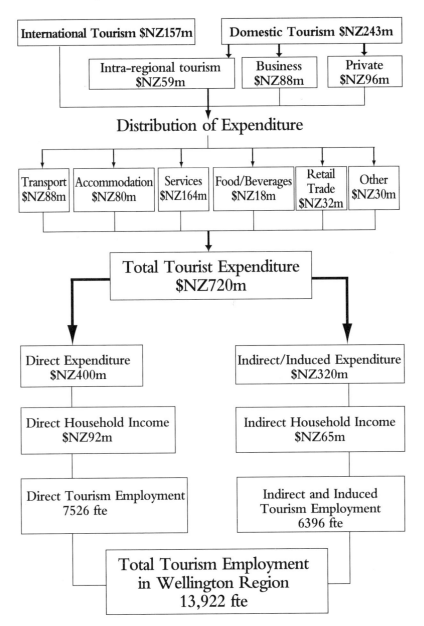

Figure 19.1: The significance of tourism to the Wellington economy

that the region's tourism appeal is related to its position as a hub of both land, air, and inter-island transportation networks which make it popular with transit tourists. As a political and cultural centre, Wellington has also been able to develop particular niches in both domestic and overseas markets. Hallmark events (Kennedy 1989) have also contributed to the domestic tourism market. However, the supply of tourism is based on a 'diverse range of attractions both natural and built. . . .They have only recently been tapped . . . by commercial operators' (Wellington Regional Council 1991).

The Wellington Regional Council is responsible for strategic tourism issues in the Wellington region. This is related to a statutory requirement to be proactively involved in tourism, especially through marketing and publicity (Wellington Regional Council 1986). Wellington City Council (hereafter WCC) and other district authorities have also supported Public Relations Offices to assist visitors and the dissemination of publicity material. But one of the fundamental problems facing the city's tourism industry is the lack of a distinctive product and identity beyond its role as a short-stay destination for business travel. The prospect of unifying the region's available resources through an emphasis on heritage and cultural tourism may offer one possible direction for the city in the promotion of a quality tourism experience for discerning visitors. The assessment of 'strategic alternatives' and the range of possible 'growth scenarios' for tourism did not fully acknowledge the significance of the planned redevelopment of the waterfront and its potential for providing a much-needed focal point for tourist activity in the city. In contrast, the more progressive WCC Public Relations Department (which is responsible for tourism in the city) has established a Heritage Subcommittee and promoted the concept of a heritage week—through the 'Discover Wellington. Our Heritage. Our Place' initiative (Williams 1991). This identified the range of historic buildings (Rainbow 1991), and the city's cultural resources such as the performing arts and heritage-based tourism attractions as part of a long term strategy to encourage the domestic tourism and local leisure markets (Appendix A). Running parallel to this local government marketing initiative is the much larger scale redevelopment of Wellington's waterfront where future heritage-related tourism development is planned.

The Lambton Harbour Development Project and Heritage Tourism

Following the relocation of Wellington's port facilities in the early 1970s and the associated decline of port-related functions on the city's waterfront, 20 ha of redundant land and buildings were created. The pressure for

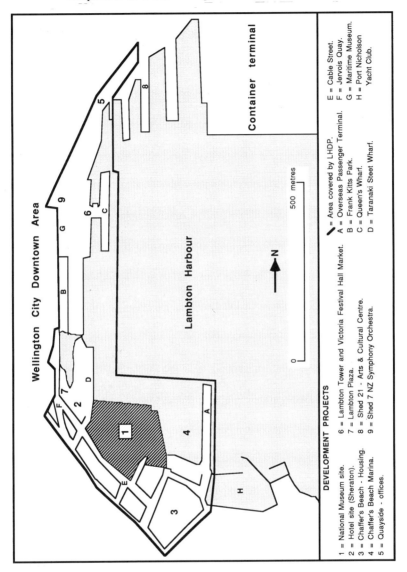

Figure 19.2: Wellington City downtown area

redevelopment largely resulted from the Harbour Board's desire to realize the area's commercial and recreational potential (Lambton Harbour Management Limited 1989). In relation to heritage tourism, the LHDP is interesting since the national government bolstered business confidence in the waterfront redevelopment with its planned NZ$179 million (at 1985 prices) National Museum of New Zealand project, which will form the dominant tourism attraction on the waterfront. The Lambton Harbour 'Concept Plan' to guide the development of the waterfront emphasized the importance of tourism, particularly in relation to the city's heritage, as the LHDP 'includes many places, buildings and artefacts of special interest. . . they are, or will become, part of the heritage of Wellington and the country. Many of the port buildings and industrial relics are of considerable value historically and are tourist attractions' (Gabites Porter and Partners 1987: 5). Future development projects planned for the waterfront area (Figure 19.2) include parks, plazas, squares, tourist facilities, shopping complexes, an international hotel, residential and commercial projects (e.g. offices), and the Museum project which will itself perform an important role in leading the development of heritage tourism on Wellington's waterfront.

The National Museum of New Zealand Project: A Catalyst for Heritage Tourism on Wellington's Waterfront?
The funding, development and planning of the new National Museum and Art Gallery of New Zealand were based on the findings of a project team set up to review the future of the National Museum, given the constraint of space within the existing building, opened in 1936. The Project Development Team report (1985) raises questions on the role of the state in funding museums, the arts, and culture. For example, to what extent should an economic rationale underpin the development of the nation's heritage and culture to promote tourism and leisure spending and consumption?

The Role of the State in Funding the Arts, Culture and Heritage in New Zealand
The establishment of a Ministry of Arts and Culture in New Zealand and the debate over its role (Department of Internal Affairs 1989) provided a timely review of the role of the state in funding the arts and cultural activities at both national and local level. It is interesting to note that the existing National Art Gallery and Museum was the one of the major elements of state expenditure whilst a significant commitment had also been made to the Museum project. The Museum project appears to have a contradictory role in the preservation, interpretation and marketing of the nation's heritage. While the Museum project may act as a vehicle for asserting the nation's cultural heritage and identity (Project Development Team 1985: 7), an ulterior motive is evident

from emphasis on the economic value of cultural heritage:

> [it] is difficult to separate out cultural policy from social and economic policy . . . it is clear that cultural diversity and an innovative society are necessary ingredients for economic development. There is a strong argument for the government's involvement in the arts and cultural area on economic grounds alone (Department of Internal Affairs 1989: iii).

This point was reaffirmed by Paragon Arts (1989) who argued that the arts alone could generate a potential NZ$200 million in foreign exchange revenue, assisting the New Zealand economy to expand. But this exploitation of heritage may not always be compatible with authenticity, integrity, and historical veracity. Thus, the Museum project has to be viewed within the context of domestic and overseas tourist spending through the consumption of heritage and culture (Hughes 1987, 1989). Furthermore, the Museum has to achieve a delicate balance of integrating commercial objectives and achieving a meaningful and authentic representation of the past. But how will the Museum project stimulate interest in heritage tourism and what type of visitor experience is envisaged?

The National Museum and Art Gallery of New Zealand Project: Its Impact and Visitor Experience

The concept guiding the Museum project is that it should seek to bring together the nation's different cultures and traditions, emphasizing the bicultural heritage of the nation in a Museum complex of three display-curatorial elements, with linked buildings to represent the structure, unity and distinctiveness of New Zealand culture in a continuum of exhibits. There are three guiding concepts which will be embraced in the work of the National Museum:

- Papatuanuka: the representation of the earth, sea, flora and fauna of New Zealand;
- Tangata Whenua: those who belong to the land by right of first discovery will be interpreted, including the Māori and Pacific Island population; and
- Tangata Tiriti: the heritage of those who belong to the land by right of the Treaty of Waitangi will be interpreted in terms of the cultural identity of Māori, Pacific Islanders and more recent settlers (Museum of New Zealand 1989).

These guiding concepts will be developed across the Museum in relation to the visitor experience, based on the three proposed components of the Museum; the National Art Museum (the existing National Art Gallery enlarged in scope); a new Museum devoted to Māori and Pacific art; and the National Museum of Human Society and the Natural Environment based on the existing collections of the National Museum. To achieve a focus, each of these new Museums in the complex will draw on elements from the National Collections whilst sharing common professional, technical and storage services based on a special Museum Support Centre. Thus, the underlying rationale was for 'a series of allied museum institutions, each with the resources to present a lively perspective on New Zealand and its place in the Pacific and the wider world' (Project Development Team 1985: 3).

The scale and impact of such a project highlights the potential effect of this development for heritage tourism as a 'focal point for the people of Wellington, as well as visitors and tourists, within which there are special focal spots, the main one of which should be the National Museum' (Project Development Team 1985: 20). Therefore, a powerful and effective Museum complex has 'considerable economic benefits, both in the short and long term' (Project Development Team 1985: 7) since the development site (the trans-Tasman shipping terminal) alone was expected to cost NZ$11.4 million at 1985 prices. This has to be set against a forecast sale price for the existing 1936 museum site and building of NZ$7 million in the late 1990s, although demand for such a property is less than assured given its location and maintenance costs. The Museum Project Development Team (1985) envisaged that this new visitor experience could increase the city's volume of tourism to rival both Auckland and Christchurch, although such estimates are somewhat optimistic since a Museum alone will not attract large audiences. Instead, a series of waterfront attractions are needed which are interactive, entertaining and varied rather than additional museums. Nevertheless, the expectation was that the the Museum could have a direct tourism benefit of NZ$8.3 million in 1992–93 increasing to NZ$23.3 million in 1999–2000, thereby providing a net addition to GDP from tourism expenditure of NZ$5 million in 1992–93 rising to NZ$14 million in 1999–2000. Yet these monetary benefits also have to be set against the educational and cultural benefits to the nation in relation to the museum experience provided.

The significance of interpretation and design of the Museum complex indicates that it can play an important educational role as well as providing culture for the masses (Hooper-Greenhill 1987; Merriman 1991). Recent developments in museum communication (e.g. interactive exhibits, new relationships with the public as audiences rather than passive observers, and the use of discovery galleries) have made the provision and presentation of heritage and material culture to visitors a more lively experience (Pearce 1989). The design of the visitor facilities, exhibitions policy, and marketing are all important elements shaping the appeal and success of such projects. As Uzzell (1989: 6) argued, the 'heritage industry is . . . [also] . . . in the business of mass communication and . . . the boundary between museums and media, and that between reality and fantasy, between myth and mimesis in both sets of institutions and practices is becoming increasingly blurred'. Yet if the National Museum and Art Gallery is truly to 'open windows on the natural world, human society, the evolution of technology and science, and the material culture of mankind as represented by the arts and crafts' (Museum Project Development Team 1985: 13), it will need to find exciting ways of communicating with the public so that cross-cultural interpretation is achieved (Upitis 1989). Both the educational, cultural and tourist function as a broadly based heritage attraction will only be maintained if the diverse range of factors motivating tourist and leisure visits are recognized, so that different beliefs and ideas can be accommodated without too many conflicts of interest. In the Museum complex, interpretive and educational programmes will need to bridge the biculturalism of the project so that different beliefs, values and attitudes are presented with a degree of empathy whilst providing an enriching cultural experience for the visitor.

Conclusion

The relocation and expansion of the National Museum and Art Gallery is one of the largest state-funded projects in New Zealand. In terms of heritage interpretation and management, economic criteria are being used to assess the likely benefits to the population, the economy of Wellington and foreign exchange earnings from tourism. The Wellington Regional Tourism Strategy may have identified the extent of heritage buildings along the waterfront but it has not recognized the need for an innovative and ambitious visitor and attraction-based strategy for the future tourism development of the waterfront. The management and organization of tourism in Wellington has largely been concerned with the bureaucratic dimensions of planning and the duplication of marketing efforts by different public sector agencies in the city. The Museum project alone will need to be carefully promoted to develop the expanding heritage tourism market to its full potential; and the city will need to coordinate both public and private sector investment in the development of additional attractions and heritage resources. Tourism planners will need to consider how they can create a heritage experience using the waterfront as a central component of a product which will be unique within a New Zealand setting. Only a far-sighted and innovative long-term assessment of Wellington's future prospects for heritage tourism and a determination to be a market leader by the mid 1990s will enable the waterfront revitalization and Museum project to fully exploit the potential of the city as a visitor destination in its own right. The National Museum Project is one of the most important examples of interpreting the material culture of New Zealand in the 1990s. It offers great scope for innovative and varied forms of interpretation, but its success will depend on careful marketing and management strategies to ensure a successful museum experience is created.

Acknowledgements

I would like to acknowledge the support provided by Christ Church College, Canterbury towards the research reported in this case study. In addition, I am grateful to Ms S. Williams, Public Relations Office, Wellington, the editorial office of *Architecture New Zealand*, and the Museum of New Zealand Project Office for providing information.

References

Department of Internal Affairs 1989, *A Proposed Ministry of Arts and Culture: Discussion Paper*, Department of Internal Affairs, Wellington.

Esser, J. and Hirsch, J. 1989, 'The crisis of fordism and the dimensions of a postfordist regional and urban structure', *International Journal of Urban and Regional Studies*, vol. 13, pp. 417–37.

Gabites Porter and Partners 1987, *Lambton Harbour Combined Scheme: Scheme Statement, Codes of Ordinances and Planning Maps*, Vol. 2, Gabites Porter and Partners, Wellington.

Henry, I. and Bramham, P. 1990, 'Leisure politics and the local state', unpublished paper, Loughborough University, Department of Leisure, Recreation and Physical Education.

Hooper-Greenhill, E. 1987, *Museum and Gallery Education*, Leicester University Press, Leicester.

Hughes, H. 1987, 'Culture as a tourist resource—a theoretical consideration', *Tourism Management*, vol. 8, no. 3, pp. 205–16.

Hughes, H. 1989, 'Tourism and the arts: a potentially destructive relationship', *Tourism Management*, vol. 10, no. 2, pp. 97–9.

Kennedy, M. 1989, 'Wellington City Motor Race: A Partial Impact Study', Unpublished report, Victoria University of Wellington, Graduate School of Business and Government, Wellington.

Lambton Harbour Management Limited 1989, *Lambton Harbour Development Project*, Lambton Harbour Management Limited, Wellington.

Mayson, R. and Williams, S. 1989, *Them and Us: Visitor Views—A Profile of Wellington*, Wellington Public Relations Office, Wellington.

Merriman, N. 1991, *Beyond the Glass Case*, Leicester University Press, Leicester.

Mitchell, I., Hall, C. M., and Keelan, N. 1991, 'The cultural dimensions of heritage tourism in New Zealand: issues in the development of Maori culture as a tourist resource', in *Ecotourism,* ed. B. Weiler, Bureau of Tourism Research, Canberra.

Mullins, P. 1991, 'Tourism urbanisation', *International Journal of Urban and Regional Research*, vol. 15, pp. 326–43.

Museum of New Zealand 1989, *A Concept for the Museum of New Zealand*, Museum of New Zealand Project Office, Wellington.

New Zealand Tourist and Publicity Department 1989a, *New Zealand International Visitor Survey 1988/89 General Report*, New Zealand Tourist and Publicity Department, Wellington.

New Zealand Tourist and Publicity Department 1989b, *The Economic Review of Tourism in New Zealand*, New Zealand Tourist and Publicity Department, Wellington.

Page, S. 1989, 'New Zealand: Changing patterns of international tourism', *Tourism Management*, vol. 10, no. 4, pp. 337–41.

Page, S. and Piotrowski, S. 1990, 'A critical evaluation of international tourism in New Zealand', *British Review of New Zealand Studies*, vol. 3, pp. 87–108.

Paragon Arts 1989, *New Horizons for the Arts Business: The Foreign Exchange Potential of the Arts in New Zealand*, New Zealand Trade Development Board, Wellington.

Pearce, D. G. 1990, 'Tourism, the regions and restructuring in New Zealand', *Journal of Tourism Studies*, vol. 1, pp. 33–42.

Pearce, D. G. 1992, *Tourist Organisations*, Longman, London.

Pearce, S. 1989, *Museum Studies in Material Culture*, Smithsonian, Leicester.

Project Development Team for the National Museum of New Zealand 1985, *Treasures of the Nation: National Museum of New Zealand—A Plan for Development*, Department of Internal Affairs, Wellington.

Rainbow, S. 1991, 'City's disappearing heritage', *Evening Post*, 25 September, Wellington.

Upitis, A. 1989, 'Interpreting cross-cultural sites', in *Heritage Interpretation, Volume 1: The Natural and Built Environment*, ed. D. Uzzell, Belhaven, London, pp. 153–60.

Uzzell, D. 1989, 'Introduction', in *Heritage Interpretation. Volume 2: The Visitor Experience*, ed. D. Uzzell, Belhaven, London, pp. 1–16.

Weiler, B. and Hall, C. M. (eds.) 1992, *Special Interest Tourism*, Belhaven, London.

Wellington Regional Council 1986, *Greater Wellington Regional Domestic Tourism Marketing Plan*, Wellington Regional Council, Wellington.

Wellington Regional Council 1991, *Wellington Regional Tourism Strategy: Summary Document*, Wellington Regional Council, Wellington.

Williams, S. 1991, 'Discover Wellington—Our Heritage, Our Place—Heritage Week 1991', unpublished report to Economic Development and City Promotion Committee, Wellington City Council, Wellington.

Young, B. 1989, 'Maori tourism—a launch pad', *Tourism Management*, vol. 10, no. 2, pp. 153–6.

Zeppel, H. and Hall, C. M. 1991, 'Selling art and history. Cultural heritage and tourism', *Journal of Tourism Studies*, vol. 2, pp. 29–45.

Appendix A

Wellington's Heritage Week Concept Plan, April 1990 (adapted from Williams 1991)

AIM: To raise awareness of Wellington's unique history or heritage consistent with the Public Relations Office Plan objective 1: that is,

To promote the city as an attractive place for residents and to evoke civic pride among citizens, by organising and supporting special promotions, events and projects that enhance Wellington's image and attractiveness as a city.

The specific goal that relates to this is:

To research and develop the validity of producing an historic week in early 1991.

'Heritage' may be defined as 'that which we have inherited'; therefore, all those aspects of society, culture, landscape, building and environment that have contributed to what we, as Wellingtonians, are today.

TARGET GROUPS:
1. The people of Wellington generally and directly.
2. Domestic visitors.
3. International visitors.

STRATEGY:
1. To hold a special week devoted to looking at our heritage.
2. To generate publicity for the week so that as many people as possible are aware of the event.
3. To organise and coordinate activities relating to Wellington's heritage by involving different sections and groups in the community e.g. museums, libraries, community arts, schools, archives and historical societies.
4. To liaise with organisations running similar events in New Zealand, e.g. Auckland Heritage Trust.
5. To seek cooperation and participation from other council departments which have components compatible with such a theme e.g. Parks and Recreation, the Art Gallery, Libraries and Wellington City transport for special displays, tours and events.
6. To identify activities/events/happenings that will highlight and therefore promote the week—either as an opening, during or closing the week specified.
7. To produce promotional material such as a poster and brochure to provide a unifying element to the week.

20

Hobson Wharf
A New Museum

T. L. Rodney Wilson

This chapter is an account of one of those rare developments, the creation of a new museum, with new attitudes, new services, new collections and, in large measure, a new public. As a project born during the worst New Zealand recession since the 1930s, it has had to be finely honed in terms of the value it provides for dollars spent, in jobs and opportunity created, in civic and community relevance, as well as its significance to New Zealand culture.

Hobson Wharf is a national institution, concerning itself with all aspects of New Zealand's maritime history, excluding only the history of our Navy (and that is the subject of the New Zealand Naval Museum at HMNZS Philomel, across the harbour from the Wharf). Hobson Wharf is located in Auckland, New Zealand's largest port, the historic centre of shipping in the southwest Pacific, and a maritime city extraordinaire. There can be few cultural institutions more closely attuned to the ethos of the city in which they are located than Hobson Wharf. Indeed, despite the fact that New Zealand has largely ignored its maritime history in the past, there are few cultural common denominators which more powerfully link our principal communities. The Māori, the Polynesian cultures, the British and Dutch, who make up the largest ethnic groups in New Zealand, are all great navigator cultures.

Hobson Wharf is the final outcome of a long-held ambition to create a maritime museum in Auckland. In November, 1981, a Trust Board was formed, drawing together interests of various individuals and groups, and in the mid-1980s the Trust Board came close to building a relatively small shipping museum on Princes Wharf in the downtown port area. Overtaken first by larger Port redevelopment plans, and then by the October 1987, share market crash, that project was virtually abandoned by mid-1988.

In early 1989 I joined the maritime museum project with a different concept for the museum which the Trust Board adopted. The new concept required a much larger museum, one which was both active and interactive, with functioning vessels and workshops, national in scope, and much more lively in character. It sought to discharge all the heritage management, scholarship, collection preservation, education, and other functions of the classic museum, but it set out to do this in a more exciting, more engaging, more popular and more recreational way. In short, it sought to turn the cultural and educational experience into recreation without compromising any of the value or quality of those prime and traditional museum functions.

The project could not have been launched in more difficult times and under more difficult circumstances. The economy was in poor condition, local government amalgamation was around the corner, and the new Auckland Port Company had just been formed. Commercial property interests in the waterfront were competitive and unwilling at first to embrace the museum project, and there was great uncertainty about the needs of an America's Cup defence should the court cases surrounding KZ1's defeat in San Diego go New Zealand's way. Furthermore, there was a change of central government looming. New Zealand confidence had taken a battering and few people were inclined to make firm decisions. To some extent Auckland wallowed in self pity and civic uncertainty. The Trust Board and its staff of one (at the beginning) had their supporters, but they certainly had their detractors as well.

It is a measure of the strength of the Hobson Wharf project and its public relevance, that it has fought its way through three-and-a-half years of obstacles to become a reality. As I write, the contractors build, the shipwrights are driving caulking, and the display designers are designing and building a range of innovative environments which will surprise and delight the museum's audience (Plate 20.1).

Content and Interpretation

Hobson Wharf is a museum committed not only to material culture, but oral culture and human skills as well. Oral history will feature in a designated display, as well as being integrated into other exhibits throughout the museum. Oral communication in teaching, and the sharing of knowledge and experience will be employed extensively in Hobson Wharf's programmes. A total of eight workshops, some of them trading commercially, make up a 'trades village' within the site. The skills of the boatbuilder, the sail-maker, the rigger, the blacksmith and engineer, the model-maker, a woodcarver and scrimshander will all be on display; and evening class, weekend, holiday and summer school programmes will permit the Hobson Wharf visitor to learn and acquire these craft and trade skills. From time to time, special projects will also be launched aimed at rediscovering and retaining traditional skills. The first of these is currently under way with the building of the first full-size, fully traditional sailing scow to be built in New Zealand in seventy years.

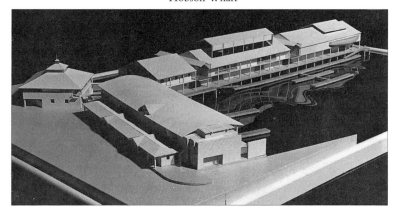

Plate 20.1: A view of the model of Hobson Wharf, Stage 1, Auckland, New Zealand

A fleet of active vessels ranging from a brigantine and the scow to steam vessels, yachts, centreboarders, powerboats, and rowing craft will operate from the museum's marinas. These offer the casual visitor the opportunity to experience a range of traditional sailing and power craft, but they also offer the volunteer crews a potent training vehicle for the programmed acquisition of seamanship skills, and even formal qualifications.

Many of the display galleries invite participation. Innovative sound and audiovisual technologies will be employed and many interactive elements are included, but all of these are designed only to provide context and information in support of the collections being displayed, and to enhance understanding. Strong as the themeing of galleries and the contextualising of objects will be, great care is being exercised to ensure that context does not take over from the experience of the objects.

Before beginning developed design of the exhibits, the design team (comprising Hobson Wharf staff and their consultants) produced a statement which sought to encapsulate the overall interpretation planned for Hobson Wharf, and to define some basic attitudes (Appendix A). The Statement of Philosophy and Heritage Interpretation notes that the Wharf will be the 'first museum to address New Zealand's maritime history in its widest sense' and aims to 'show what is singular about New Zealand's maritime heritage, and to set it within a wider context—looking at the physical geography, maritime traditions and international history which have shaped events here'. In addition, five themes (A Pacific People; Migration Across the Sea; Europe enters the Pacific; Sport and Recreation; and The Maritime Future) are used to integrate the museum's activities.

The Hobson Wharf Site and the Audience's Various Uses of it
Hobson Wharf's public will be diverse and will bring wide-ranging expectations. Whilst the local Auckland audience will comprise a large portion of the Hobson Wharf public, the very nature of the museum and its location at the bottom of the Auckland City CBD (in the centre of a developing recreational sector of the old port) ensures that it will be a major national tourism destination. Indeed, it is conservatively estimated that at 1989–90 levels Hobson Wharf will produce an additional $8,250,000 tourism revenue for the city annually. However, Hobson Wharf will have to meet a range of visitor intentions ranging from participation in a navigation class or sailing school to having lunch in the museum's tropical brasserie-cafe.

Inbound tourist visitors will vary in nationality, ethnicity, social background, and interests. They will range from those who seek a 'thirty minute, highlights only, and dash through the shop' visit to the special interest traveller. Domestic tourists and local visitors will, of course, also come with divergent expectations and needs, but where the inbound tourist is looking to discover something about another culture, the domestic visitor will come to discover his or her own. Therefore, the story Hobson Wharf tells must be capable of being both looked in on from outside, and 'discovered' from within by New Zealanders.

Some Benefits to the Community

Gone are the days when museums, hiding behind the cloak of academic respectability, could assert an unchallengable right to public resources because of their scientific, scholarly and educative value, because of their (all too often undiscriminating) 'treasure house' repository role. Today, the benefits of scholarship and education are required to be quantifiable and publicly accountable. The value of the repository must be demonstrable. The willingness of Government and Local Government to shoulder the financial burden has dramatically diminished.

Whilst we may endlessly debate the politics of public and governmental agencies acting as providers of museum services, Hobson Wharf could not have been achieved had it required public funding for its core services. As a consequence, its structure and its activities reflect the need for it to earn its own way. To the best of my knowledge it will be the only major museum in New Zealand to operate without funding support from the public purse. That is not to say, however, that specific future programmes for Hobson Wharf may not be targeted for funding from the government sector.

One of the major advantages that has emerged for the museum is that it has become a catalyst for the long-awaited redevelopment of the Auckland

City waterfront. As upgrading of this area will inevitably result in turning around the recent decline in harbour-edge property values, the museum has achieved political support and Auckland Regional Council funding commitments, for example, can be seen simply as astute strategic investment.

The museum also creates sustainable employment in an employment market which has contracted severely in recent years. From its own small staff and its licensee operations it creates more than 44 full-time and 27 part-time jobs. But the increased tourism revenue expected will add statistically another 190 full-time equivalent jobs in the Auckland community.

Whilst Hobson Wharf has been greeted warmly and widely for the scale, quality and seriousness with which it will preserve and interpret New Zealand's maritime heritage, its strategic importance in advancing further harbour-edge redevelopment, in creating a sophisticated high-quality tourism destination, in its funding independence from government, and in its creation of jobs, have been major advantages in these 'tough times'.

In the end affordability and demonstrable public advantage are yardsticks against which all state or civic activities must be measured. Museums are no exception and the rigorous justification and moulding of Hobson Wharf to maximize these advantages may be expected to become commonplace in the future. However, it is no accident that these processes have assisted Hobson Wharf to fulfil its prime cultural and educational tasks.

Appendix A

A Statement of Philosophy and Heritage Interpretation

Hobson Wharf will be the first museum to address New Zealand's maritime history in its widest sense, ranging from the Polynesian voyaging canoe to the passenger steamer and the P-Class yacht. In doing so, it will make a bold statement about New Zealanders as a people of diverse origins, but sharing a common heritage and island home.

The Concept

The museum's aim is to show what is singular about New Zealand's maritime heritage, and to set it within a wider context—looking at the physical geography, maritime traditions and international history which have shaped events here. It addresses a broad span of history, from Pacific voyaging more than 2000 years ago through to recent international yacht races. It is national in its scope, revealing Auckland as the principal maritime centre of New Zealand and of the southwest Pacific. It is targeted at the general public, but will have ample depth to interest a specialist audience. Above all, it will be accessible, informative and rewarding.

The core of Hobson Wharf will be a series of themed displays, in which vessels, boats, models and equipment from the museum's collection feature prominently.

Some of these will be presented in a classical museum style, whilst others will be shown within 'walk-in' settings which dramatically evoke the past. A range of small craft and larger vessels berthed in the water-basin beside complement the interior displays, and offer experience on the water. The museum is also reviving and sustaining a range of skills through the construction of waka, boats and ships, and through workshops on site, which will be fully operational and open to the public.

Through its displays, collection and programmes, Hobson Wharf will make a bold cultural statement. It offers a positive, encompassing vision of New Zealand people by drawing attention to their shared maritime heritage. It suggests that New Zealanders can confidently celebrate their diversity by recognising a common tradition: their forbears all crossed the sea to reach here, in migrations made possible by the skill of navigation cultures. It also suggests that New Zealand's island and oceanic environment has helped shape the collective identity of its people, and their keen sense of challenge when looking out on the world.

Hobson Wharf will transcend being a collection of ships, boats, models and artefacts. It will do so by 'taking the raw materials of information and artefacts and weaving them into patterns that are orderly, beautiful and true' (King 'The Theme Park experience' *Futurist*, Nov. 1991). It will present information in inviting and informal ways that are 'classy but not elitist, populist but not tawdry, didactic but not pedantic'. It will provide an 'experience of enduring value'.

A Pacific People

New Zealand is a nation of islands in the world's largest ocean. This setting shapes every aspect of our maritime past and present. The people of New Zealand are islanders, and are inextricably linked to the sea. It shapes their culture and mentality, is a local and global highway, a source of food, and a place of recreation. The New Zealand archipelago is part of a larger oceanic region in which human life has been continually shaped by ocean voyages and coastal seafaring, both in the distant past and in more recent history.

Migration Across the Sea

The islands of New Zealand are, in a symbolic sense, canoes cast adrift from a larger mainland. The archipelago emerged from a supercontinent called Gondwana, some 60 million years ago, and became an ark carrying a unique cargo of flora and fauna. However, like other Pacific islands it was devoid of human life—to reach here would require an ocean journey.

The colonisation of the Pacific was a remarkable event in world history. It took place roughly during the period 1500 BC to 1000 AD and is generally believed to have begun in the island region lying between southeast Asia and the Solomon Islands, spreading from there to Western and Eastern Polynesia. Sailing in fast voyaging canoes, people made landfall using sophisticated, non-instrument techniques of navigation, some of which are still in use today. Generally they explored by sailing against prevailing east winds, which could carry them home as required; some scholars believe that the Polynesians sailed as far east as South America. The discovery and colonisation of New Zealand was a striking demonstration of the skill of Polynesian navigators.

Polynesian oceanic voyaging diminished throughout the Pacific after each of the major island groups had been colonised, and at some point it ceased between home islands and larger, more remote islands, such as New Zealand. Here the Polynesian migrants became selfcontained, developing a sophisticated tribal society. However, oceanic travel—with its themes of origins, voyaging and arrival—remained an important part of their historical consciousness.

The tribes remained closely bound to the sea and to the inland waterways, which served as transport routes and sources of food. Maori developed a variety of canoe designs in response to abundant timber stocks and the marine conditions of the islands; and European visitors of the eighteenth and nineteenth centuries were particularly struck by the size and speed of waka taua (war canoes). Maori seafarers quickly made use of the opportunities presented by the arrival of Europeans. Some made journeys abroad to explore the new world which had intruded into their homeland and to find markets for trade, while others joined European whaling operations. Later, Maori sailors operated a fleet of canoes and ships supplying food to new European settlements.

Europe Enters the Pacific

Europe's maritime nations had begun expanding the edges of their world in the fifteenth century. Developments in shipping and navigation made it possible for them to undertake long sea voyages in search of trade opportunities and scientific knowledge. A variety of European expeditions ventured into the Pacific and some explored New Zealand, the earliest known (to date) being the Dutch in 1642. However, it was the voyages of England's Captain Cook which paved the way for much wider European contact with New Zealand and its people.

Sealers, whalers, and traders were the first to come in the wake of the explorers, as part of a Pacific-wide search for raw materials and cargoes. Along with the missionaries, some of them began rudimentary settlements within the Maori world, and this cultural contact paved the way for a more general migration of European people. Successive waves of immigrants made the long voyage to the 'new land' and for many it was a formative colonial experience. Most came from Britain and Ireland, but other peoples came too, notably the Dutch, Chinese, Dalmatians, and later people from other islands in the Pacific. As with Maori, the voyage and the homeland were to remain prominent in the historical consciousness of the migrants.

Like Maori, Europeans in the last century were closely linked to the sea. Ships, ferries and boats were the main way of transporting people and goods around the country, especially in harbour regions such as Auckland. A local fishing industry emerged, as did a strong boat-building industry, whose craftsmen adapted vessels and designed new ones to suit local conditions.

The maritime culture of Europeans differed from that of Maori people in a fundamental respect, though. European society was recently established and dependent on close links with its trading partners in the Pacific region and especially with Britain, the major market for agricultural exports. International shipping was to be critical in New Zealand's development, and the fact that its main customer was located halfway around the world posed a particular challenge for the developing nation.

New Zealanders looked overseas for cultural inspiration as well as for trade. A sea voyage 'home' to Britain or to Europe was a popular holiday, and the tradition endured into the 1960s, although by then many young people found that leaving New Zealand gave them a strong sense of belonging there. Today, modern communications and fast air transport make the world seem smaller, but New Zealanders remain acutely aware of their position as a small, secluded nation. The oceanic distances that surround us are a reminder of our isolation but they also provide a sense of security, freedom and solidarity.

Sport and Recreation

New Zealand's seas have been a place of recreation as well as of transport and trade. The earliest recorded water sports were races in canoes, whaleboats and trading vessels but pleasure craft were soon introduced. Yachting, which originated in Europe and North America, was established here in the late nineteenth century, and New Zealanders have since made significant contributions to yacht design, construction and racing, both in small and larger craft. Power boating became popular from the turn of the century, and the Hamilton jet propulsion unit stands as a classic example of 'Kiwi' backshed engineering. Generally the twentieth century has seen an explosion of marine sports—canoeing, swimming, scuba diving, surf-lifesaving and surfing, to name a few.

The coast has also been a place for more passive forms of leisure. Beach picnics were enormously popular during the first half of this century, with harbour ferries providing much of the transport, particularly in the Auckland region. The availability of the motor car and new prosperity after World War Two enabled many people to make a regular pilgrimage to the beach and the bach, which became symbols of a particular New Zealand ethic in an increasingly urbanised society.

The Maritime Future

As New Zealand enters the twenty-first century, it still retains close links with the sea. Nearly all its cities are seaports, and many of its lesser towns are on the coast. Passenger travel is by road and air now, but ships remain vital in carrying New Zealand goods to the world and our newer markets amongst Asian nations and the Middle East. Older shipping routes to Britain, the United States, Australia and Pacific nations continue, and New Zealand's fishing industry has become internationalised too.

The changes in shipping and trade are part of a wider reorientation of New Zealand's economy and society in the latter half of this century, and commercial and cultural dependence on Britain has declined while the influence of Pacific Rim countries has strengthened. Amidst an emerging global economy and electronic culture, New Zealanders are reassessing who they are and where they have come from. Maori and other indigenous Pacific peoples have looked to their history and traditions as sources of cultural renewal, while people of European descent have been reshaping their identity too, and increasingly locating it within a Pacific context. Hobson Wharf will no doubt contribute to these processes.

New Zealand's status as an island nation continues to shape the life and character of its people. This is most apparent in Auckland, a Polynesian and European metropolis linking two harbours and two seas. Its container port is a major trading link with the world, while its harbours are the home of a fishing fleet and thousands of recreational craft. And it is in Auckland, and at Hobson Wharf, that the diversity of New Zealand's maritime heritage will be seen. Amidst coastal traders and international ships will be found waka, outrigger canoes, state-of-the-art racing yachts, and a profusion of other boats that New Zealanders simply like to mess about in.

Future Directions
Strategic Heritage Management

21

Strategic Planning for Visitor Heritage Management

Integrating People and Places through Participation

Simon McArthur and C. Michael Hall

Introduction: The Importance of Strategic Planning

Earlier chapters have stressed the need for strategic planning as one of the critical ingredients of heritage management. Strategic planning is one of the mechanisms required to integrate visitor and heritage management. Much of conventional heritage management planning fails to give adequate consideration to the visitor, and particularly ignores the fact that there is no such thing as a typical visitor. The nature of both heritage and the visitor market is dynamic. Consequently, heritage management objectives need to shift from a resource dimension to one which balances visitor and conservation concerns. Therefore, objective setting at all levels of heritage management agencies must take on an additional level of significance. Two recent and comprehensive examples of this approach are the Wet Tropics of Queensland (Chester and Roberts 1992; Wet Tropics Management Authority 1992) and the Australian Alps (Australian Capital Territory, New South Wales, and Victoria) (Mackay and Virtanen 1992), which are used throughout the chapter to illustrate some of the products of strategic planning.

One of the central themes of this book is managing heritage through visitor management. Heritage values are people values. Many of the problems of heritage conservation do not usually lie in the physical resource itself but in the interaction of people and the resource. Problems, like heritage, are based on people's values. For example, fire is regarded by many as a 'threat' to a forest, even though it may be a part of the normal ecological process. Similarly, the demolition of parts of an historic site or the erection of barriers for 'safety reasons' may reduce the heritage value of a site to the point where it also reduces the visitor experience. Heritage is often treated as being static, yet the resource and its associated values are constantly changing. Therefore, we need to develop management strategies which can accommodate change. This chapter will address the formulation of such strategies.

Strategic Heritage Planning

Strategy is a means of achieving a desired end, i.e. the objectives identified for the management of heritage (Chaffee 1985). As far as heritage managers should be concerned, the 'strategy' is the use of appropriate visitor management and interpretive practices in order to achieve two basic strategic objectives: ensuring the conservation of heritage values and enhancing the experiences of the visitors who interact with it. Strategic analysis combines three different types of analysis (Richardson and Richardson 1989):

- Environmental analysis which assists planners and managers to anticipate short- and long-term changes in the operational environment.
- Resource analysis which helps the heritage manager to understand the significance of the site's physical and human resource base to successful ongoing environmental adaptation.
- Aspirations analysis which identifies the aspirations and interests of the major stakeholders in the heritage site and assists management to formulate their own strategic objectives in light of the desires and interests of others.

As Richardson and Richardson (1989: 58) observed: 'If performed effectively, strategic analysis can generate tremendous insight (particularly for first time users) into the factors which underpin present success/failure levels and into the organizational changes which make greatest sense in the context of the anticipated future'. Indeed, strategic analysis is part of the process by which heritage management agencies and site management can be turned into 'learning organisations' that can constantly adapt to the demands of their stakeholders (Garratt 1987; Tweed and Hall 1991). Therefore, measures which heritage managers can take to evaluate the strategic basis for heritage management might include (Richardson and Richardson 1989):

- An aspirations analysis to determine who the important stakeholders are/will be and to ascertain their power positions, aspirations and propensities for or against alternative potential developments;
- An environmental analysis for the insight this might stimulate on questions of organizational restructuring as well as potential product/market competitive developments;
- Pertinent market segmentation exercises;
- Analysis of the present and potential competitive market structure in order to identify the inherent attractiveness of the markets, and the openings

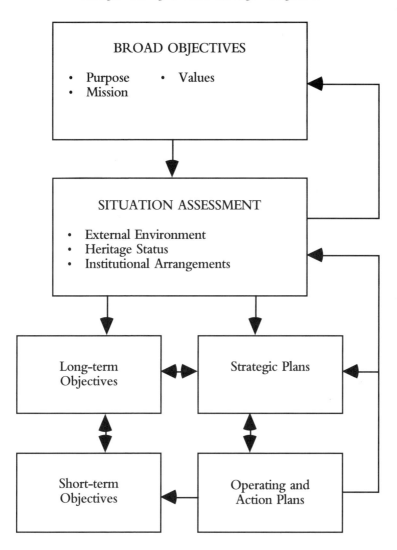

Figure 21.1: A broad strategic framework for heritage management

Heritage Management

which might exist for managers to exploit;
- Analysis of the wider and more futuristic environment in order to anticipate futures which the event might seek to exploit, change or avoid as necessary;
- Rank opportunities and threats in order of their perceived significance; and
- Conduct a resource analysis including an audit.

Following this strategic analysis and evaluation, management can then proceed to generating the strategic developments that will make heritage management a success.

Chapter 2 outlined a strategic approach to visitor management through interpretation. Figure 21.1 provides a broader strategic framework for heritage management. The model outlines a number of stages in the strategic planning process. As noted in Chapter 2, objective setting is a critical component in heritage management because it determines what we are attempting to achieve. Therefore, heritage managers need to note the broad mission of their agency or organization, its purpose and the set of values it reflects. The values and ambitions of a heritage management agency can be set in a vision statement which provides the direction necessary to guide organizational and project goals, objectives, policies, strategies, implementation, and evaluation. An agency's vision is often communicated both internally within the organization and externally to its clients and the broader community within a mission statement. For example, after taking into account information gained from a community consultation process in the case of the development of a Wet Tropics World Heritage area management plan, the Wet Tropics Management Authority developed a vision statement:

> The management of the Wet Tropics of Queensland World Heritage Area will be an example and inspiration to Australians and other nations. Maintaining and restoring the World Heritage values of the Area will be paramount. The management will reflect a sense of community ownership and serve a function in, and contribute to, the community. People will be encouraged to use and enjoy the Area and appreciate its World Heritage values, but in ways that do not jeopardize those values. The values will be presented in ways that help develop better appreciation, understanding and community support for ongoing protection of the Area's unique qualities. The Authority will seek to establish harmonious relations with land holders and management agencies within, and neighbours adjacent to, the World Heritage Area, to ensure management will protect World Heritage values. The impact of essential infrastructure and facilities will be minimized. The Authority will undertake to increase appreciation, awareness and understanding of the Area's cultural values and will encourage participation by the community, in particular Aboriginal people, in the management of the Area. Degraded areas will be rehabilitated

and threatening influences such as pollutants, weeds, feral animals and diseases will be controlled. Scientific research will be encouraged to increase the knowledge and understanding of the World Heritage Area and facilitate better management. The values of the Area must be preserved for future generation to treasure and enjoy (Wet Tropics Management Authority 1992: 7).

Situation assessments are conducted to identify information and issues relating to the external and internal environments, heritage status, and the institutional arrangements by which heritage is managed. For example, in the case of the preparation of the Wet Tropics management plan, in addition to an extensive community consultation process, the Authority conducted a number of specific consultancy studies to rapidly acquire specific information for the development of detailed strategies (Chester and Roberts 1992: 180). Situation assessments included those focusing on:

- Community attitudes;
- Tourism;
- Aboriginal cultural tourism;
- Recreation;
- Current levels and patterns of visitor use;
- Scenic resources;
- Building siting and design;
- Town planning;
- Transport and services; and
- Economic contribution of tourism to the Daintree/Cape Tribulation area.

After conducting the situation assessment, managers need to determine goals, long- and short-term objectives, strategic plans, and their implementation through operating and action plans. The majority of management plans and programmes prepared by heritage management agencies in Australia and New Zealand only set generalized long-term goals rather than obtainable, measurable objectives with a predetermined time frame. By setting measurable objectives it is possible to indicate the effectiveness of any management programme.

Goals are statements of intent outcome expressed in broad terms. For example, the primary goal established by the Wet Tropics Management Authority is 'To provide for the implementation of Australia's international duty for the *protection, conservation, presentation, rehabilitation and transmission to future generations* of the Wet Tropics of Queensland World Heritage Area, within the meaning of the World Heritage Convention' (Chester and Roberts 1992: 178). In contrast, objectives are the ends towards which agencies or programmes are directed. They are the statements of conditions that an organization or programme seeks to attain, expressed in such a manner that progress towards or divergence away from them can be measured

(Lipscombe 1992). Therefore, both long- and short-term objectives should:
- be specific;
- be able to be evaluated;
- be attainable;
- have specific time limits;
- have language able to be clearly understood by those responsible for its achievement;
- produce results which can be clearly and concisely communicated; and
- where appropriate, be integrated with the objectives of organizations which share a common interest with a heritage area and/or a visitor market.

Even some of the most innovative strategies for heritage management have failed to distinguish clearly enough between the various levels of strategic planning and goal and objective setting. An example of the setting of objectives which are not clearly measurable is provided in the Memorandum of Understanding (MOU) between the Commonwealth of Australia, Australian Capital Territory, New South Wales and Victoria for the management and conservation of the Australian Alps. The MOU established formal mechanisms and processes for cross-border collaborative nature conservation, environmental and recreation management programmes for a number of protected areas. According to Mackay and Virtanen (1992: 159) the 'key objectives' for the management of the Australian Alps were:
- Protection of the landscape;
- Protection of plants, animals and cultural values;
- Provision of recreational opportunities to encourage the enjoyment and understanding of the alpine environment; and
- Protection of mountain catchments.

However, these are not objectives but goals. Examples of clear objectives would be:
- To eliminate all recreational activity in alpine areas within Tongariro National Park by the end of the current financial year.
- To survey and assess the distribution and status of buttongrass (*Gymnoschoenus sphaerocephalus*) within Cradle Mountain National Park before the end of the current financial year.
- To survey and assess the level of Tasmanian Aboriginal support for the continued burning of peatlands within Southwest National Park, within eighteen months of the release of this park management plan.

(Please note, the above are fictitious!).

Strategic plans must contain a statement of action, which conveys how each objective will be achieved. Actions are far more specific than objectives. Actions provide a direct guideline to *how* we will implement the objective.

As in the case of the setting of objectives, considerable problems emerge in concept definition. In the case of the draft Wet Tropics management plan, some of the actions were ill-defined and are probably closer to being an objective. For example, in the case of the conservation of vegetation communities, the action was defined as to 'determine the level and types of disturbance of these rare rainforest communities and assess during 1992/1993 their need for conservation and/or rehabilitation' (Wet Tropics Management Authority 1992: 63). In contrast, an example of an action would be 'to allocate three staff members to measure the density of seedlings for known disturbed and undisturbed rare rainforest communities' *(fictitious example)*.

Why are statements of action usually left out of management plans? One reason may be fear of being tied to an action regardless of changing circumstances in the internal and/or external environment, e.g. a new minister. Nevertheless, if the strategic planning process is appropriately formulated, the feedback mechanism will enable heritage managers to adapt and respond accordingly. A more cynical observation would be that some heritage managers are scared of setting performance standards which can be assessed by all stakeholders throughout the planning process. However, heritage managers must realize that it is those very same performance standards and clear definitions of output that will make the management process both more effective and efficient and provide extra weight in the search for funding. It is the successful meeting of performance standards which will provide support for the goals of heritage management.

Evaluation is the assessment of performance standards. Unfortunately, evaluation is typically ignored in heritage management, perhaps partly because it is a form of judgement at both a collective and individual level. Nevertheless, it is crucial that heritage managers determine whether or not a programme was a success in the light of the initial objectives. Indeed, it may well be the case that some goals and objectives were met while others remained unfulfilled. The success or otherwise of heritage management will only remain hearsay and conjecture unless a formal evaluation occurs. Furthermore, evaluation is a continuation of the control function of management and helps develop management processes and procedures for future programmes. Evaluation is therefore a valuable means to learn from the mistakes and the successes which have been realized throughout the management process, while also providing important information to use in further lobbying for government or private industry support in future years. Ongoing evaluation also allows the development of a body of knowledge and information as to the effectiveness that a programme may have in meeting its objectives. Something that was successful five to ten years ago may not be appropriate now and therefore it becomes necessary for heritage managers to adapt to the new management environment. A number of methods are available for evaluating the success of a heritage management programme, e.g. cost-benefit analysis, goals achievement matrix, environmental and social impact assessment, limits of acceptable change, and internal and external structured focus groups (see Chapter 22). However, the selection of an evaluation technique must be based to measure the performance of the action against the specific objective.

While some readers may regard a distinction between goals, objectives, and actions and evaluation as pedantic, it must be emphasized that the success of any strategic planning exercise (and hence heritage management) is dependent upon a clear understanding of terms and issues. Moreover, as the following section indicates, there are a number of other advantages in adopting a strategic approach to heritage management.

Advantages of Strategic Planning for Heritage Management

Table 21.1 outlines a number of advantages which strategic planning offers to the heritage manager. First, it provides a sense of purpose and the foundation of criteria for the formulation of new projects. Second, it stresses the need for both short- and long-term objectives which can accommodate changing circumstances, e.g. a change of government. Third, it gives stakeholders a clear indication of the current and long-term level of support required for heritage management programmes. Fourth, it provides for potential integration of stakeholder objectives into an organizational or programme strategy, thereby increasing the likelihood of success. Fifth, it encourages strategic thinking and an increased receptiveness to opportunities in the external environment. Sixth, the strategic planning process can give staff a sense of ownership and involvement in an organization's goals and objectives with a consequent likely increase in morale and performance. Finally, effective strategic planning can make organizations more effective and efficient in attaining programme and/or organizational goals.

The 'Total Approach' to Strategic Planning

This book has consistently advocated a broadening of heritage management concerns to integrate the visitor within the management process. The strategic planning approach advocated in this and other chapters allows agencies to accommodate changing heritage values and visitor characteristics, thereby avoiding unnecessary strain on existing management practices. The development and success of 'Total Catchment Management' (TCM) in a number of land uses, such as agricultural and forestry, came from the integration of the needs of all stakeholders. We now need to adopt the same

Table 21.1: The advantages of a strategic approach to heritage management

Strategic planning perspective provides	Setting requires	Example
Strategic thinking at the upper management level and in specialist functions, e.g. interpretation, facility management, and archaeology	Staff at all levels to be involved in the strategic heritage planning process plus the involvement of community groups and site visitors	Awareness of strategic information and its communication to relevant managers, e.g. an interpretation officer who receives negative feedback regarding the relevance of heritage information signs
The significance of visitor and owner objectives	Attention to the range of interests involved in heritage management	Providing experiences for a range of visitor preferences and abilities, e.g. provision of child-orientated activities and facilities for the disabled
		Incorporating the perspectives of special interest groups in the heritage planning process, e.g. historical societies and conservation and outdoor recreation groups
Precise objectives which offer clear direction for future actions	The delineation of long-term objectives which allow for flexibility in achievement of an agency's mission statement	The interpretation of the cultural heritage components of a national park and reserve system
	The identification of short-term objectives which establish immediate goals for the agency to accomplish	The completion of a specific interpretation project within a set time frame
New major projects	Experimentation and modifications of existing plans	Use of project proposals
	Anticipation of the changing circumstances within which heritage management occurs	Review of the effectiveness of relevant previous and currently operating projects
		Identification and evaluation of the expectations, motivations, and values of new and potential user groups
Mid- to long-term commitment of resources	The integration of a succession of short-term projects in a comprehensive heritage management strategy	The undertaking of a number of interpretive projects at selected sites within a co-ordinated regional framework

philosophy and process into heritage management. In TCM the outcome is improved land values; in strategic heritage management the outcome is improved visitor experiences and conservation of heritage values. The overall structure and process advocated in this chapter applies the same principles as the visitor management/interpretation flow diagram in Chapter 2.

Effective heritage visitor management requires the development of and adherence to long-term strategies. Managers and agencies must strive to provide quality visitor experiences that are individual, enjoyable, educational and sympathetic to the environment. Finally, we must begin to manage our heritage and associated interpretive facilities together at a strategic level, and that means better strategies, planning, management, and evaluation.

References

Chaffee, E. E. 1985, 'Three models of strategy', *Academy of Management Review*, Vol.10, No.1: 89–96.

Chester, G. and Roberts, G. 1992, 'The Wet Tropics of Queensland World Heritage Area: the planning challenge', in *Heritage Management: Parks, Heritage and Tourism, Conference Proceedings*, Royal Australian Institute of Parks and Recreation, Hobart, pp. 177–84.

Garratt, B. 1987, *The Learning Organisation*, Fontana, London.

Lipscombe, N. 1992, 'Communication or confusion: the terminology of planners', *Australian Parks and Recreation*, vol. 28, no. 3, pp. 29–35.

Mackay, J. and Virtanen, S. 1992, 'Tourism and the Australian Alps', in *Heritage Management: Parks, Heritage and Tourism, Conference Proceedings*, Royal Australian Institute of Parks and Recreation, Hobart, pp. 159–65.

Tweed, D. M. and Hall, C. M. 1991, 'The management of quality in the service sector: an end in itself or a means to an end?', in *Australian and New Zealand Association of Management Educators Conference Proceedings*, Bond University, Queensland.

Richardson, B. and Richardson, R. 1989, *Business Planning: An Approach to Strategic Management*, Pitman, London.

Wet Tropics Management Authority 1992, *Wet Tropics Plan: Strategic Directions*, Wet Tropics Management Authority, Cairns.

22

Evaluation of Visitor Management Services

Simon McArthur and C. Michael Hall

Introduction

Previous chapters have stressed the role of feedback in improving planning and delivery of services and have indicated the need for evaluation as a vital tool for any visitor management programme. A number of evaluation projects have been conducted in both Australia and New Zealand but their level of success has been largely dependent upon individual skills and the level of management support (Beckmann 1988). This chapter will attempt to assist readers in improving both skills and support levels. The principles of visitor service evaluation are briefly addressed before dealing with the selection of evaluation techniques. The emphasis will be on using the most appropriate balance of tactical and applied research to offer short- and long-term solutions. The chapter features an analysis of interpretive programme evaluation and, in particular, the ability to attract and hold attention spans; to transmit knowledge versus understanding; and finally, to change behaviour. The chapter will conclude with the challenge of marketing evaluation programmes to management.

The Role of Evaluation Within Visitor Management

There are few people involved in the various aspects of visitor management who deny the value of evaluation or do not recognize the need for more (Chanowitz and Langer 1980; Zube 1981; Krumpe and Brown 1982; Roggenbuck and Berrier 1982; Pearce and Moscardo 1985; Beckmann 1988; Bitgood 1989; Manfredo and Bright 1991). Chapter 2 outlined the way that promotion of heritage sites with high conservation significance has tended to increase and modify visitor numbers and profile. The effective management of heritage sites requires influencing visitor values and behaviour. Visitor expectations have increased (McArthur and Gardner 1992). The gradual realization that heritage is inherently owned by the community rather than its day-to-day managers has intensified these expectations (see Chapter 1). Compounding this situation are limited funds, staff and time. There is less room for managers to make mistakes, and fewer opportunities to call them learning opportunities. Therefore, evaluation is critical as a means of obtaining performance feedback, as justification to continue or modify existing programmes, and as a basis for the implementation of new ones.

A recent example of the sort of vital feedback gained through visitor evaluation was outlined by McArthur and Gardner (1992). The research indicated that visitors to most Tasmanian State Forest failed to recognize that it had been previously logged, believing they had in fact passed through a national park (Plate 22.1). The consequence of this for the Forestry Commission had been a failure to demonstrate that forestry was in fact being managed in sustainable manner, which tended to restrict the level of community support for forestry in general. The information provided the basis to refocus the planning and provision of interpretation.

Principles for Evaluation of Visitor Management Service

Visitor evaluation is 'as an amalgam of two components . . . a study and analysis of the demographic and psychological profiles of those people who come to a particular tourist site or environment [and] the visitor's appraisal of a given site, environment or display' (Pearce and Moscardo 1985: 282). Visitor evaluation is not an examination of visitor impact, which refers to the physical and social effects that result from the inflow of visitors to a specific site.

Research and monitoring are essential components of evaluation. Research is typically undertaken within the heritage management process as an important element of the planning/policy development process. Monitoring is typically used as a technique for assessing long-term trends affecting the resource, the visitor experience, or the profile of visitor, or as a method of assessing particular issues of management concern, such as visitor impact (Wet Tropics Management Authority 1992). However, most evaluation of visitor management programmes is unfortunately conducted within comparatively short periods which may make the results unrepresentative. Nevertheless, by following a number of principles for the evaluation of a visitor management service (Table 22.1), the standard of evaluations may be improved.

Evaluation of Visitor Management Services

What's all the fuss about these Southern Forests? ... they haven't even been logged yet!

Plate 22.1: Most visitors to the Tasmanian State Forest fail to recognize that it has been previously logged

Table 22.1: Principles for the evaluation of a visitor evaluation service

Principles	Explanation
• Set measurable objectives	Clear, precise objectives for the service itself. If a visitor management service has clearly defined objectives, then much of any evaluation programme is merely about confirming that these are being met. Too often the evaluation programme must await management to define the original purpose for a service already in operation.
• Define the problem	What actually needs to be evaluated. Rigidly stick to issues which management are likely to accommodate.
• Set up a hypothesis	Attempt to predict the result.
• Pre-determine final product	Consider how you would like to enter and interpret results and what you wish to do with them afterwards. Many projects allow a great deal of information to be wasted because in reality it was never needed or could not be adopted to assist with management decisions. Given the dynamic nature of both resource and visitor, results which stagnate quickly lose their relevance and utility.
• Select techniques	Clearly define techniques considering available time and resources (further comments on techniques below).
• Run a pilot programme	Test techniques to ensure they are appropriate (for visitors, usually 5–10% of intended sample size).
• Run controlled programme	Stick to a regular method (review if method changes—it will influence the results).
• Analyse results	Browse to detect trends. Identify likely success of programme (any data-handling problems). Enter and summarize data. Re-determine trends versus hypothesis. Manipulate data.
• Present data	Produce in a format that reflects the needs of the audience (different sized reports, verbal presentations, posters, and various media).
• Consider implications	Reliability and scope of results.
• Consider alterations	What can be done to improve the situation.
• Review methods	Determine worthiness of evaluation programme and comment on future improvements.

Techniques for Evaluation of a Visitor Management Service

No matter which technique is selected to evaluate a visitor management service, a balance between applied and tactical research should be attempted (assuming that pure research is a luxury that few managers can afford). Applied research has an outcome in mind and applies techniques to a commercial or institutional application—the Tasmanian Forestry Commission example above is largely of this nature. Tactical research is focused to achieve a specific solution without considering other areas, such as the monitoring of visitor numbers at a particular site. Ideally, a sound evaluation program will use a blend of the two.

There are considerable demands made by management for quick fix answers, yet these can often do more damage than good. Visitor surveys by the Tasmanian Forestry Commission during the summers of 1990/91 and 1991/92 reported conflicting visitor demands for facilities (McArthur and Gardner 1992). While the first year suggested widespread demand for more facilities, more detailed questions in the second year discovered that it was an issue of quality, not quantity (saving the Commission many thousands of dollars). Therefore, in almost any evaluation program, there is a vital need to gain understanding through experimentation and long-term monitoring.

The evaluation technique(s) adopted depend primarily on the type of information required, but available resources also play a major part. The following sections will discuss evaluation techniques for three main areas of visitor service evaluation: visitor numbers, visitor profile, and interpretation programmes.

Visitor Numbers

The most frequent form of evaluation of visitor management service comes in the form of monitoring usage. Visitor numbers are undoubtedly the easiest to collect since they require minimal staff time. However, they are also the easiest to accept on face value and frequently offer little information from which to make critical decisions.

While visitor numbers are obviously a key factor in attempting to determine carrying capacity, with just two more components, entry time and duration of stay, managers can begin to look at ways of modifying use. Barrow (1991) used these two factors to create the 'Design Day approach', a technique which 'represents the days in the year when the site will be at full capacity at some point in the day'. Such techniques can assist with both the lowering and raising of visitation levels. However, quantitative analysis and techniques such as the Design Day approach do not immediately resolve issues of ecological and social carrying capacity. To collect meaningful information about visitors and their behaviour requires more extensive research in qualitative techniques. Table 22.2 indicates some of the most regularly used techniques for determining visitor numbers and profiles. While extrapolation from other sources is the quick and cheap way of gaining base-grade information, it requires sound networks with other colleagues. A certain degree of goodwill must be reciprocated upon demand for this technique to be successful in the long term.

Visitor Profile
Traditional demographic profiles such as age, sex, residence, and income have decreasing utility for visitor management. Key psychographic profiles now required for visitor management include motivations, expectations, experience and perceptions of key issues. For example, profiles created as a result of market research, such as 'indulgers', 'pioneers' and 'anti-tourists' (Department of Tourism, Sport and Recreation 1990), have significant implications for visitor management practice.

There are three main techniques used to detect visitor profile: observations, surveys, and interviews. Observations can be quick, cheap and good for indicating trends or providing hints on how to conduct a survey or interview. Observations may include:
- Group size;
- Form of transportation;
- Type/amount of equipment;
- Clothing;
- Overall and specific uses of time (activities and settings);
- Maps of where they go and what they do (flow diagrams); and
- Behaviour (including language, noise level, attentiveness, and organization).

Surveys are the most often used because their cost is between that of observations and interviews. They can be produced in written and verbal formats and range from a small group of 60 visitors to a sample of thousands from the general community (polling).

Interviews tend to be slower, labour-intensive, and require well-trained staff. However, they are ideal to get a more in-depth study following a trend-indicating survey. Extended interviews using a selected number of individuals delve deeper yet and are known as focus group discussions. These require extensive knowledge to be run properly and are usually the time when professional expertise is sought out. Those considering the use of a survey or interview should:
- Be sure of precisely what needs to be known and why it needs to be known;

Table 22.2: Techniques for determining visitor numbers and profiles

Techniques	Forms
Determining quantity of visitors	
Counters	• Counters for vehicles, turnstiles, doorways and tracks (compressed air tubes, pressure pads, spring-loaded switches, and infra-red beams) • Observations of numbers and/or group size
Administrative	• Bookings • Visitor books • Receipts and income • Number of enquiries and amount of information (publications) distributed
Impact assessment	• Noting vehicle tracks, trampling, amount of waste, resource consumption (e.g. wood and water)
Determining profile of visitors	
Observation	• Visitor flow diagrams • Type and order of visitor experiences • Timing experience • Recording use of facilities (individual or photographic e.g. video and audio—time-lapse or motion/sound triggered) • Recording behavioural characteristics (as above)
Computers	• Programmes that record visitor choices made on interactive devices
Surveys/interviews	• Written, oral, and behavioural
Focus groups	• Selected small groups in lengthy discussions
Polling	• Phone, post, and personal
Visitor numbers and profile	
Extrapolation from other sources	• Numbers at neighbouring sites • Past studies • General number of enquiries and complaints (written and verbal)

- Consider all the alternatives and never copy another survey;
- Find a balance between knowing a little about a lot, or a lot about a little;
- Consider the first survey as a pilot and not try to discover too much at once;
- Constantly think about the audience, because they are easily confused;
- Remember that the visitor is helping in their own time and deserves attention; and
- Inform the visitor of the benefits of the evaluation to them, ensuring appropriate co-operation.

A survey is like a scientific experiment and it requires appropriate respect. To be successful, a survey does not have to provide all of the information you originally were after, but it does have to justify itself for more than just a learning experience.

Evaluating Interpretation Programmes

There are three dimensions to the evaluation of interpretive programmes:
1. Self-evaluation (assessing one's own professional standards of quality);
2. Peer evaluation (assessment by other interpreters); and
3. Visitor evaluation (objective assessment of visitor reaction).

Self-evaluation should be the very first form of assessment conducted on any programme, and needs to be done in the proposal stages. Self-evaluation is a form of front-end evaluation, since it encourages the individual proposing the programme to ask some hard questions about audience and message *before determining technique*. Some of the audience-related questions involve defining the existing visitor's understanding, misconceptions, interests, and demands. In addition, serious thought needs to be given to latent demand, since interpretive programmes often change visitor profiles over time. Message questions must relate to the issues pertaining to the immediate and surrounding area, likely changes in issues, overall goals of management, and what is already in operation or is planned. Front-end evaluation is becoming more and more necessary in seeking approval and funding for visitor management programmes. The essential ingredient to a proposal is a clear statement of measurable objectives of the programme (see Chapter 21) .

Other self-evaluation components reflect the identification and assessment of selection criteria. These criteria make it possible to measure the ability of the programme to meet its objectives. Aside from audience and message, some of the criteria which need to be objectively assessed include (Pennyfather 1975):
- Cost (initial and operating);
- Simplicity;

- Ease of installation;
- Reliability;
- Relationship to other media and degree to which it must be isolated;
- Flexibility (how adaptable the medium is to change); and
- Durability (resistance to wear and tear, including vandalism).

One of the techniques available to heritage managers is a Goals Achievement Matrix (GAM). This involves listing and weighting the relative importance of clearly defined project criteria. The proposal(s) are then scored firstly for their direct ability to satisfy the criteria (out of 3 or 5). This figure is then multiplied by the appropriate weighting to determine a final score. Scores for different proposals/techniques can then be compared and ranked. An example of this technique can be found in the Tasmanian rainforest case study (Chapter 6, Table 6.2). The matrix provides an objective assessment less prone to personal bias. Nevertheless, GAM is only an indicator, the ultimate choice often resting on unforeseen circumstances (including politics).

Peer evaluation has long been used as a means of seeking input during the planning, design and maintenance of interpretive exhibits. However, given the significant personal involvement in interpretive programmes, peer evaluation can be a threatening and self-destructive process if not carefully and sensitively managed.

Both self-evaluation and peer evaluation are sometimes known as formative evaluation, since they test the preparation stage of the proposal before it is actually in place. Formative evaluation usually involves the use of mock-ups and trials on a sample audience, which may include peers. Both forms of evaluation draw on extensive guidelines to assess interpretive content and presentation. Two simple principles include the need to make sentences short, positive and active and leave out jargon and technical terms. There is extensive literature on assessing the readability of text and a number of simple formulae are widely available, even as part of standard computer word programs. One of the more popular in Australia is the Fry test, which involves a series of calculations and graph reading. The Forcast test involves subtracting 20 from the number of one syllable words in a 150-word passage, then dividing by 10. Most interpretive text should come out at a reading year level of six or seven (11 or 12 years old). There is extensive research into the ergonomics of exhibit design. The last point worth mentioning in this area is the height of text which is frequently displayed outside the recommended half a metre above and one metre below eye level (Stansfield 1981).

Assessments of cost and effectiveness are also within the visitor evaluation realm. Unfortunately, some heritage managers assess cost on its own and use this as a measure of effectiveness. However, few attempts have been made to assess the cost-effectiveness of different interpretive programmes (Beckmann

1988) because of the obvious difficulty of comparing between message, audience, and media. Gauging the cost to set up a programme can be done but only adds one component of the larger need of measuring overall cost-effectiveness. Assessing the 'cost per contact' of some programmes is a quick method of contrasting value for money. The Tasmanian Department of Parks, Wildlife and Heritage use this technique annually to compare the cost of their personal interpretation programme, the Summer Ranger Programme, with that of non-personal services. Nevertheless, the technique obviously comes unstuck without other dimensions being considered. For example, while personal services may cost twice as much per contact as non-personal, they may be twice as effective at communicating their message (twice as many concepts, understanding held for twice as long and twice as many proactive reactions to experience).

One of the simplest and most popular forms of evaluating interpretation is the assessment of an exhibit's ability to attract and hold visitor attention. Most popular in museums and some visitor centres, this technique mainly involves monitoring the number of people who either look, stop, admire or read an exhibit. Timing provides some form of scale to the attention span, and this is often compared against a 'model time' measured by the evaluator. McManus (1989) argued that 'although people may not appear to be reading, their tape-recorded verbal behaviour suggests otherwise' referring to high proportions of 'text-echo' (the label content used in conversations with group members) as proof. Other behavioural trends include visitor flow to and around the exhibit, body language, interactions with other visitors, and even the number of finger and nose prints has been counted! The large amount of research done in this area has provided interpreters with clear principles for the presentation of exhibit-based information (Bitgood 1989).

Timing tests conducted on various interpretive walks in Tasmanian forests confirmed that trails 'which were designed to incorporate an element of discovery, privacy and intimacy (varied surfaces) were more successful than those using more traditional approaches' (McArthur and Gardner 1992). Furthermore, signs which used more interactive, emotive techniques were more successful at gaining visitor attention. There were also clear indications of the number of signs and length of text which visitors can be expected to be attracted to long enough to read and absorb the message. Most visitors to a typical interpretive trail of less than fifteen minutes would read no more than eight interpretive signs, and were unlikely to read more than five to six sentences. Though some visitors requested the use of scientific names, tests showed that fewer than half read them.

Visitor evaluation conducted in the Cradle Mountain Visitor Centre in Tasmania was used to modify visitor flow, and the design and use of exhibits

(Saunders and Mumbray 1990; Saunders and McArthur 1991). It also used timing to conclude that interactive displays were far more popular than static forms (visitors staying for nine as opposed to two minutes). Nevertheless, in commenting on these results, Saunders (1992) emphasized the limits of such techniques and commented that while they may suggest the experience is popular, they do not necessarily indicate the effectiveness of the interpretation. Studies undertaken in 1992 confirm that the Centre is not succeeding in this capacity (Mumbray, pers. comm.). Indeed, Pearce and Moscardo (1985) stress the value of running such simple programmes over a number of years, enabling managers to detect trends in popularity of various exhibits and attractions.

Affective testing is used to find out how a visitor feels about the interpretive experience. They can be carried out using written/verbal surveys or tests, but are ideally done using less 'formal' methods. Many visitors are unable to verbalize feelings and ideas about their experience, and the range of responses makes objective collation difficult. Ideally, affective tests need to employ standardized psychological tests such as the semantic differential and agreement scaling tests. One simple technique is to represent emotion using visual expression, such as asking visitors to represent their feelings via a series of faces showing different expressions, or bodies with different postures.

Determining the 'performance' of interpretation in assisting visitors to attain knowledge usually involves cognitive testing which examines the responses of visitors to a written/verbal questionnaire or quiz. One popular technique involves one random sample completing the questionnaire before experiencing the interpretation and another random sample completing it afterwards. A comparision of the average scores calculated for the two groups gives an indication of the 'performance' of the interpretation.

There have been numerous evaluation programmes conducted to detect visitor recollection of knowledge (Borun 1977). Unfortunately, most programmes in Australia and New Zealand have focused on testing orientation-based information. For example, a programme run at Namadgi Visitor Centre in the Australian Capital Territory evaluated the 'effectiveness' of the orientation displays. Results suggested that 92 per cent of the 150 groups evaluated could point out on a map the correct route they should take, while 82 per cent could reasonably estimate the time it would take to reach their destination (Tatnell 1991). However, the recollection of knowledge is inherently related to a visitor's individual needs and interest levels, and this tends to be reflected in their 'performance' in tests of this nature. Evaluation programmes conducted in Tasmanian forests found that less than 10 per cent of visitors remembered any of the scientific plant labels they had passed (McArthur and Gardner 1992).

While retaining knowledge is useful in aiding visitor management during the experience, it is disadvantaged because of its reliance on contact between visitors and evaluators. Visitors who know in advance that they will be tested cannot be seen as truly representative. Furthermore, there is no guarantee that this knowledge is transferred to the next heritage experience. In building up awareness, managers may well have to start all over again.

As noted above, one of the reasons for a shift from information to interpretation has been the need to change a visitor's perspective. It is known that attitudes have an affective, behavioural and cognitive component. Showing how a change in attitude is related to the person's needs is effective in changing attitudes. Flemming and Lewis (1978) observed that:

- Active participation produced greater attitude change than passive reception of information;
- A positive and rewarding experience with an object will foster a positive attitude, participatory exhibits, particularly interactive forms, being the most successful; and
- Interpretation successful in creating attitude change usually illustrated how a change was important to the visitor.

Many involved in the evaluation of visitor services point out that assessing changes in attitude and behaviour can be extremely expensive and may only confirm staff intuition. Furthermore, the techniques of evaluators may pose a threat to a visitor's confidence, intelligence and standing within a group. Therefore, there is a critical need for a well-defined and accepted implementation process for the evaluation of an interpretive programme. Table 22.3 provides an insight into a number of stages undertaken to evaluate the effectiveness of an interpretive walk.

There are a number of different ways to ask questions within a survey (Table 22.4). As part of a survey, some visitor managers of heritage have used some innovative methods to subtly detect changes in attitude. One of these has been the use of tasks such as filling in missing words that make up sentences within a paragraph, or underlining words or phrases that emphasize the visitor's attitude on a subject (Figure 22.1). The results from this research suggested that almost two thirds of visitors surveyed were able to detect most inappropriate actions, with variation providing useful direction for future management changes (Huxtable and Beckmann 1989).

It is incorrect to assume that a change in attitude will be followed by a positive change in behaviour. Consider, for example, the lack of substantial success in drink/driving campaigns specifically aimed at 18 to 25 year olds. One alternative, coercion, can substantially impact an individual's freedom to experience heritage. In commenting on Australian environmental education programmes, Prior (1992: 14) claimed that 'regulated behaviour

Please read this story and <u>underline</u> anything that you would do differently from Ted.

Ted visited the National Park every holiday. This summer he pitched his tent at the camp site and collected dead wood for a camp fire from the nearby forest. He <u>gave his food scraps to the brushtail possum and grey kangaroo</u> that visited his tent. On some days he went for a <u>walk on the heathland</u> to take photographs of the views and wildflowers. He kept mostly to the track, <u>except when he saw a good short-cut</u>. Sometimes he got a lift to the beach with his campsite neighbours who had a four-wheel drive. He liked that, especially when they <u>went down a track marked "Revegetation area"</u> which took them onto an uncrowded beach. Once <u>they ran over a snake</u>—Ted was glad because it made the park safer for visitors like him.

Source: Victorian Department of Conservation & Environment 1988/89.

Figure 22.1: Extract from a survey to assess the effectiveness of a summer programme in changing attitudes

change can be successful, provided that there is strong public support for such regulations, that they are very carefully explained, and that those affected have some say in the ways in which regulations are put into operation'.

It is extremely difficult to determine exactly to what extent interpretation has changed visitor behaviour, and there is limited Australian research in this field. The most frequent evaluation technique has been through direct observations while the visitor is still on-site, e.g. do visitors leave the track or interfere with an artefact? Surveys have also been used to attempt to detect an intention to change behaviour as a result of an interpretive heritage-based experience. For example, despite confirming success in some interpretive programmes (such as detecting more correct answers following a personal interpretive experience), less than half 'identified possible changes to their

Table 22.3: Implementation process for the evaluation of interpretation

Stage	Example
1. Define problem(s) and prioritize	Uncertain of the effectiveness of existing interpretive walk. (a) Is it attracting target audience? (b) Is it holding attention? (c) What message has audience learnt? (d) Does audience enjoy experience? (e) Does audience have any difficulties?
2. Define the specific objectives	• To establish proposed hypotheses to be investigated and contrast profile of user group with actual profile. • To determine behavioural reactions to the interpretive experience. • To contrast understanding before and after interpretive experience. • To define and contrast the level of enjoyment of interpretive experience. H1: Experience is predominantly attracting target audience. H2: Target audience understand key messages of interpretation. H3: Target audience distinguish experience as enjoyable.
3. Identify constraints to programme	• Staffing: one staff member available for up to two months. • Limited budget of $ 1000. • Most visitation occurs between Thursday and Sunday. • Need results three weeks after monitoring period.
4. Define time frame for programme	• Programme design—two days. • Pilot test and review—two days. • Training—two days. • Production of materials and equipment (counter and survey forms)—two days. • Monitoring—three weeks. • Compilation of results and write up—two weeks. • Presentation of results—two days.
5. Select techniques	• Track counter. • Observations (break-up of duration, group size, behaviour). • Interviews (pre and post).
6. Pilot test and review	Test methods on site.
7. Train staff member	Take out to site and attempt final test.
8. Produce materials and equipment	Install counter, print survey forms.
9. Conduct monitoring	Implement techniques outlined above.
10. Compile results and distribute	Two levels of reports for two levels of readership.
11. Present results verbally	Summary of most relevant implications.

Table 22.4: Different questioning techniques to evaluate visitor responses to interpretation

Techniques	Examples
• Open-ended questions	
—without direction	'What is your opinion of these signs?'
—with direction	'Do you think these signs are effective at getting their message across?'
• Closed questions	
—neutrality	'Are these signs fun to read?' Yes / No
—bias	'These signs are fun to read' Yes / No
• Multiple-choice questions★	'How would you describe these signs?' a Interesting and different b Enjoyable c Fairly plain d Dull to boring e Other _____
• Ranked preferences	In order of your enjoyment, number the following interpretive walks from 1 to 3 • Sandspit ___ • Weldborough Pass ___ • Julius River ___

★ Requires background knowledge or good hunches to anticipate categories, though you can include open-ended component in case you have misjudged the categories.

personal behaviour and/or attitudes which had been directly or indirectly suggested to them by the interpretation activity' (Huxtable and Beckmann 1989). Figure 22.2 represents one technique that not only tries to detect commitment to a cause, but the level of commitment in monetary terms.

Assessments made after leaving the site obviously become more difficult, e.g. do visitors now use a resource more wisely or approach a culture with more respect? To monitor this change requires a more holistic approach to evaluation that may cross over many different settings and activities, requiring a level of co-operation between the visitor and various agencies.

Some recent work on the evaluation of visitor information delivery has been done by Manfredo and Bright (1991). The authors' theorized that behaviour change was a 'function of message elaboration which is measured

> *Imagine that a private forest area, which is home to several rare species, is going to be heavily logged. Would you be willing to donate any money to any (one or more) of the following activities, and if so, how much?*
>
> (a) A job creation program for forest workers so that the area can be left unlogged   No   Yes   amount $
>
> (b) Research to find out just how rare the species are   No   Yes   amount $
>
> (c) A fund to buy and protect half the forest, allowing logging in the other half   No   Yes   amount $
>
> (d) A media campaign to support the logging   No   Yes   amount $
>
> (e) A media campaign to protest against the logging   No   Yes   amount $

Figure 22.2: Extract from a survey to assess willingness to undertake behavioural change and financial commitment as a result of a summer interpretation programme

Source: Victoria Department of Conservation & Environment 1988/89

using three variables: number of thoughts generated, acquisition of new beliefs, and changes in old beliefs' (1991: 1). After testing their theory on visitors' use of brochures for a wilderness area, they found that their results supported other research which suggested that the less experience visitors had with a heritage site, the more likely they were to be influenced by interpretation (Krumpe and Brown 1982; Roggenbuck and Berrier 1982).

Given that a change in behaviour is directly affected by a combination of a visitor's prior knowledge and the credibility of the information, visitor management must respond in two ways. First, interpretation must be highly targeted towards the audience most in need of behavioural change. The more experience that the audience possesses, the more care must be taken in the content and delivery of interpretation. It may be better to either ignore a secondary audience, or provide an alternative form of communication, than to attempt using the same medium. Second, interpretation must clearly demonstrate whose values are being represented. Visitors will not change their own behaviour if a similar practice is not clearly represented by management. Such a principle is frequently broken, particularly in the name of 'practicality' by maintenance staff.

Marketing Evaluation to Managers

The greatest challenge in implementing evaluation is to persuade senior administrators and professionals that part of the organization's resources should be allocated towards a long-term programme. The budget for every exhibit or interpretive facility should include an allocation for evaluation and feedback and, where appropriate, for the modification of the facility. Most agencies spend less than one per cent on evaluation, yet an individual project should adopt a figure between five and ten times this. In a recent survey of the major Australian park management agencies, respondents stated that evaluation was a low priority, primarily because of the perceived cost of evaluation (Beckmann 1988).

There appears to be more interest in the production of new programmes rather than the examination of old ones. This perhaps reflects a catch-22 attitude of visitor managers: as they instinctively recognize the old programmes as 'poor performing', they want nothing more than their replacement. However, this denies them solid evidence with which to argue for one particular programme over another. The long-standing reliance on 'gut feelings' is being overdone and cannot be seen as reliable in the dynamic world of the visitor. The cost of not evaluating limits the effectiveness of any interpretive programme. Any programme running below its capacity represents poor investment and severely damages the performance of other programmes, as well as the general reputation of management (McArthur and Gardner 1992). The strategy is not a matter of arguing whether or not to evaluate, but in establishing the cost of not evaluating. This tactic must be presented in a clear and preferably measurable form: some scenarios are presented in Table 22.5.

The emphasis needs to be on using evaluation to detect poor interpretive programmes and thus allowing the implementation of improvements, thereby saving management resources. If an evaluation programme is built into a project before it is implemented, rather than being added on afterwards, it is easier and cheaper to run. For example, the Tasmanian Forestry Commission has a policy that ensures that each progressive stage of a project is dependent upon a positive evaluation of the previous stage (Cornford 1992; Forestry Commission 1992). Programme justification should be inherently linked with the need to test whether those measurable objectives (stipulating desired audience, message, and behaviour), mentioned above, are being achieved.

Table 22.5: Marketing evaluation to managers: hidden issues and implications of not using evaluation

Situation	Possible result	Implication	Time and Cost
• Lack of management presence • Poorly located track • Small text on interpretive signs • Poorly worded interpretation	• Poor management identity • Meandering and deviation • Visitors don't read signs • Misunderstood message	• Impact on heritage • Poor planning • Additional demand on limited management resources	• Unforeseen expenditure • Loss of productivity • Loss of financial support • Loss of stakeholder support
• Untargeted interpretation	• Lack of visitor interest	• Failure to meet visitor needs	• Inefficient use of resources
• Unidentified audience • Inappropriate audience • Negative impact upon resource	• Unguided visitor management • Visitors don't enjoy experience	• Failure to meet stakeholder needs • Failure to support management and its objectives	• Reduced staff morale • Delay of future projects • Continuation of inappropriate strategies

An example of the positive contribution which evaluation makes towards visitor management can be illustrated from the application of the five stages of the travel experience to the way in which visitor management is effectively implemented. Visitation has five stages: decision-making and anticipation, travel to heritage site, on-site experience, return travel, and recollection of the experience. The recollection will draw on all the other stages and feed back to the motivations and expectations for visits to other heritage sites (see Figure 1.1). Consequently, altering one experience will influence choice and behaviour of subsequent experiences. The five-stage model was used to formulate an information strategy for visitors to Tasmanian forests (Forestry Commission 1992). This strategy identified four stages to the visitor information strategy, that of motivation, strategic information, enhancement and reinforcement/extension (Table 22.6). Existing services and products were then identified and allocated to these stages.

Many promotional publications offer images that are not representative of most visitors' experiences. Identifying the nature of promotional tools (publications) from the visitor's perspective allows for a more co-ordinated, focused approach. Non-representative publications relating to experiences managed by the Forestry Commission tended to confuse perceptions of the agency's role in providing heritage experiences. Feedback from users (McArthur and Gardner 1992) revealed that full-colour publications quickly fell out of date and had an over-emphasis on motivational rather than strategic information. By using the five-stage travel model, the Forestry Commission modified the content, design, marketing, and distribution of all its pre-visit publications. The focus of publications were changed from a national parks image to that of a production forest manager. Even the title of publications were modified to reinforce the emphasis, e.g. from *Southern Forest Reserves* to *Visiting Forests in Southern Tasmania*. The changes also allow for considerable reduction in production, the savings being redistributed to other products.

Conclusion

Evaluation does not dictate the solutions, it provides information and insights to make decisions. Aside from the chronic need for more effective evaluation of interpretation, the future emphasis in visitor evaluation must be in accurately assessing motivations. By understanding why visitors visit heritage sites, evaluation can assist management to solve visitor problems such as crowding, littering, and physical impacts. Accommodating specific visitors with specific experiences assists the goals of visitor management to be achieved.

Table 22.6: Forestry Commission Information Strategy

VISITOR SERVICE INFORMATION STRATEGY

Step 1: Sales & motivation	Step 2: Strategic information	Step 3: Enhancement & education	Step 4: Reinforcement & extension
experience/interest (planting ideas)	working info to access and experience activity/destination (travelling to site)	(making experience more meaningful)	(further application of experience and further opportunities for learning)
Techniques (a) Publications —Progression to joint full-colour brochures (extensive marketing and distribution) except where current stocks are significant or tenure/activity-related —Joint promotional posters between Tourism & FC or Tourism & PWH	Techniques (a) Publications that are strategic and cost-effective —computer format for easy and regular updating —quality maps, deeper focus on experience e.g. G. W. Tiers and Arve Rd	Techniques (a) Interpretation —interpretive signage and brochures —self-drive tours —personal guided tours/walks —activities (Summer Ranger etc.)	Techniques —notesheets (tree species, birds etc.) —posters/postcards —children's books —audios / videos —games —guidebooks
Techniques (b) Media —Joint theme promotions e.g. Summer Forest Discoveries e.g. Rainforest walks	Techniques (b) Strategic signage —orientation signage —information signage e.g. booths (general theme introduction) (assists in corporate identity)	Techniques (b) Education —seminars, workshops —education camps	
Techniques (c) Staffing —Staff training for those handling public enquiries (inter-agency level) —Specialist for travel centre(s)	Techniques (c) —Recreation data base		

Table 22.6 *continued*

	FUNDING		
Mainly inter-agency funding	Combined funding for some of (a) and (c) Single agency funding for (b)	Single agency funding	Single agency funding
$ Saved	$ Redirected and invested	$ Invested	$ Saved

	CORPORATE IDENTITY		
Lowered in publications Increased in staff	Increased in (b)	Increased	Strengthened

Source: Forestry Commission 1992.

References

Barrow, G. 1991, 'Spreading the load', *Environmental Interpretation*, (October), pp. 14–16.

Beckmann, E. 1988, 'Interpretation in Australia—current status and future prospects', *Australian Parks and Recreation*, vol. 23, no. 6, pp. 6–14.

Bitgood, S. 1989, 'Deadly sins revisited: a review of the exhibit label literature', *Visitor Behaviour*, vol. 4, no. 3, pp. 4–8.

Borun, M. 1977, *Measuring the Immeasurable*, Association of Science Technology Centres, Washington, D. C.

Chanowitz, B. and Langer, E. 1980, 'Knowing more (or less) than you show: understanding control through the mindless–mindfulness distinction,' in *Human Helplessness*, eds. J. Garber and Seligman, Academic Press, New York.

Cornford, D. 1992, 'Teepookana Visitor Strategy', unpublished report, Forestry Commission, Hobart.

Department of Tourism, Sport and Recreation 1990, *The Implications for the Emerging Market for Tasmanian Tourism*, Department of Tourism, Sport and Recreation, Hobart.

Flemming, M. and Lewis, W. H. 1978, *Instructional Message Design*, Educational Technology Publications, Englewood Cliffs.

Forestry Commission 1992, 'Communication Strategy for Education and Visitor Services Branch', unpublished report for Forestry Commission, Hobart.

Huxtable, D. and Beckmann, E. 1989, 'Holiday programs in Victoria—an evaluation', *Australian Ranger Bulletin*, vol. 5, no. 3., pp. 35–7.

Krumpe, E. and Brown, P. J. 1982, 'Redistributing backcountry use through information related to recreation experiences', *Journal of Forestry*, June, pp. 360–2, 364.

Manfredo, M. J. and Bright, A. D. 1991, 'A model for assessing the effects of communication on recreationists', *Journal of Leisure Research*, vol. 23, no. 1, pp. 1–20.

McArthur, S. and Gardner, T. 1992, *Forestry Commission Visitor Manual*, Forestry Commission Tasmania, Hobart.

McManus, P. 1989, 'A summary of how museum visitors read labels and interact with exhibit texts', *Visitor Behaviour*, vol. 4, no. 3, pp. 174–89.

Pearce, P. L. and Moscardo, G. 1985 'Visitor evaluation: an appraisal of goals and techniques', *Evaluation Review*, vol. 9, no. 3, pp. 281–306.

Pennyfather, K. 1975, *Guide to Countryside Interpretation, Part Two: Interpretive Media and Facilities*, Countryside Commission, Edinburgh.

Prior, M. 1992, 'Responding to threat, psychology and environmental issues', *Habitat Australia*, April, pp. 12–14.

Roggenbuck, J. W. and Berrier, D. L. 1982, 'A comparison of the effectiveness of two communication strategies in dispersing wilderness campers', *Journal of Leisure Research*, vol. 14, no. 1, pp. 77–89.

Saunders R. and Mumbray T. 1990, 'Visitor Reaction to Cradle Mountain Visitor Centre (Easter 1990)', unpublished report, Department of Parks, Wildlife and Heritage, Hobart.

Saunders, R. and McArthur, S. 1991, 'Visitor Reaction to Cradle Mountain Visitor Centre (Summer 1990/91)', unpublished report, Department of Parks, Wildlife and Heritage, Hobart.

Saunders, R. 1992, 'Voices in the wilderness: interpreting Tasmania's World Heritage area', *Australian Parks and Recreation*, vol. 28, no. 1, pp. 16–19.

Stansfield, G. 1981, *Effective Interpretive Exhibitions*, Countryside Commission, Cheltenham.

Tatnell, A. 1991, 'Visitor centres—Big Brother's substitute for real experiences?', *Australian Parks and Recreation*, vol. 28, no. 2, pp. 16–17.

Wet Tropics Management Authority 1992, *Wet Tropics Plan: Strategic Directions*, Wet Tropics Management Authority, Cairns.

Zube, E. H. 1981, *Environmental Evaluation: Perception and Public Policy*, Brooks/Cole, Monterey.

23

Towards Sustainable Heritage Management?

C. Michael Hall and Simon McArthur

As we move round the galleries, Griffin is candid about the shortcomings of the place—the static glass cases, ancient dioramas, uninspiring slabs of text and the incongruously small front entrance. He is itching to make over the all-important Aboriginal gallery, now nearing the end of a reasonable lifespan for a semi-permanent gallery, and wants even more emphasis placed on contemporary Aboriginal Australia. The gallery should begin with the present, he says, not the past. 'That's the standard museum treatment—to treat them as if they're about to die out. Well, they didn't die out—they survived' (Interview with Des Griffin, the Australian Museum's director, in Hall 1992).

Heritage has long contributed to the appeal of tourist destinations. However, in recent years 'culture' and 'nature' have been increasingly promoted in order to attract those travellers seeking aesthetic and enriching tourist experiences (World Tourism Organization 1985; Weiler and Hall 1992). The growth in heritage-oriented tourism can be attributed to an increasing awareness of the economic value of culture and nature, higher levels of education, greater affluence, more leisure time, greater mobility, and increased access to the arts. Along with these important factors influencing travel trends, there has been growing recognition of arts activities, heritage sites, and cultural facilities as tourist attractions (Hall and Zeppel 1990, 1992; Hollinshead 1990; Moulin 1990). Many regions are considering the potential of heritage tourism as a source of alternative and sustained tourism development. However, despite the perceived employment and economic benefits of heritage, the increase in the number of visitors that tourism brings to a region can have negative impacts on the integrity and quality of heritage sites. Therefore, management mechanisms need to be put into place that will ensure the maintenance of the values of the heritage resource while also ensuring a positive visitor experience, and the subsequent benefits that heritage tourism can bring. As Davies (1987: 104) observed:

Towards Sustainable Heritage Management?

Trends for the 1990s are likely to be concerned with adding and enhancing the visitor experience, forging a closer merger with the non-commercial and commercial sectors with many non-commercial tourist attractions being forced to adopt a commercial approach. . . it is likely that heritage tourism—with adequate interpretation and information—will be one of the emerging trends. And if heritage is to be preserved, it certainly needs the profit generated from a sound commercial approach. Marketing, market research and new product development will be paramount. Revenue and product generation will be much more closely examined and re-investment in tourism as market conditions change will be a more complex process.

This book has attempted to provide a range of management processes that can assist in the maintenance of heritage values. It has noted that heritage management requires the adoption of sound business and management principles, particularly strategic management and marketing techniques. However, the adoption of such principles does *not* mean the crass commercialization and commodification of heritage. Rather it refers to the appropriate use of management techniques by those responsible for the maintenance of heritage values and the satisfaction of visitor experiences. For example, as Chapter 3 noted, heritage marketing is not concerned with 'selling', but instead it strives to find an appropriate match between the values of the heritage site and the visitor.

The search for 'site-friendly' forms of visitation lies at the heart of notions of sustainable tourism. Unfortunately, tourism and recreation have often been seen as two different forms of site use, with the former being commercial and the later being non-commercial (Hall 1991). However, tourism and recreation should be seen as two ends of the visitation spectrum. Indeed, the supposed differences between them are becoming increasingly blurred, as heritage sites, such as national parks or historic homes, find themselves having to charge visitors in order to maintain site qualities.

A sustainable approach to heritage management is concerned with visitation being appropriate to the values attached to a heritage site, particularly the maintenance of the site's 'sense of place', i.e. the qualities which provide for uniqueness and which provide for people's personal attachment to that place. However, such an approach does not mean that visitation should be prevented. Instead, it becomes essential for heritage managers to identify and develop a heritage product which satisfies the visitor and management objectives. Indeed, in the present economic environment, support for heritage preservation can only be ensured if we do encourage visitation. Yet, visitation needs to be part of a win–win situation which ensures that both local values are maintained and satisfied and visitor motivations are met. As Helber (1988: 20) observed:

We are intrigued and fascinated by unusual and scenic natural environments and the different lifestyles and characteristics of people outside our communities. It is these differences that motivate large numbers of people to travel to both domestic and international destinations. A very basic strategy then, in tourism development, is to retain and preserve these aspects which make our community or region uniquely different from all others.

As this book has indicated, a number of planning principles need to be applied in heritage management. First, for visitation to be sustainable it must be at a scale appropriate for the specific location and should produce no permanent degradation of the values associated with the heritage site. Second, visitation must be placed within a strategic planning framework which identifies values, goals, objectives and appropriate actions for heritage management and site visitation. Third, and most critically, it is apparent that local communities must be involved in the heritage management process.

In order to make heritage management sustainable it is essential that all the stakeholders involved in visitation become involved. For example, many nature-based tour operators have neglected the concerns of local people, particularly indigenous peoples. The natural environment is a cultural resource, a factor of particular significance when the rights and heritage values of indigenous peoples have often been ignored. A fundamental maxim for the heritage manager is that heritage values are people values. To be able to manage heritage you have to be able to manage values, therefore you have to be able to manage people.

Heritage managers need to be able to adopt the strategic planning principles noted in Chapter 21. Managers must adopt public participation measures on more than a once-off basis, and instead must establish an ongoing community consultative process which encourages stakeholder involvement and 'ownership'. Furthermore, managers need to identify markets which meet community goals in order to link the heritage product to the market. In this setting, interpretation therefore becomes essential, as it is interpretation which adds value to the heritage product, provides satisfying visitor experiences, and aids visitor management—thereby establishing a win–win situation for management, the local community, and the visitor.

As this book demonstrates, there are a number of encouraging developments in the adoption of strategic planning and management principles in cultural and natural heritage management in Australia and New Zealand. The management of the Wet Tropics of Queensland (Chester and Roberts 1992; Wet Tropics Management Authority 1992) and the Australian Alps (Mackay and Virtanen 1992), and non-traditional heritage managers such as the Tasmanian Forestry Commission, have attempted to match products with markets and involve stakeholders in the heritage management process in a manner which is quite new to Australia. In New Zealand, the Department of Conservation and other heritage management agencies are beginning to respond to demands for sustainable resource management and the supply of visitor experiences for a growing tourism market. In both Australia and New Zealand innovation has occurred in heritage management agencies primarily because of a range of pressures, including stakeholder demands, unfavourable publicity surrounding the institution, or changed funding regimes. Indeed, it is the increasingly uncertain external environment within which heritage management operates that will determine future management practice.

The Future

This book has advocated the adoption of a strategic approach to heritage management that emphasizes goal and objective setting, stakeholder participation, appropriate marketing, and interpretation as a visitor management tool. However, most of all, it stresses the role of values in heritage management. Yet values are not static, the meanings and attachments associated with a particular site are dynamic and change over time. Therefore, heritage managers need to adopt process-oriented management techniques which can adapt to changing circumstances and values.

Sustainable heritage management requires strategic planning which can identify issues and determine appropriate management responses. While each heritage site has its own set of local issues which will need to be addressed, a number of broad issues which will affect heritage management in Australia and New Zealand can be identified:
- First, the growing attraction of heritage sites for domestic and overseas tourists;
- Second, the increasing demand of Aborigines and Māori for control over their heritage;
- Third, the recognition of heritage values other than ecological values, including the legitimacy of cultural practices, such as high-country grazing, as a form of heritage appropriate to national parks and reserves;
- Fourth, the growth of a user-pays philosophy in government approaches towards heritage management;
- Fifth, the development of a sustainable development ethic which integrates heritage sites with a broader conservation framework.

The above range of issues will determine the future of heritage management in the two countries. It is to be hoped that this book will contribute, if only in a small way, to the establishment of management strategies that will meet the demands placed upon heritage and provide a greater understanding of the complex values which heritage managers seek to satisfy.

References

Chester, G. and Roberts, G. 1992, 'The Wet Tropics of Queensland World Heritage Area: the planning challenge', in *Heritage Management: Parks, Heritage and Tourism, Conference Proceedings*, Royal Australian Institute of Parks and Recreation, Hobart, pp. 177–84.

Davies, E. 1987, 'Shaping tourism trends—the commercial perspective', *Tourism Management*, vol. 8, no. 2, pp. 102–4.

Hall, C. M. 1991, *Introduction to Tourism in Australia: Impacts, Planning and Development*, Longman-Cheshire, South Melbourne.

Hall C. M. and Zeppel, H. 1990, 'Cultural and heritage tourism: the new grand tour?', *Historic Environment*, vol. 7, no. 3/4, pp. 86–98.

Hall C. M. and Zeppel, H. 1992, 'Arts and heritage tourism,' in *Special Interest Tourism*, eds. B. Weiler and C. M. Hall, Belhaven Press, London.

Hall, S. 1992, 'Showtime for Terry and Des', *The Australian Magazine*, September 26–7.

Helber, L. E. 1988, 'The roles of government planning in tourism with special regard for the cultural and environmental impact of tourism', in *The Roles of Government in the Development of Tourism as an Economic Resource*, ed D. McSwan, Seminar Series No. 1, Centre for Studies in Travel and Tourism, James Cook University, Townsville, pp. 17–23.

Hollinshead, K. 1990 'Cultural tourism', *Annals of Tourism Research*, vol. 17, no. 2, pp. 292–4.

Mackay, J. and Virtanen, S. 1992, 'Tourism and the Australian Alps', in *Heritage Management: Parks, Heritage and Tourism, Conference Proceedings*, Royal Australian Institute of Parks and Recreation, Hobart, pp. 159–65.

Moulin, C. 1990, 'Cultural heritage and tourism evolution', *Historic Environment*, vol. 7, no. 3/4, pp. 3–9.

Weiler, B. and Hall, C. M. (eds.) 1992, *Special Interest Tourism*, Belhaven Press, London.

Wet Tropics Management Authority 1992, *Wet Tropics Plan: Strategic Directions*, Wet Tropics Management Authority, Cairns.

World Tourism Organization 1985, *The State's Role in Protecting and Promoting Culture as a Factor of Tourism Development and the Proper Use and Exploitation of the National Cultural Heritage of Sites and Monuments for Tourism*, World Tourism Organization, Madrid.

Index

Aboriginal and Torres Strait Islander Commission 108
Aboriginal and Torres Strait Islander Heritage Protection Act 1984–86 (Aust.) 107, 108
Aboriginal and Torres Strait Islander Heritage Protection Amendment Act 1987 (Vic.) 109
Aboriginal heritage
 land rights 140
 management issues 103–18, 138–46
 and tourism 103–6, 112, 138–6
Aboriginal Heritage Act 1972–1980 (W.A.) 108
Aboriginal Heritage Act 1988 (S.A.) 109
Aboriginal Land Rights Act (Aust.) 107
Aboriginal Relics Act 1975 (Tas.) 109
Aboriginal sites
 contemporary perspectives 110–13
 legislation and administration 106–10, 188
Acropolis (Athens) 132
Adelaide (S.A.) 132
advertising 27
Agathis notabilis (kauri) 12
albatross 12, 197
Alexandra (N.Z.) 205
alpine areas 85, 246
America's Cup 232
Aniwaniwa (N.Z.) 67
Antiquities Act (N.Z.) 171, 173–7, 178, 184
Aoraki 99
Aotearoa *see* New Zealand
Archaeological and Aboriginal Relics Preservation Act 1972–1984 (Vic.) 109
Archives Act 1975 (N.Z.) 182, 184
Art Deco 209–17
Art Deco Trust (Napier) 211–17
Arthur Ranges (Tas.) 22, 86
Atihaunui a Paparangi 67
Auckland (N.Z.) 6, 205, 219, 226, 231–8
Australia *see also under individual states and territories*
 concepts of heritage 2–4, 10–11, 130, 133, 138, 277
 European heritage 7, 10–11, 147–56, 157–65, 188–96

indigenous *see* Aboriginal heritage
natural heritage 12, 15, 23, 24, 41, 70–81, 82–91, 141–2, 157–65
Australia ICOMOS 147, 148, 159, 191
Australian Alps 41, 44, 241, 246
Australian Capital Territory 84, 91, 106, 109, 241, 246, 261
Australian Heritage Commission 108, 138
Australian Heritage Commission Act 1975 (Aust.) 107, 108
Australian National Parks and Wildlife Service 141
Australian National Rainforest Conservation Program (ANRCP) 71
Australian Tourism Commission Act 1987 145
authenticity 144
Ayers Rock *see* Uluru National Park

Ballarat (Vic.) 148
Bath (U.K.) 132
Bay of Islands Maritime and Historic Park (N.Z.) 11
Bay of Plenty (N.Z.) 6
Blackwood (Vic.) 148
Brisbane (Qld.) 10
Bungal Forest (Vic.) 148
Burra Charter *see* Australia ICOMOS
Byron Bay (N.S.W.) 132

campfires 82–3, 85–9
Canadian ICOMOS 164
Canadian Parks Service 35
Canberra College of Advanced Education 184
Canterbury (N.Z.) 6
Cape Tribulation (Qld.) 245
Carnarvon Ranges (Qld.) 26
Catlins District (N.Z.) 200–1
central Deborah mine (Vic.) 147
Central Land Council 104
Central Plateau (Tas.) 24
Chester (U.K.) 132
Cheviot Beach (Vic.) 150
Christchurch (N.Z.) 10, 12, 205, 219, 226
Clutha River (N.Z.) 203
Coal Mines (Tas.) 189, 193
commercial tour operators 90

279

Index

Commonwealth of Australia 246
community planning *see* public participation
conservation 1, 59–74, 70–81, 141, 147–56, 158–61, 188–96, 199–201, 215–16
see also heritage management
Conservation Act 1987 (N.Z.) 179–80, 184, 199
Conservation Commission of the Northern Territory 108, 141
Conservation, Forests and Lands Act 1987 (Vic.) 148
Cradle Mountain (Tas.) 157, 158
Cradle Mountain–Lake St Clair Board 158, 164
Cradle Mountain–Lake St Clair National Park (Tas.) 84, 88, 157–65 *see also* Overland Track; Waldheim Chalet
Cradle Mountain Visitor Centre 260–1
cross–country skiing 202
Crown Lands (Reserves) Act 1978 (Vic.) 147
Cultural Conservation Advisory Council (NZ) 171, 183–4, 186
cultural heritage *see* heritage
cultural landscapes 53–5
Cultural Record (Landscape Queensland and Queensland Estate) Act 1988 (Qld.) 109
cultural significance *see* heritage: significance
cultural tourism *see* heritage tourism

Daintree National Park (Qld.) 37, 245
Darlington (Tas.) 189
Deinacrida (giant weta) 12
Deloitte Ross Tohmatsu 6, 16
Department of Aboriginal Affairs (Vic.) 109
Department of Arts, Sport, the Environment and Territories (Aust.) 108
Department of Conservation (N.Z.) 61–8, 120, 123, 124, 126, 179, 180, 186, 200, 203
National Heritage Interpretation Plan 62–8
Department of Conservation and Environment (Vic.) 263, 266
Department of Conservation and Natural Resources (Vic.) 147, 150, 153
Department of Environment and Conservation (Qld.) 109
Department of Environment and Planning (S.A.) 109
Department of Internal Affairs (N.Z.) 176, 177, 186

Department of Lands and Survey (N.Z.) 60
Department of Lands, Parks and Wildlife (Tas.) 109
Department of Parks, Wildlife and Heritage (Tas.) 82–91, 188–95, 260
Department of the Environment, Land and Planning (A.C.T.) 109
Dunedin (N.Z.) 10, 197, 205–6
Dunedin City Council 200, 201

East Coast (N.Z.) 97
East Gippsland (Vic.) 148
Eastwoodhill Arboretum (N.Z.) 10–11
ecotourism 27, 143 *see also* heritage tourism
education 33, 88–91
Eiffel Tower (Paris) 133
Entally (Tas.) 189
environmental history
administrative history 55–7
cultural landscapes 53–5
field 51–2
reconstruction 52–3
Environmental Protection (Impact of Proposals) Act 1974–1975 (Aust.) 108, 109
Environmental Protection Agency (Commonwealth) 108
evaluation 15–16, 32, 46, 80, 251–73

facilities 24, 78–80
Federated Mountain Clubs (N.Z.) 203
feral fauna and flora 201, 202
Fiordland National Park (N.Z.) 12, 60
Fordism 218–20
Forestry Commission (Tas.) 15, 27, 33–5, 38, 255, 267, 269, 270–1, 272
Forests Act 1958 (Vic.) 148
Fort Nepean *see* Point Nepean National Park
Fox Glacier (N.Z.) 60, 125
Franz Josef Glacier (N.Z.) 60, 65
Fraser Island (Qld.) 26

Garvie Mountains (N.Z.) 203
gastroenteritis 82, 84–5
Geeveston (Tas.) 21
Gellibrand Hill Park (Vic.) 148, 155–6
Gisborne (N.Z.) 6
Goals Achievement Matrix (GAM) 259
Gordon River (Tas.) 23
Great Barrier Reef Marine Park 12
greenstone 122
Grey Valley (N.Z.) 124
Guggenheim's cottage (Vic.) 148

280

Index

Gulf Station farm (Vic.) 147
Haast (N.Z.) 65
Hamilin Pool (W.A.) 12
hardening 21, 23
Hastings (N.Z.) 215
Hawkes Bay (N.Z.) 6, 209
Hawkes Bay Regional Council (N.Z.) 181, 186
heritage
   and identity 1, 3, 5, 8, 119–29, 130–4
   nature and characteristics 2–4, 119–20, 130–6, 138
   reconstructed 158–9, 193–5
   significance 1, 4–12, 119–29, 148–9, 159–61, 170, 188–96, 234–5
   values 13–16, 188–96, 241–2, 244, 275–7
Heritage Conservation Act 1991 (N.T.) 107, 108
heritage management *see also* institutional arrangements; interpretation; visitor management
   future 277
   heritage visitor management system 13–16, 241–50
   paradox of management 2, 274–8
   planning 30, 32, 241–50, 251–73
   regional 197–208
   role of government 171–3, 184–5, 214–15, 218–29
   site management 70–81, 147–56, 157–65, 188–96, 214–16, 220–9, 241–50, 251–73
   sustainable 274–8
heritage marketing 40–7, 130–6, 137–46, 267–9 *see also* visitor management
   benefits 42, 137
   definition 40
   evaluation 46
   internal analysis 41–3, 267–9
   management 46, 139–40
   market segmentation 41–3, 142
   objectives and strategies 43–5, 137
   situation analysis 41–3
   strategic marketing 40–6, 138–40, 267–9
Heritage Objects Act 1991 (A.C.T.) 109
heritage tourism 5–8, 67–8, 80, 95–7, 100–2, 103–6, 122, 140–6, 188–96, 197–9, 200, 207, 211–17, 218–29, 274–8
Hermitage Hotel 60
Highfield (Tas.) 189, 192, 194–5
Historic Articles Act (N.Z.) 173

Historic Buildings Act 1981 (Vic.) 148
Historic Charleston Foundation (U.S.A.) 211
Historic Places Act 1980 (N.Z.) 171, 177–9, 181, 184
Historic Places Bill 1992 (N.Z.) 181–2, 184
Historic Places Trust *see* New Zealand Historic Places Trust
Historic Savannah Foundation (U.S.A.) 211
Hobart (Tas.) 11, 13, 194
Hobson Wharf (N.Z.) 231–8
Hokitika (N.Z.) 124
Holt, Harold 150
Huon pine 23

impacts *see* visitor management: impacts
indigenous peoples *see* Aboriginal heritage; Maori
institutional arrangements 14, 15, 169–187
interpretation 18–38, 59–69, 123, 147–56, 157–65, 182–4, 231–4, 251–73
   educational component 33
   evaluation 80, 258–67
   objectives and philosophy 27, 58–9, 235–8
   planning 31, 32, 71–3, 161–3
   site-based 74–5, 147–56, 157–65, 188–96
   Tasmanian rainforest 70–81
   Victorian historic sites 147–56
   Waldheim Chalet 157–65
Ironbridge Gorge Museum (U.K.) 193

Japanese Cultural Properties Protection Law 185

Kahungungu iwi 67
kaimoana 68
Kakadu National Park (N.T.) 3, 6, 37, 104, 137
kauri 12
Kawarau River (N.Z.) 199, 203
Keogh's Creek (Tas.) 21

Lake Pedder (Tas.) 75, 76
Lake St Clair *see* Cradle Mountain–Lake St Clair National Park
Lake Wanaka (N.Z.) 198
Lakes District (N.Z.) 203
Lal Lal Blast Furnace (Vic.) 148
Lampton Harbour Development Project 222–8
Lambton Harbour Management Limited 219

Index

Land (Planning and Environment) Act 1991 (A.C.T.) 109
Land Conservation Council (Vic.) 148
land tenure 15, 170
Larnach's Castle (N.Z.) 206
legislation *see under individual acts*
Leiopelma (native New Zealand frog) 12
Liffey Falls (Tas.) 15
Lincoln College 61
Lord Howe Island hen 12

Macleay's swallowtail butterfly 76, 77
Macquarie Harbour (Tas.) 189
Makarora (N.Z.) 65
Maldon (Vic.) 11, 151–152
Maldon Historic Reserve (Vic.) 151–152
Manawatu (N.Z.) 6
Māori
　heritage 95–102, 125, 127, 169–88
　perspectives on DOC interpretation 66–7
　sacred sites (wahi tapu) 98–9
　tourism 94–6, 100–2
Maori Antiquities Act 173
Maori Arts and Cultural Institute 26
Maori Land Court 98, 175
Maria Island (Tas.) 189
marketing *see* heritage marketing
Mataura River (N.Z.) 203
Melbourne (Vic.) 148
Miami Design Preservation League (U.S.A.) 211
Midlands (Tas.) 194
Milford (N.Z.) 99
Milford Sound (N.Z.) 132
Milford Track (N.Z.) 21, 26, 60
minimal impact bushwalking 82–91
mining 126
Ministry of Cultural Affairs (N.Z.) 172, 177, 183, 185
Ministry of Tourism (N.Z.) 214
Moeraki Boulders (N.Z.) 99, 200
Mootwingie (N.S.W.) 110
Mount Aspiring National Park (N.Z.) 204
Mount Buffalo Chalet (Vic.) 148
Mount Buffalo National Park (Vic.) 148
Mount Cook (N.Z.) 99
Mount Cook National Park (N.Z.) 60
Mount Ruapehu (N.Z.) 65 *see also* Tongariro National Park
Mount Tarawera (N.Z.) 60
Mount Wellington (Tas.) 13
mountain bikes 202

Museum of New Zealand 172, 182–183, 218–28
Museum of New Zealand Te Papa Tongarewa Act 1992 (N.Z.) 182–3, 184
museums 6, 7, 172, 182–3, 184, 218–29, 231–8

Namadgi Visitor Centre (A.C.T.) 261
Napier (N.Z.) 178, 209–17
National Estate 3, 9, 107, 138
National Library Act (N.Z.) 182
National Parks Act (N.Z.) 60
National Parks Act 1975 (Vic.) 147, 148
National Parks and Wildlife Act 1967–1974 (N.S.W.) 106, 109
National Parks and Wildlife Service (N.S.W.) 109
national park management 51–8, 59–74, 140–6
National Trust (Australia) 9, 189, 193
Native American Grave Protrection and Repatriation Act 1990 (U.S.A.) 185
Native and Historic Objects and Area Preservation Ordinance 1955–1960 (N.T.) 106
natural heritage *see* heritage
natural significance *see* heritage: significance
Nelson (N.Z.) 6
Newcastle (N.S.W.) 111
New Orleans (U.S.A.) 133
New South Wales 84, 91, 106, 109, 241, 246
New Zealand 7, 21, 169–87, 197–208, 209–17, 218–29, 231–8
　concepts of heritage 95–102, 119–20
　European heritage 205–7, 209–17, 218–29, 231–8
　indigenous *see* Māori
　natural heritage 59–69, 197–205
New Zealand Archaeological Association (NZAA) 182, 186
New Zealand Coastal Policy Statement 201
New Zealand Historic Places Trust 9, 171, 178–9, 184, 201, 206, 207, 214
New Zealand Natural Heritage Foundation 62
New Zealand Lotteries Board 183
New Zealand Tourism Board 67
Ngāi Tahu iwi 68, 96, 99, 200
Ngāti Porou 97–8
Ngāti Rakai 97–8
Ngāti Tuwharetoa 60
Niagara Falls (Canada/U.S.A.) 132

Index

Norfolk Bay (Tas.) 193
North America 6, 65, 120
Northern Land Council 104
Northern Territory 106, 107, 108–9
Northern Territory Aboriginal Areas Protection Authority 109
Northern Terriory Aboriginal Sacred Sites Act 107, 109
Northern Territory Tourist Commission 142, 146
Northland (N.Z.) 6

Oamaru (N.Z.) 197, 200, 206–7
O'Brien, C. 27, 39
off–road vehicles 24, 202
Olveston (N.Z.) 206
Oparara Caves (N.Z.) 12
Organpipes National Park (Vic.) 12
Otago (N.Z.) 6, 12, 197–208
Otago Boys High School 206
Otago Conservation Board 204
Otago Goldfields Park 199, 203
Otago Harbour Planning Study 201
Otago Peninsula Trust 199–200
Otago Regional Council 201, 205
Overland Track (Tas.) 21, 84–8, 158 *see also* Cradle Mountain–Lake St Clair National Park

Paparoa National Park (N.Z.) 65
Paragon Arts 225
park history *see* environmental history
penguins 12, 197, 200
Phillip Island (Vic.) 12
planning 43, 141, 214–216 *see also* public participation; strategic planning
Point Nepean National Park (Vic.) 26, 149–51
Port Arthur (Tas.) ix, 6, 10, 188, 189, 190, 193
Port Arthur Management Authority (Tas.) 189, 192
Port Phillip Bay (Vic.) 149
pounamu (nephrite jade or greenstone) 122
Protection of Movable Cultural Heritage Act 1986 (Aust.) 108, 109
public participation 141
Punakaiki (N.Z.) 65
Pureora Forest (N.Z.) 12

Queen Elizabeth II Arts Council (N.Z.) 172
Queensland 91, 106, 109
Queenstown (N.Z.) 203, 205

rainforest 12, 70–81, 85
recreational fishing 23
Recreation Opportunity Spectrum (ROS) 204
recreational succession 21
Red Square (Moscow) 132
Reefton (N.Z.) 124, 125, 126
Register of the National Estate *see* National Estate
Resource Management Act 1991 (N.Z.) 119, 171, 178, 180–11, 182, 184, 185, 199, 214
Richmond (Tas.) 194
Rocks, the (Sydney, N.S.W.) 11, 133
Rotorua (N.Z.) 26, 60, 100
Rotorua Thermal Reserve (N.Z.) 12
Routeburn Track (N.Z.) 204
Royal Forest and Bird Protection Society (N.Z.) 201

Salamanca Place (Tas.) 11
San Antonio Conservation Society (U.S.A.) 211
Sarah Island (Tas.) 189
SAVE Britain's Heritage 192, 196
Scenery Preservation Board (Tas.) 158
sense of place 8, 119–29, 130–6
Shotover River (N.Z.) 203
South Australia 106, 107, 109, 133
South Island (N.Z.) 68, 95, 99
Southern Alps (N.Z.) 125
Southland (N.Z.) 6, 99
South-west New Zealand 37, 65, 204
South-west Tasmania 37
South-West Tasmanian National Parks (Tas.) 3, 12, 22, 75–80
sponsorship 189
Stanley (Tas.) 189, 192, 194–5
strategic planning 30, 32, 241–50
sub-Antarctic Islands 26
sustainable resource management 18, 180, 274–7
Sydney (N.S.W.) 11, 133
Sydney Opera House (N.S.W.) 132

Tahakopa (N.Z.) 201
Taiaroa Head (N.Z.) 12
Tainui iwi 96
Takitimu Range (N.Z.) 99
Taneatua (N.Z.) 67
Taranaki (N.Z.) 6
Tasman Peninsula (Tas.) 11, 189, 192
Tasmania 21, 22, 23, 75, 106, 109, 157–65, 188–95, 252, 253, 261

Index

Te Atau 97
Te Kuiti (N.Z.) 10
Te Runanga o Ngatihine 181, 187
Te Urewera National Park (N.Z.) 67
Tongariro National Park (N.Z.) 60, 67
Total Catchment Management (TCM) 249–50
tourism *see* heritage tourism
Tourism South Australia 135, 136
Travis Swamp (N.Z.) 12
Treaty of Waitangi 61, 62, 66, 67, 68, 169, 176, 177
Treble Cone (N.Z.) 198
Trollope, Anthony 153
Tuhoe iwi 67
tussock grasslands 202–3
Tuwharetoa iwi 67

Uluru National Park (N.T.) 6, 26, 104, 132, 137–146
UNESCO Convention on the Means of Prohibiting the Illicit Import, Export and Transfer of Ownership of Cultural Property 176, 177
United States National Park Service 61
University of Otago 184, 198
urban conservation *see* conservation; heritage management

VAMP (Visitor Activity Management Programme) 35
Van Diemens Land Company 195
Victoria 24, 84, 91, 106, 109, 147–56, 241, 246
visitor behaviour 28
visitor management 13–16, 18–38, 241–73
  see also heritage management; heritage marketing; interpretation
  evaluation 251–73
  framework 35–7, 241–50
  impacts 18, 19, 20
  practice 22–6, 189, 191–2, 255–8
volunteers 189

Waikato (N.Z.) 6
Waipapa Ecological Area (N.Z.) 12
Waipiro Bay (N.Z.) 98
Waitangi (N.Z.) 10

Waitangi Tribunal 98
Waitomo Caves (N.Z.) 60, 65
Waiuta (N.Z.) 125
Waldheim Chalet (Tas.) 157–65
Walhalla Historic Area (Vic.) 153–5
Walls of Jerusalem National Park (Tas.) 88
Wanaka (N.Z.) 203, 205
waterfront redevelopment 218–29, 231–2
Weindorfer, Gustav 157–65
Wellington (N.Z.) 6, 11, 205, 218–29
Wellington City Art Gallery (N.Z.) 3, 17
Wellington Civic Trust (N.Z.)
Wellington Regional Council (N.Z.) 219, 222, 229
Werribee Park mansion (Vic.) 147
West Coast (N.Z.) 6, 60, 120–9
West Coast (Tas.) 24
Western Australia 91, 106, 108
Western Australian Museum 108
Westland *see* West Coast (N.Z.)
Wet Tropics (Qld.) 241, 244, 245
Wet Tropics Management Authority 244–5, 247, 252, 276
Whakapapa (N.Z.) 65 *see also* Tongariro National Park
Whakarewarewa geyserfield (N.Z.) 60
Whanganui River 60
Whitestone Civic Trust 206
Wild 83
wilderness *see* heritage
Wild South Ltd. 200
Willandra Lakes (NSW) 26
Wilson's Promontory National Park (Vic.) 24
woodchipping 80
Woodlands Homestead complex (Vic.) 148, 155–6
Woolnorth (Tas.) 195
World Heritage 3, 15, 23, 33, 65, 75, 85, 120, 123, 126, 141, 162, 204, 244
World Heritage Convention 3, 141

Yellow Eyed Penguin Trust (N.Z.) 200
Yellowstone (U.S.A.) 132
York–Avon Valley (W.A.) 11
Yosemite (U.S.A.) 132
Yulara Tourist Village *see* Uluru National Park

Praise for
Rebuilding Relationships in Recovery

"*Rebuilding Relationships in Recovery* is an invaluable resource for anyone seeking to mend and strengthen their relationships post addiction. It offers a balanced mix of personal anecdotes, practical advice, and emotional support, making it a must-read for individuals committed to personal growth and recovery. Janice's emphasis on patience, self-awareness, and resilience provides a hopeful and encouraging roadmap for navigating the complexities of relationship repair and personal development throughout the recovery journey."

—RYAN OSCAR, CCRC, CCAC, host of the *From Darkness to Life* podcast and director of operations and education at Our Collective Journey

"This book is a must-read for anyone struggling to repair and rebuild their relationships in recovery. It is a beautiful and sensitively written guide to help readers navigate the broken bonds often left in the wake of addiction. Janice's voice is free of judgment but full of grace and honesty. She offers actionable and realistic steps and tactics for healing and reconciling, supported by her candid account of her own experience. She is as encouraging as she is relatable and offers hope to those intimidated by the challenges to come. This book is a gift to the sobriety community, providing both education and inspiration on an often-overlooked topic."

—HADLEY SORENSEN, author of *The Dirty Truth on Social Drinking*

"*Rebuilding Relationships in Recovery* is the most important book I have ever read about addiction issues and how to repair connections during sobriety. Dowd offers an enormous number of strategies and ways to move forward as people battling with this disease fight to reclaim their lives. Dowd beautifully describes the steps and emotions that survivors and family members experience throughout the healing process. I will be recommending this book to clients and colleagues, especially those who have been stuck in unaddressed grief and are looking for a resource that helps them understand how to acknowledge their pain and reconnect with loved ones, in sobriety."

—SHARI BOTWIN, LCSW, therapist, trauma expert witness, law and crime network guest expert, media contributor, and author of *Stolen Childhoods*

"Janice Dowd has written a masterpiece of a book. This is a manual for all recovering people, which I believe should be placed in the hands of graduates of treatment programs everywhere as a guidepost, and available wherever possible to the public at large. Covering disease concept formation, the inception of Alcoholics Anonymous, and addressing the overarching and personalized aspects of a recovery program, Ms. Dowd bares her truth on the pages of this manuscript in the hopes of sharing her journey plainly to help the entire addictive system. . . . Personally, I cannot wait to share this book with my clients to aid them with their own path because I believe its effectiveness will be exponential."

—MAGGIE W. BANGER, LPC-S, therapist